Seamus Mullen's HERO FOOD

HOW COOKING WITH DELICIOUS THINGS CAN MAKE US FEEL BETTER

Andrews McMeel Publishing, LLC

Kansas City • Sydney • London

Know the farmer and the farm. It's the best way to ensure the freshest produce. Here, Patty Gentry's organic Early Girl Farm on Long Island.

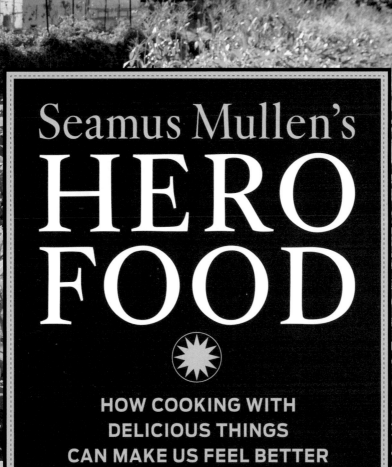

Seamus Mullen's
HERO
FOOD

HOW COOKING WITH DELICIOUS THINGS CAN MAKE US FEEL BETTER

PHOTOGRAPHS BY COLIN CLARK

Q 641
Mullen

Andrews McMeel Publishing, LLC
an Andrews McMeel Universal company
1130 Walnut Street, Kansas City, Missouri 64106

www.andrewsmcmeel.com

www.seamusmullen.com

12 13 14 15 16 WKT 10 9 8 7 6 5 4 3 2 1

ISBN: 978-1-4494-0758-2   756590860

Library of Congress Control Number: 2011932647

Produced and edited by Dorothy Kalins Ink, LLC
Design by Don Morris Design, New York
Photographs by Colin Clark

DEDICATION

TO MUTTI

My darling grandmother, Valerie Rachel Mullen,
this book is for you.

My happiest childhood memories are with you.
You have taught me so much about integrity,
compassion, kindness, courage, independence, and
curiosity. You might have been a rather unorthodox
grandmother (dragging me to anti-war protests and
narrowly escaping arrest when I probably should
have been in school, or riding chicken busses with
me in Central America when grandmothers your
age consider going to the movies an adventure),
but you have been a tremendous friend and an
inspiration to everyone who's come to know you.
Thank you so much for everything you've given me.

AN INTRODUCTION..x
SEASON I: WINTER IN BARCELONA..............6

CHAPTER 1: OLIVE OIL.......................................12
A NOTE ON...Spanish Olive Oil.............................16
Preserved Artichokes...18
Quick-Cured Lemons...18
All i Oli...21
My Favorite Vinaigrette...21
TECHNIQUE: Smoked Olive Oil...........................22
Eggs Poached in Olive Oil....................................22
Crispy Fried Artichokes...27
Minted Yogurt...27
Sweet Potato Chips and Whipped Salt Cod..............28

CHAPTER 2: DRIED BEANS..............................30
A NOTE ON...Soaking Beans................................33
A NOTE ON...Salting Beans.................................33
TECHNIQUE: Making Dried Beans
    in a Pressure Cooker.......................................35
Verdina Bean Salad...35
Tolosa Bean Soup..36
A NOTE ON...Black Beans...................................36
Cazuela of Mongetes and Cockles.........................39
Truffled Lentils and Eggs......................................40
A NOTE ON...Ibérico Ham...................................43
Flageolets with Autumn Greens and Fresh Bacon.....45

CHAPTER 3: ALMONDS......................................46
Ajo Blanco with Sardine Confit.............................50
Pork and Almond Stew...52

Grilled Asparagus and Leeks
    with Romesco Sauce...54
TECHNIQUE: Making Romesco Sauce.....................55
Salbitxada..57
10 THINGS to Do with Almonds..........................58
Almond Sablé...59

CHAPTER 4: GRAINS...60
TECHNIQUE: Grating Tomatoes...........................64
TECHNIQUE: Making Sofrito................................65
Risotto of Irish Oats..66
Farro Salad with Preserved Tuna...........................69
Creamy Grits with Slow-Cooked Pork Loin.............70
TECHNIQUE: Cleaning Squid...............................73
A NOTE ON...Bomba Rice....................................73
Rice with Squid and Green Beans..........................74

CHAPTER 5: ANCHOVIES..................................76
TECHNIQUE: Cleaning Anchovies.........................81
Homemade Potted Anchovies................................82
A NOTE ON...Preserving Anchovies......................82
Anchoas y Escalivada, or Anchovies and
    Charred Vegetables..85
Lightly Smoked Sardines on Toast.........................86
A NOTE ON...Smoking Sardines...........................86
Caramelized Cauliflower with Anchovies.................87
Ensalada of Preserved Anchovies..........................89
Flash-Fried Anchovies
    with Crispy Lemons and Sage...........................89
Two Kinds of Anchovies, One Kind of Flatbread....90
Grilled Flatbreads...90

SEASON II: SPRING ON MY ROOFTOP..........92

CHAPTER 6: GOOD EGGS...................................98
Gently Scrambled Eggs with Wild Vegetables.........103
Deviled Eggs..104
Five-Minute Eggs with Romesco.............................104
TECHNIQUE: Deep-Frying an Egg in Olive Oil......107
Fork-Crushed Sweet Potatoes with
   Sobrassada and a Fried Egg..........................108
A NOTE ON...Sobrassada.....................................108
Soft-Cooked Gribiche
   with Pickled Anchovies on Toast......................108
Tortilla Española 111
Lamb Tartare with Spring Pullet Eggs...................112

CHAPTER 7: GOOD BIRDS................................114
A NOTE ON...Chicken Stock................................117
Poached Long Island Duck Breasts
   with Farro..119
TECHNIQUE: Cutting Up a Duck..............................120
Duck Liver Toasts and Pickled Raisins....................122
Homemade Duck Sausage.....................................124
TECHNIQUE: Cutting a Quail Egg............................126
Quail en Escabeche with Fried Quail Eggs.............127
TECHNIQUE: Escabeche for Pickling
   Poultry or Fish...127
Caldo del Día...128
Sopa de Enfermos..128
Sunday Roast Chicken...130
Crispy Guinea Hen...131
A NOTE ON...Paella..132
Chicken and Seafood Paella...............................134

CHAPTER 8: SWEET PEAS................................136
A NOTE ON...Blanching..139
Pea Tendrils a la Catalana....................................141
TECHNIQUE: Cooking Garbanzo Beans...................141
Simply Sweet Peas..142
Sugar Snap Pea Salad...142
Squid with Baby Favas, Mint, and Basil...................144
Whole Black Sea Bass with Pea and Butter Sauce....146
A NOTE ON...Txakoli...147
Chilled Sweet Pea Soup.......................................147
Lightly Cured Wild Salmon with Pea Salad.............148
Kefir Vinaigrette..148
A NOTE ON...Torn Herbs......................................148

CHAPTER 9: PARSLEY.....................................150
Parsley Juice...155
Salsa Verde..155
A Real Smoothie..155
TECHNIQUE: Pickled Shallots................................156
Salad of Marble Potatoes......................................156
White Bean Salad
   with Preserved Tuna and Parsley Vinaigrette.....159
Parsley Vinaigrette...159
TECHNIQUE: Cooking Octopus...............................160
Octopus and Parsley Salad....................................160

CHAPTER 10: BERRIES....................................162
Mutti's Blueberry Boy Bait....................................167
Strawberry Ice Cream..168
Raspberries and Yogurt With Buttermilk Crêpes....168
Blackberry and Almond Crumble 171
Currant Glaze For Pork...171

SEASON III: SUMMER ON THE FARM.........172

CHAPTER 11: CARROTS......................................178
A NOTE ON...Pickling..181
Salt-Baked Carrots and Beets.................................182
Pickled Carrots..185
Vegetable Pickling Liquid.......................................185
Chilled Carrot Soup with Yogurt and Tarragon.......186
Ice-Cold Carrots, Radishes, and Beets
    with Potted Anchovy and Lemon Butter.............189

CHAPTER 12: CORN...190
10 THINGS to Do with Corn...................................193
Corn and Crab Salad...195
Steamed Corn with Clams and Bacon.....................196
Best Grilled Corn, in the Husk................................198
Crispy Fried Hominy...199

CHAPTER 13: STONE FRUIT..........................200
Confit of Duck Legs with Plums.............................204
Lightly Cured Fluke with Pickled Plums.................204
Pickled Plums...207

Fruit Pickling Liquid...207
Stone Fruit Gazpacho with Scallops.......................208
White Peaches, Pistachios, Honey, and Ricotta.......211
Spiced Stone Fruit Preserves..................................212
Plum Cake..212

CHAPTER 14: GOOD FISH..............................214
TECHNIQUE: Curing Raw Fish...............................218
Lightly Cured Summer Bonito.................................219
Pan Roast of Arctic Char with Sorrel Sauce...........220
Line-Caught Atlantic Cod with Picada....................223
TECHNIQUE: Preserving Tuna................................224
A NOTE ON...Trout...226
Trout a la Navarra..229
Mutti's Pan-Fried Troutlings...................................229
TECHNIQUE: How to Smoke a Trout......................230
Warm Smoked Trout with Pickled Onions..............231
Gently Roasted Brown Trout
    with Summer Squash..232
TECHNIQUE: Desalinating Salt Cod.......................235
Salt Cod with Garbanzo Beans
    and Spinach...236

SEASON IV: AUTUMN IN VERMONT...........238

CHAPTER 15: SQUASH...............................244
Autumn Squash Salad.................................248
Roasted Winter Squash 251
Stuffed Spaghetti Squash............................254
Butternut Squash Soup with Smoked Trout.............254

CHAPTER 16: MUSHROOMS...........................256
A NOTE ON...Cleaning Mushrooms........................259
Warm Mushroom Salad................................261
Warm Mushroom Vinaigrette..........................262
Flatbreads of King Oyster
    and Shitake Mushrooms...........................262
Pickled Mushrooms..................................265
Cremini Mushrooms al Ajillo........................265
Pickled Chanterelles with Mackerel
    in Escabeche....................................266

CHAPTER 17: GREENS..............................268
Spicy Rapini with Almonds.........................272

TECHNIQUE: Steaming Greens..................................272
Crispy Tuscan Kale on the Grill............................275
Sorrel Sauce...276
Xató Salad...276
Pan-Roasted Brussels Sprouts...............................279
Chard Croquettes...280

CHAPTER 18: GOOD MEAT............................282
Slow-Roasted Lamb Shoulder.................................287
A NOTE ON...Lamb...288
Homemade Lamb Bacon
    with Kale and an Egg...................................290
Lamb Meatballs in Tomato Sauce with Ricotta.......293
Lamb Loin Wrapped in Caul Fat and Herbs............294
TECHNIQUE: Brining Meat and Poultry.................297
English-Cut Pork Chops with Borlotti Beans.........298
Spice-Rubbed Hanger Steak on the Grill 301
Roasted Marrow Bones...............................302

ACKNOWLEDGMENTS..............................304
INDEX...306

AN INTRODUCTION

SPANISH LESSONS

I fell in love with Spain by accident. On the 40-minute drive from our Vermont farm (right), to my seventh grade class, my dad was teaching himself Spanish from Berlitz tapes, unwittingly subjecting me to learn the language. I hated it. I wanted to listen to The Cure and The Clash, not some canned voice with a Castilian accent: *"El ruido de la calle no me deja dormir."* Fast forward: I'm 17, thousands of miles away from rural Vermont and living with a host family in Burgos in the heart of Castilla y León. I'm learning more Spanish lessons, like drinking wine from a wineskin, sucking the juice from the heads of langoustines, downing shrimp (shells and all), and swallowing whole squid. Little did I know I'd return years later to work in some of the best kitchens in the country, immersing myself in the world of Spanish cuisine.

THE WOMEN WHO MADE ME COOK

My career as a chef most likely began at age six when I caught an eight-inch brook trout in the Ompompanoosuc River and proudly brought it home. My grandmother, Mutti, who grew up in London and studied at the Cordon Bleu in Paris, showed me how to clean and cook my little trout (page 229). From there I spun into summer jobs cooking in local restaurants. When I went off to college in Michigan and had to work part time,

it only made sense it would be in a restaurant.

The tiny little International Café was near campus and always busy. One day I saw the chef, Kiki Babeluc, mumbling to herself, embracing some customers and screaming at others. I instantly liked her. Kiki became my first real mentor in the kitchen. Her fiery, stubborn character reminded me of my grandmother. We quickly became quite fond of each other. Kiki was an intense workaholic with a very solid repertoire of very dated, classic French cuisine.

I became increasingly less interested in academics and more drawn to food. I preferred to work at the restaurant or in my apartment, where I baked bread and made pasta. By the time I finally finished school, I had a mountain of debt and I needed to find a job. Badly.

I was a bit lost. I had an expensive and relatively useless degree in Spanish literature. Mutti sensed that I needed to get my life in order. As a graduation present, she took me on a wine-tasting tour of Sonoma. The more we drank, the more candid she became: "Seamus," she told me, "you are happiest when you cook. It's what you do best. Embrace it."

MORE SPANISH LESSONS

After several years of cooking in some of the best restaurants in San Francisco and New York and just as I was turning 30, I decided to return to Spain. Young cooks work for free as a *stagier* in all the good kitchens there, and I figured that no one would turn down free labor. So I saved my money and tried to find a *stage* in Spain, with no luck. I was intrigued by the then-two-star restaurant Mugaritz, near San Sebastián in the Basque Country. I decided I wanted to work there. After endless phone calls and unanswered emails, one day I packed my bags, jumped on a plane, and managed to talk my way into a *stage*. Over the next two years I worked in some of the best kitchens in Spain, first for free, then for pennies, and eventually for a meager, but livable, salary. I made many friends, and learned much, but eventually it was time to return to New York.

IN A NEW YORK STATE OF MIND

Back in the United States, Spain was hot, but people only seemed to know about so-called "molecular gastronomy"—foams and spheres—or paella and sangria. Americans knew little of the deep traditional Spanish culinary roots of all that modern food. It was those roots I loved—the little fried anchovies, the creamy chilled almond soups, the grilled octopus, meaty sausages, and baked rice dishes. In 2006, I was approached by the owner of an upscale Spanish restaurant interested in collaborating on another place, something more than just a simple tapas bar. In nine months, we raised capital, found a location, and opened Boqueria, a 60-seat restaurant in the Flatiron District of Manhattan, named for one of my favorite markets in the world, La Boqueria in Barcelona.

On November 1, 2006, Frank Bruni gave us a glowing review in *The New York Times*. It sent

"The more we drank, the more candid Mutti became: 'Seamus, you're happiest when you cook. It's what you do best. Embrace it.' "

our kitchen into a tailspin. One minute we were serving 60 guests a night and the next, 260. I had never experienced anything like it. I was working the fish station and calling tickets to other cooks and the tickets just kept coming until they were floating all over the kitchen, drowning in chicken stock, catching fire in the broiler. Somehow we managed to survive. The more we practiced, the better we got at managing the hunger New Yorkers seemed to be acquiring for our Spanish food.

A SPANNER IN THE WORKS

Eight months after we opened, the stress of running an incredibly busy kitchen caught up with me. I was exhausted. I remember calling my mom and telling her I felt like my body was broken and I needed a new one. Then I woke up in the middle of the night with an excruciating pain in my hip. I called 911 and spent the next three days in the hospital while doctors tried to figure out what on earth was going on.

After testing for everything they could think of, the doctors decided to give me an MRI. Suddenly it became clear why I was in so much pain: my hip was full of fluid, causing tremendous pressure on my sciatic nerve. A quick culture showed that my white blood cell count was through the roof, but there was no sign of infection in my hip. They couldn't figure out why I would have such extreme inflammation without infection. A few days later, my file made its way into the hands of Dr. Harry Fischer, the head of the Department of Rheumatology at Beth Israel

Medical Center. He told me that he suspected I was suffering from a flare-up caused by rheumatoid arthritis. The minute he left my bedside, I Googled "rheumatoid arthritis" and quickly learned that this auto-immune disease causes the body to over-produce white blood cells and attack itself, leading to extremely painful, often debilitating inflammation. The more I read, the more I freaked out: What if I was not able to cook again?

Over the next few months I learned how the disease behaved—how an attack could come out of nowhere or be brought on by stress—and tried to wrap my mind around ways to moderate my lifestyle and adapt to significant change. In the years since that diagnosis, I've come to understand a very, very important part of my disease and that is the effect food has on overcoming the discomfort of my RA. As a chef, I've always been aware of the role that food can play in our health, but I never understood just how crucial it was to my own wellness.

I became adamant that I would not let RA stand in the way of my career. In 2008, we opened a second Boqueria restaurant, this time in SoHo. Following the success of the two restaurants, in 2009 the Food Network asked me to be a contestant on *The Next Iron Chef,* an eight-week TV battle. The show, an intense experience in cooking as a competitive sport, took me back to my high school soccer matches. I did very well and made it to the final three out of ten original competitors. While we were shooting in Japan,

"And here's the good news: In that great fatalist way of Mother Nature, what I like turns out to be good for me!"

I had a severe RA attack. I couldn't move well around the set and was eliminated. I returned home in a wheelchair. At 35 years old, I realized that I had to make some major changes in my life or RA would get the best of me. That's when I made the commitment to write *Hero Food* and focus on well-being—mine and yours.

MY HEROES

I do not believe that what we eat can cure illness, but I do believe that eating well and mindfully can improve our sense of well-being. There is so much talk about how ingredients like turmeric are anti-inflammatory but I wonder, how much of the stuff do I have to eat to make a real difference? A pound a day? I agree with the nutrition expert Marion Nestle who writes in *What to Eat:* "You are better off paying attention to your overall dietary pattern than worrying about whether any one single food is better for you than another."

I know there's no silver bullet, but I have discovered that some foods can make dramatic differences. These foods—18 of them in this book—have become my Heroes. Parsley, for example. In the endless hours I've spent in research looking for some legitimate lifestyle guidance for treating RA, I learned that the folate in parsley (and other vegetables) could play a role in clearing out the buildup of uric acid in my joints that causes me so much pain. One morning, when my hands hurt so badly I could barely tie my shoelaces, I put a handful of parsley with some lemon

juice and an apple in the Vitamix, buzzed it up, and drank it. Within a couple of hours, my hands felt noticeably better. We all have achy joints, I thought. This delicious discovery that worked for me should be shared.

When I was first diagnosed with RA, I tried "elimination" diets, focusing on what *not* to eat. But I have come to understand that rather than eliminate foods from my diet, it's much more helpful to *add* more Heroes, like parsley.

I've experimented with many other ingredients, to varying degrees of success. While there is a direct correlation with some ingredients and the relief of joint pain, with others there's more of what I like to think of as an emotional understanding that these foods are helping me. One of my real-life heroes was Dr. David Servan-Schreiber, author of *Anticancer: A New Way of Life*. His book is full of emerging scientific research leading to his conclusion that certain foods can affect our well-being. But he also believed that a positive mental state can help our bodies heal. Not that you can meditate your way out of disease, but the more you can do to take the psychic load off your immune system, the better prepared it will be to do its job and protect you from disease. When I deal with pain, it saps so much of my energy. I know it's crucial to lessen stress and to have faith that I'm doing the right thing for myself. So if I believe that eating a bit of ginger every morning is doing the right thing, then by all means I'll eat a bit of ginger every morning!

I know that omega-3s matter—there's some evidence of their effect on inflammation. I take fish oil each day and when I forget to take it, I'll feel it in my joints. Since anchovies and sardines are loaded with omega-3s, it only makes sense that they be an integral part of my diet. And here's the good news: in that great fatalistic way of Mother Nature, *what I like turns out to be good for me!*

My Heroes are real food. Elemental things like Good Meat, Good Birds, Eggs, Carrots, Greens, and Berries. I believe that Michael Pollan is right when he says in *In Defense of Food:* "Instead of worrying about nutrients, we should simply avoid any food that has been processed to such an extent that it is more the product of industry than of nature."

When I cook, I'm aware of much more than recipes. I'm obsessive about the way a pig is raised, about the provenance of my chickens, and in turn, their eggs. I fret about how my vegetables are grown, about how my fruit is treated, about the freshness and sustainability of the fish I use. All that adds up to why *Hero Food* is good for you. But my hope is that you will eventually forget about why these recipes are good for you and make them just because they are good.

I am not a nutritionist—I'm a chef. And I'm unwilling to let so-called health food take the place of great food. In this book, I do not promise instant cures or make outlandish health claims, nor do I pretend that what works for me will work for everyone; we all react differently to different foods. And like me, you'll have to pay real attention to what you eat and then monitor how

your body likes it. *Hero Food* doesn't make breakthrough claims. Instead my goal is to provide delicious alternatives to incorporate in your daily meals. Much of this stuff we already know, but we don't always know what to do with it.

There's a lot of faux-science out there—confusing claims and much of it wildly subjective. But I have developed a gut sense about what's really good for me. The more I learn, the more I discover research that supports my conclusions. It's not quite as simple as an *Eat This, Not That!* world. But my hope is that you'll embrace all my Heroes as part of your healthy eating pattern.

A NEW CHAPTER BEGINS

This past year has been one of the most exciting of my life. After years of working together, my partner and I decided we'd be happier moving on. I left Boqueria to focus on other things—this book and taking a much-needed break from working long hours to learn, to grow, to plan. As I write, I'm about to open a new restaurant in New York's Greenwich Village with my brother and a team of trusted colleagues. Tertulia, inspired by the convivial cider taverns of Northern Spain, will serve seasonal Spanish food with an emphasis on the highest quality ingredients. This is the realization of a longtime dream: a restaurant that fulfills my vision for food and hospitality without compromises. When you read these words, we'll be well on our way. There will be many new stories to tell. But I know I won't be able to do it without my Heroes.

WINTER

IN BARCELONA

CH. 1: Olive Oil FRUITY ✳ DELICATE ✳ VOLUPTUOUS

CH. 2: Dried Beans CREAMY ✳ ROBUST ✳ ELEMENTAL

CH. 3: Almonds CRUNCHY ✳ VERSATILE ✳ NUTRITIOUS

CH. 4: Grains NUTTY ✳ ANCIENT ✳ TOOTHSOME

CH. 5: Anchovies BRINY ✳ SHINY ✳ ESSENTIAL

7

VERAT / CABALLA

3'50

PVP

Clockwise from bottom left, an-impromptu soccer match in an alley of the Born neighbor-hood where I lived. Fried artichokes from one of my favorite restaurants, La Cova Fumada in la Bar-celoneta. A hidden courtyard opposite the Picasso Museum, perfect for morning coffee. Fresh green olives in the Boqueria market.

Gambas de Paramós at La Cova Fumada are as expensive as they are delicious, above; I love the succulent juices from their heads. Legs of *jamón Ibérico* in a local bar; little cups catch the dripping fat as the ham cures.

WINTER

A spectacular Barcelona view, sunset over Tibidabo Mountain, above, as seen from the apartment where we photographed much of the food in the Winter chapters. Sunday lunch, right, can take the better part of a day at my friend Jordi Vilà's neighborhood restaurant, Vivanda, in the hills above Barcelona. I love his spicy grilled snails and tiny flatbreads of *escalavida* (see page 85 for a version you can make).

Left, the bar at the elegant tapas restaurant Ciudad Condal at the bottom of the Rambla Catalunya. Above, Condal's uncomplicated little sandwich of *salchichón Ibérico*; just slim, crusty bread and the world's best sausage. Shopkeepers at the historic Colmado Quilez, above right, with the most incredible selection of gourmet canned goods I've ever seen.

LA CASA DEL BACALA

A tiny *xató* salad at Vivanda, (recipe, page 276), above. With my friend Jordi Vilà, right, at his Pizzería Saltimbocca. I worked at his first place, Alkimia, and learned so much about Catalan food.

WINTER

Above, buying salt cod at La Casa del Bacalao, which has the best selection and quality in the city. Right, my first stop whenever I hit town, La Boqueria market.

chapter one

OLIVE OIL

FRUITY

✳ ✳ ✳

DELICATE

✳ ✳ ✳

VOLUPTUOUS

PEOPLE ARE ALWAYS ASKING ME which kind of olive oil to use. I certainly understand their confusion when they walk into a store and confront shelves and shelves lined with cool-looking bottles. Oils, for me, fall into two separate categories: oils to cook with, and oils for finishing dishes or for delicate applications where they're not exposed to high temperature. Making olive oil is a process of extracting oil from the olive

juice pressed from fresh fruit; extra-virgin oils still have the floral delicacy of the olive in them. However that flavor is destroyed when the oil is overheated. The little flavor bits burn. It's as simple as that.

So it's silly to cook at high heat with really expensive olive oil. Not only do you lose the flavor, but you lose the beneficial elements of the fruit that are lost in the high heat. Oils to drizzle over a dish are unrefined, cold-pressed, extra-virgin or virgin olive oil (the main distinction between them is that extra-virgin has lower acidity). I do use these good olive oils for cooking as long as I don't heat them above 150°. In fact, for gently sweating vegetables or for poaching fish or meats, they add a beautiful aromatic flavor. Virgin oils can be unrefined as well, but have a higher level of acidity than extra-virgin.

For anything that requires a hot sear, like caramelizing meat, I use "pure" or "blended" olive oil, sometimes sold simply as "olive oil." This is generally a blend of virgin and refined olive oils; it can be heated to a higher smoke point and is more consistent. In the recipes in this book, I call for extra-virgin

"Olive oil is the glue that holds good food together from a flavor point of view, but it turns out to be equally high in things that are good for us."

olive oil where I think it matters most and otherwise ask for "olive oil."

Olive oil is the glue that holds good food together from a flavor point of view, but it turns out to be equally high in things that are good for us. In the world of nutrition, there is still much to be learned about the health values of many foods. Olive oil, however, is one of the few things that most people agree is good for you. Even the Food and Drug Administration gets behind it and allows a qualified health claim on labels that replacing just 2 tablespoons of saturated fat with extra-virgin olive oil may reduce the risk of cardiovascular disease. This is not to say that we should be slugging pints of the stuff. But there is compelling evidence that replacing artery-clogging saturated fats with the healthier monounsaturated fats (and olive oil, with its 75 percent of monounsaturated fats, has the highest amount of most any oil) may lower the risk of heart disease.

For me, the most important aspect of olive oil—besides its deliciousness—is its potential anti-inflammatory effect. The way I understand it, inflammation basically results from the body's instinct to send in white blood cells to fight off infection. For people with rheumatoid arthritis (and other auto-immune diseases) our immune systems are triggered to fight off infections that may not actually exist. The monounsaturated fats in olive oil may help to reduce that inflammation. Obviously this is a rather simplistic view of the science behind it, but the essential takeaway is there are good properties in olive oil that may reduce swelling. And I deal with systemic swelling in my joints on a daily basis.

I couldn't cook the food I love if it weren't for olive oil, and as it turns out, I might not even be able to physically endure cooking without it. I wasn't sure if all this research I'd been reading about olive oil was really true, so recently I decided to completely cut olive oil and olives from my diet for two weeks. By the fourth day, my joints felt tight and painful. I returned to olive oil and instantly knew relief. Olive oil has been a bit of an unsung hero. I'm here to call it a real Hero.

A NOTE ON...SPANISH OLIVE OIL

Several years ago, when I was working at a midtown Manhattan restaurant, a lanky Spaniard walked into the kitchen with a box full of olive oil bottles. In a thick accent, he asked me if he could speak to the chef. After I answered in Spanish, he was very relieved and went on to explain that he represented Valderrama, an artisanal olive oil producer from just outside Toledo, south of Madrid, and he had some oils he wanted me to try. I'd been cooking with olive oil for years in some great restaurants, but honestly hadn't thought enough about their distinctions until I got to know Carlos. He turned me on to the four olive oils that have become my first choice to cook with: Hojiblanca, Picual, Picudo, and my

favorite (and most available here as it turns out), Arbequina. Over the years, as I've moved on to open my own restaurants, I've turned many people on to Valderrama. When we set out to photograph this book, I knew we had to go to the Valderrama olive groves where, on rolling acres with beautifully managed trees, they practice an uncommon way of growing and harvesting olives—using a Ferrari tractor specially netted to catch the fruit before it can hit the ground and bruise. It then takes less than 45 minutes to process those olives into oil. Unlike factory operations where the fruit is shaken from the trees only to languish on the ground, then is stored in warehouses for days or more, at Valderrama the juice that's used to process the oil is as fresh as can be.

Homemade condiments in Valderrama olive oil from the groves in Toledo, Spain. From left, Pickled Mushrooms (page 265), Preserved Artichokes (page 18), Quick-Cured Lemons (page 18), and Preserved Anchovies (page 82).

Preserved Artichokes

WHEN I WAS A KID I was addicted to those little jars of canned artichoke hearts. My mom would buy them to toss into salads, but inevitably every time she went to the pantry for that night's salad, she'd find empty jars. I could finish three or four jars in one sitting. I haven't lost my taste for artichokes; if anything it's just gotten a bit more refined. Once you make your own preserved artichokes, you'll never, ever go back to the store-bought kind.

Makes 4 jars

4   pounds large artichokes (8–10)
     About 4 cups extra-virgin olive oil
2   medium carrots, peeled and cut into 2-inch pieces
4   cloves garlic, peeled
     Salt
½   cup white wine
4   sprigs fresh thyme
2   bay leaves, preferably fresh
     Juice of 2 lemons

Trim the artichokes as described in Crispy Fried Artichokes (page 27), and cut lengthwise into quarters.

In a large pot, heat ¼ cup of the olive oil over medium-high heat. Add the artichokes, carrots, and garlic, season with salt, and sauté for 2 minutes. Once the carrots and artichokes begin to color, add the white wine and cook off the alcohol, about 1 minute. Add the thyme, bay leaves, lemon juice, and 1 cup water and reduce to a low simmer.

Pour in enough olive oil to cover the vegetables. Cook until the artichokes can be easily pierced with a knife but are still a little firm, about 15 minutes. Turn off the heat and carefully remove and discard the carrots.

Distribute the artichokes evenly among four canning jars, topping each jar with the olive oil. Close the lids. The artichokes will keep for a few weeks in the refrigerator.

Quick-Cured Lemons

PRESERVED LEMONS ADD A NEW DIMENSION to dishes, a delicious kind of salty sour. There are many different ways to cure lemons. Typically they take weeks or even months. Here's a great way of getting that unique flavor much faster. The two-step process involves salting lemon slices for a few days, then rinsing them and marinating them in olive oil.

I like to fold the marinated lemon slices, both the flesh and the rind, into bean or rice dishes to add a bright contrast. Slip several slices under the skin of a chicken before roasting. Or sliver them into a salad or grind a few in a mortar and pestle and use to add a new layer of flavor to a vinaigrette.

Makes 2 jars

4   sprigs fresh thyme
1   pound kosher salt
1   pound sugar
2   cloves garlic, crushed with the back of a knife
10   lemons, blanched briefly in boiling water to remove wax
2   bay leaves
1   *guindilla* pepper, or a piece of ancho chile
     About 2 cups extra-virgin olive oil, preferably Picudo or Arbequina

Remove the leaves from 2 of the thyme sprigs. Mix the thyme leaves, salt, sugar, and garlic in a large bowl. Pour a thin layer of the mixture onto a platter or deep roasting pan.

Slice the lemons into rounds and layer some on top of the salt mixture, then layer on more of the salt mixture. Continue layering until all of the lemons are covered. Cover and refrigerate for 3 days.

Rinse the lemon slices thoroughly and pat dry with paper towels. In a clean canning jar or two, layer the lemon slices, adding the remaining thyme sprigs, the bay leaves, and *guindilla* pepper. Pour in olive oil to cover the lemons completely. Marinated in the oil, the lemons will keep in the refrigerator for up to a month.

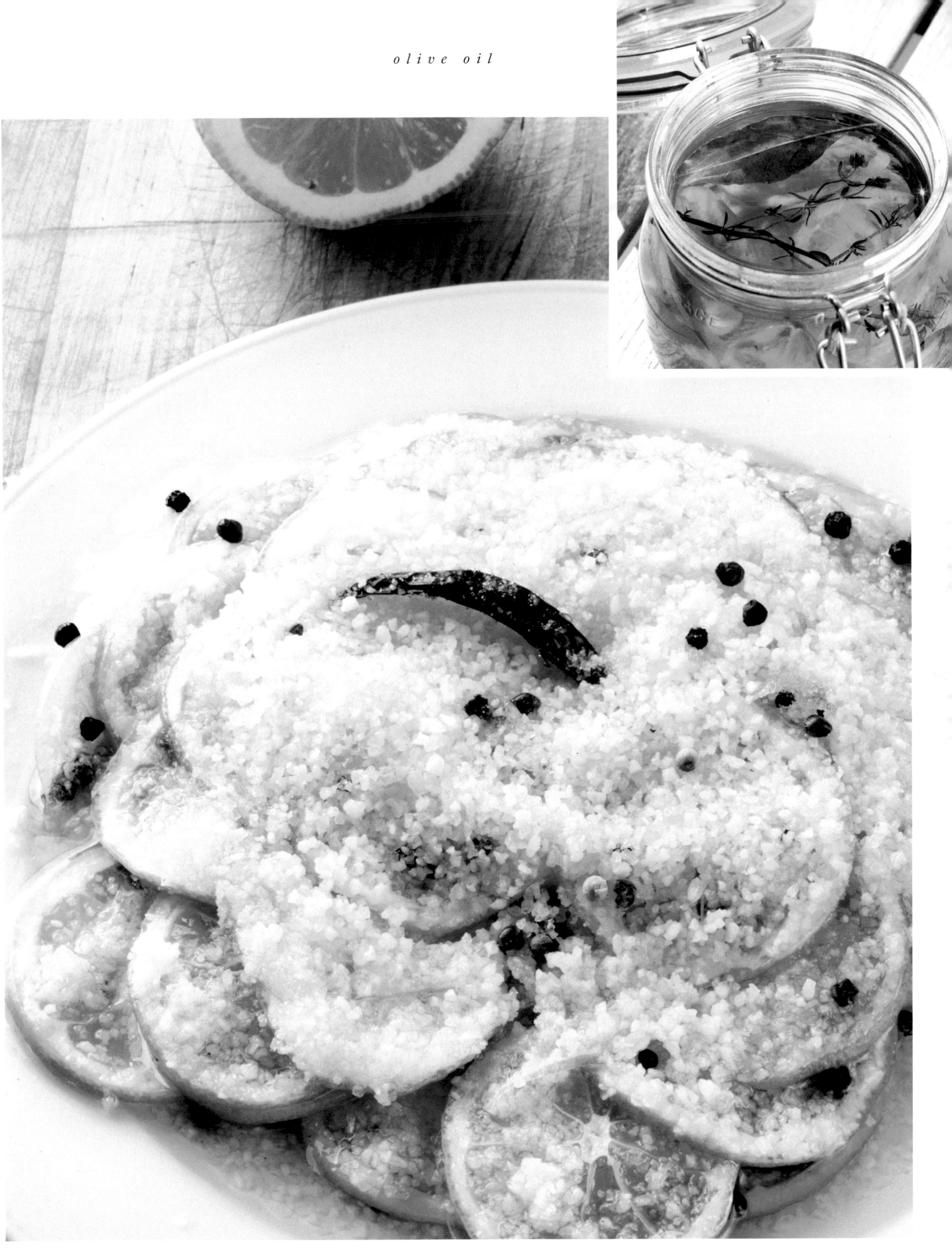

All i Oli

IF THERE COULD BE BUT ONE SAUCE in all of Spanish cooking, for me it might just be *all i oli*. The name quite simply means "garlic" (*all*) "and" (*i*) "oil" (*oli*), and that's pretty much all that's in a traditional *all i oli*. I fold it into a rice dish to add a creamy texture, or I serve it as a condiment for grilled fish and vegetables. I love to make this by hand in a mortar and pestle. It's one of the magical moments of cooking where two simple things are transformed into something so remarkably different. *All i oli* can also be made with a handheld blender (an egg yolk will help to hold it together), but if you choose the 21st-century technique over the 15th-century method, you'll want to mix ½ cup extra-virgin olive oil with ½ cup canola, grapeseed, or safflower oil. If you don't mix the oils, the blender's blade will bruise the delicate olive oil and turn it bitter.

Makes 1 cup

Small handful of garlic cloves, finely minced
1 teaspoon kosher salt
Tiny squeeze of lemon juice
1 cup extra-virgin olive oil, preferably
Picudo or Arbequina

In a large mortar and pestle, combine the minced garlic, salt, and lemon juice and grind in a clockwise motion until pounded into a paste. Add the olive oil, drop by drop, while working the pestle in circles, always in the same direction. As the sauce begins to emulsify and become creamy, start to add the oil in a steady stream until completely incorporated.

My Favorite Vinaigrette

IT MAKES SENSE THAT OLIVE OIL became an important part of my life when I lived in Spain. After all, Spain is the largest producer of olive oil in the world, with over 260 varieties of olives. I love Picudo and Arbequina for delicately finishing a sauce or dressing a salad. This vinaigrette seems to be too simple to be so good. My mother always keeps a version in a jar in a cupboard, beneath the kitchen counter. Drizzled over summertime tomatoes right out of her garden, I can't think of anything better.

Makes 2¼ cups

¼ cup good white wine vinegar
1 tablespoon honey
1 teaspoon Dijon mustard
1 clove garlic, thinly sliced
Leaves from 1 sprig fresh thyme
Salt
Freshly ground black pepper
2 cups extra-virgin olive oil, preferably
Arbequina or Picudo

Combine all the ingredients except the oil in a small mixing bowl and whisk together thoroughly. Drizzle in the olive oil slowly while whisking.

Smoked Olive Oil

ONE OF MY FAVORITE WAYS to prepare sardines is to smoke them over wood chips, but unfortunately the fish always gets overcooked before it takes on a smoky flavor. A few years ago in the restaurant we were trying to figure out a way to perfectly smoke sardines and still have them be moist and properly cooked. We came up with the idea of smoking olive oil first, and then gently poaching the sardines in the smoked oil. It worked brilliantly. We now use smoked olive oil for all sorts of things, from cooking eggs to making vinaigrettes. The process is really simple; all you need is a grill, a pot, a large bowl, and some wood chips.

Once the coals are really hot on the grill, add the wood chips to create smoke. Put a small saucepan with 2 or 3 cups of extra-virgin olive oil on the grill. Cover the pan with a glass bowl large enough to capture the rising smoke. To get a good strong smoky flavor, you'll need to smoke the oil for at least 15 minutes. Once the oil is smoked, pour it into a dark bottle (label it to avoid confusion) and store it out of direct sunlight. The possibilities for using it are endless.

Eggs Poached in Olive Oil

WHEN I STARTED WORKING AT ALKIMIA in Barcelona, one of the first things that the chef, Jordi Vilà, told me was that France has its Mother Sauces, but Spain has its olive oil! At Alkimia, each dish was sauced with a different olive oil. One dish on the menu blew me away: a duck egg deep-fried in olive oil, the whites gently folded together to form a sphere (page 107). When I moved back to New York I couldn't stop thinking about that egg. I wanted to pay tribute to Jordi, but do something a little different. So I started playing around with eggs, olive oil, and the temperature of the oil; I discovered that by keeping the oil at a relatively low temperature, the yolk and the white would congeal at the same time, resulting in a creamy, sexy, shiny, olive-y egg.
Serves 4

1   **clove garlic, peeled**
1   *guindilla* **pepper or other dried chile**
½   **cup extra-virgin olive oil, preferably Hojiblanca**
4   **small organic eggs, freshest possible (look for pullet eggs)**
    Coarse sea salt

In a small sauté pan, heat the garlic and chile in the oil to 140°. If you have a gas stove, you may need to rig up some sort of heat diffuser to keep the heat low. For testing the temperature, a good rule of thumb (pardon the pun) is to stick your thumb in the oil. If you can stand it for about 2 seconds without burning yourself, it's probably at 140°. Another option is to slip in a candy thermometer, but that's not nearly as much fun.

Crack the eggs, one at a time, into a small ramekin or coffee cup and slip each into the oil. Fresh eggs will have a very firm white that will quickly form in the oil. If you're using larger eggs, try not to add all of the white to the oil.

Cook for about 3 minutes, then remove each egg carefully with a slotted spatula and place over toast or potatoes or lentils. The eggs will be coated in a gorgeous veil of olive oil. Crush a little coarse sea salt on the yolks.

What better way to celebrate the olive than dinner in the groves? It stays light so late in southern Spain and the place was so irresistible that we pulled a table right out there among those glorious trees.

Crispy Fried Artichokes

ARTICHOKES ARE THE POET WARRIOR of the vegetable kingdom: soft, delicate hearts plated in sheets of armor. At least that's how the great Chilean poet Pablo Neruda described them. I believe that preparing artichokes is the mark of an accomplished chef. When cooks trail for a job at the restaurant, I always give them the artichoke test: turning an artichoke (peeling it perfectly with a knife as if on a lathe) takes skill, patience, and precision. Cooking one takes even more.

In Spain, Picual and Hojiblanca olives are grown in lower-lying areas than Picudo and Arbequina olives, and tend to be a bit more bitter and less fruity than more delicate varietals grown at higher altitudes. These slightly bitter oils are better for frying and cooking at high heat.

Serves 4

2   pounds artichokes (8–10 medium)
    Olive oil for frying, preferably Picual or Hojiblanca
1   cup corn flour
1   cup rice flour
1   cup semolina
    Salt
4   lemons, sliced into rounds
    Leaves from 1 large bunch fresh sage
    Minted Yogurt (recipe follows)

For the artichokes: Using a small, sharp paring knife, cut away the tough outer leaves of an artichoke and discard. Hold the artichoke in one hand and carefully turn it against the knife, almost as if the knife were a lathe. Try not to cut away all the leaves, the tender inside leaves will become crispy and delicious once fried.

Once you've cleaned away all the outer leaves, hold the artichoke upright with the stem facing down. Using the tip of the knife, cut the outer dark green skin down towards the end of the stem. This stem skin is quite bitter, so remove just enough to reveal the pale edible stem. The final result should retain the shape of the artichoke, just smaller. Don't worry if the first few don't turn out well, it gets easier with practice. Depending upon the size, cut the trimmed artichokes into halves or quarters. Now for the choke: If the artichokes are small, the fuzzy choke is so tender that it'll crisp up with cooking. For large artichokes, the easiest way to get the choke out is to use a teaspoon or a melon baller to scrape it out. Be careful not to take the beautiful meat with it.

Because artichokes discolor quickly after being turned, keep them bright in a stainless steel bowl with water, lemon juice, and parsley stems. If you're really neurotic about having perfect greenish-white artichokes (which of course I am!), then keep them submerged under the lemon water by covering the bowl with a damp cloth.

In a deep fryer or a heavy-bottomed pot, heat the olive oil to 340° on a candy thermometer. Combine the corn flour, rice flour, and semolina in a small bowl and use to dust each artichoke as you're ready to drop them into the hot oil. Fry only a few at a time, making sure not to overcrowd the pot. Fry until crispy and cooked through, about 3 minutes. With a slotted spoon, transfer the artichokes to a plate lined with a paper towel and season with salt.

Dust the lemon slices and sage leaves with the flour and fry until crispy. Divide the fried artichokes, lemon slices, and sage leaves among 4 plates. Serve with Minted Yogurt on the side.

MINTED YOGURT

1   cup plain yogurt
    Zest and juice of 1 lemon
¼   cup extra-virgin olive oil, preferably Arbequina
1   clove garlic, finely grated
    Leaves from 1 bunch fresh mint, finely chopped

Whisk all the ingredients together in a small bowl and refrigerate until needed. Scatter on a few sweet peas if you like.

Sweet Potato Chips and Whipped Salt Cod

EVERYONE HAS AN OPINION about frying in olive oil—some cooks complain that you can't get it hot enough, others think it's too expensive because they discard it after one use. But I believe that if you don't overheat the oil, and strain it after each use, not only will olive oil last as long as any other neutral-flavored frying oil, but it adds a whole new flavor dimension to fried food.
Serves 2

2½	cups olive oil suitable for frying
2	cloves garlic, peeled
2	*guindilla* peppers, or 2 pieces of ancho chile
½	pound salt cod, desalinated (page 235)
	Coarse sea salt
	Juice of 1 lemon
4	sweet potatoes, scrubbed and sliced paper-thin with a mandoline

In a large sauté pan, heat ½ cup of the olive oil over medium-low heat and add the garlic and peppers. When the garlic starts to bubble on the surface, add the salt cod and gently cook for 5–7 minutes. Using two forks, still in the pan, flake the cod apart into small pieces. Once the cod is cooked through, it should be tender and have a delicate, salty flavor. Discard the peppers and any pin bones. Drain the cod and garlic through a fine-mesh sieve; set the olive oil aside.

Place the cod and garlic in a mortar and pestle and grind into a paste. As you work the pestle, slowly drizzle the reserved cooking oil into the cod until it's completely incorporated. Season with salt and lemon juice and refrigerate.

Soak the sweet potato slices in ice water for an hour before frying. Drain and pat dry.

Heat the remaining 2 cups olive oil in a large heavy-bottomed pot until it registers 340° on a candy thermometer. Fry the chips in batches until golden and crispy. With a slotted spoon, remove the chips to a plate lined with paper towels. Salt and serve with the whipped salt cod.

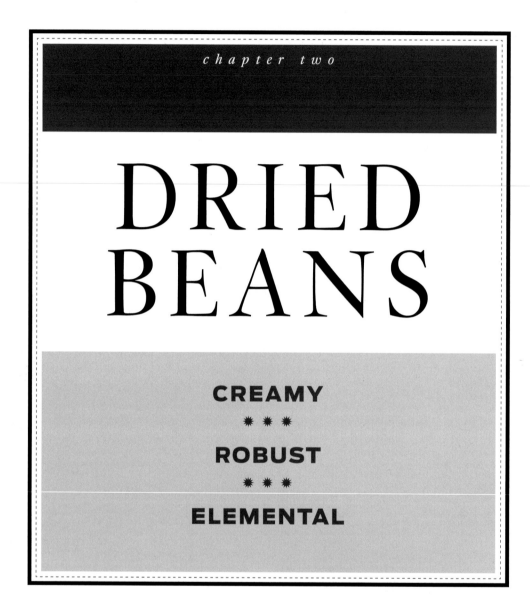

chapter two

DRIED BEANS

CREAMY

✳ ✳ ✳

ROBUST

✳ ✳ ✳

ELEMENTAL

I DISTINCTLY REMEMBER MY FIRST EXPERIENCE with dried beans. It was the end of August in Vermont and I was seven or eight years old. My mother and grandmother were harvesting pole beans—kidney beans, pinto beans, black-eyed peas—from our huge family garden, laying the whole plants they'd just pulled from the ground across the rafters of the garden shed to dry. To get out of working, I hid beneath an old pink-

"I think of beans as little nutritional bullets: They're so low in fat and so high in protein and fiber. They've become key to my cooking."

flowered quilt that we used to protect crops from frost. My grandmother kept coming into the shed, calling my name, then climbing up the stepladder and hanging the beans, completely unaware that I was crouching right below her. I don't think I'll ever forget the comforting sound of the wind rattling the drying bean shells overhead as I avoided the arduous task of picking them.

I did not fall in love with beans that summer, but over the years, as I've embraced Spanish cuisine, beans have become preeminent in my cooking. Few things are as comforting and as versatile. Beans move easily from the star of the show to a best supporting actor role. In the health war against bad things, beans are a great supply of ammunition, with minerals like magnesium for muscle contraction and relaxation, potassium, iron, phosphorous, plus some B vitamins. On a USDA list, some beans have more calcium than milk.

I think of beans as little nutritional bullets: They're so low in fat and so high in protein and fiber. Why does fiber matter? I see fiber in our bodies like the raft of

egg whites that clarifies a stock: Impurities stick to the whites, leaving behind a flavorful, nutrient-rich broth. Some types of fiber in our digestive system works like that egg raft to help move the evil stuff out so we limit the time that disease-causing bacteria thrives. Really starchy food, refined sugars, and overly processed grains (such as those in commercial white bread) move more slowly through the digestive tract than high fiber foods. Harmful bacteria in the intestine feed on the byproducts of digestion, so the more you keep that sludge in your system, the longer these pathogens can grow. Bravo fiber!

Beans are relatively easy to grow and store, and surprisingly easy to prepare. As you discover beans, you come to understand the dals of India, the cannellini of Italy, and of course the magnificent *alubias* of Spain. I love the fresh beans from artisanal growers that you find at farmers markets: not just because they are astonishingly beautiful and not just because they were raised properly, but because you know they'll cook faster and taste fresher—they haven't sat for months (or years) on some grocery shelf. The beauty of

dried beans is they retain their nutrients in ther dried state.

In about the time it takes to open a can of beans, you can rinse a bag of dried beans and start them soaking (see A Note on Soaking Beans [right]). As you cook your own dried beans, you'll develop an aversion to for the tinniness and mushiness of canned beans.

A NOTE ON...SOAKING BEANS

I come down on the side of soaking beans, even if you're using a pressure cooker. Along with fiber and protein, a bean has starch, it is porous and will absorb liquid. Unsoaked beans are often chalky when cooked. The violent action of the pressure cooker beats up the cell walls of the beans. Soaking lets the bean starch absorb water so they'll be more creamy, have a better texture, and become easier to digest.

A NOTE ON...SALTING BEANS

With most bean dishes, I like to cook them in two stages, first with aromatic vegetables and herbs and no salt. Then I pick out the large vegetables and add my additional seasonings. The jury is still out as to whether cooking beans in salted water hardens the beans. I'm not necessarily convinced. When you cook with things like bacon or ham, you are in effect, salting the beans. That said, I think it's difficult to control the seasoning in the first stage of cooking. So I prefer to wait until the second stage, when the starch in the beans has fully expanded and the beans have absorbed the cooking liquid. Then you can actually taste the cooked beans and decide if they need more seasoning.

Making Dried Beans in a Pressure Cooker

EVERYWHERE I'VE TRAVELED over the years, I've always been amazed that, the world over, no kitchen is complete without a pressure cooker. Except in the United States. My mom always used a pressure cooker to make beans—and on more than one occasion I recall the top exploding and the steam valve shooting straight up and lodging in the ceiling. Fortunately, technology has improved greatly and modern pressure cookers are far safer than those of my childhood. Nowadays, pressure cookers even have steam release valves.

Cooking in a hermetically sealed environment thoroughly saturates dried beans with the flavor of all the delicious aromatics you add. Beans that can take hours to cook will be lush and creamy in a fraction of the time.

Pressure cooking is so simple: place the ingredients and cooking liquids into the pot, cover, and lock the lid in place. Increase the heat to high until the pressure cooker begins to whistle, then lower to a simmer and cook according to the recipe. Don't be scared to check on the dish during the cooking time. Just be sure to release the steam before you open the lid. But don't stress: the safety valve will prevent you from opening the pot too soon. If, for some reason, you need to open it quickly because you suspect your food might need more liquid, run the entire pot under cold water for a minute or two and the lid should safely pop right off.

Most modern pressure cookers have two pressure settings, High and Low. I prefer to cook on Low to give the ingredients more time to get to know one another. However, if you're really under a lot of pressure(!) to get dinner out quickly, switch to the High setting, which can cut your cooking time in half.

Verdina Bean Salad

NOTHING IS MORE SPANISH than good cured ham. This dish brings ham, artichokes, and beans together in a delicate and delicious salad. In Asturias in northern Spain, they fairly worship beans. Arguably the most famous Spanish bean dish is the Fabada Asturiana with its broad, kidney-shaped white beans, pork belly, and sausage. One of my favorite beans is a little more obscure, the tiny green verdina bean from Asturias. It's like a smaller flageolet (which can be substituted), just a bit creamier in texture.
Serves 4–6

FOR THE BEANS

2	cups verdina beans, soaked overnight and drained
1	onion, quartered
1	carrot, halved
1	smoked ham hock
1	handful your favorite herbs

Combine all the ingredients in a pressure cooker and add cold water to come an inch above the beans. Fit the pressure cooker with the lid and raise the temperature to high until it starts to whistle. Reduce to the lowest setting and cook until the beans are tender, about 30 minutes. Drain the beans and discard the ham hock, onion, carrot, and herbs. Alternately, add all the ingredients to a large heavy-bottomed pot. Bring to a boil and then reduce to a simmer and cook, covered, for 1½ to 2 hours, then drain the beans.

FOR THE SALAD

4	artichokes preserved in olive oil (page 18)
	Salt
	Freshly ground black pepper
1	healthy handful wild arugula
¼	cup My Favorite Vinaigrette (page 21)
	As many slices of Ibérico ham as you can afford

In a large serving bowl, combine the drained beans and artichokes and season with salt and pepper. Gently fold in the arugula. Add the vinaigrette, gently toss, and finish with a scattering of Ibérico ham.

Tolosa Bean Soup

THE LITTLE TOWN OF TOLOSA in the Basque region of Spain is famous for its beans. So famous, in fact, that the Brotherhood of the Bean, *Cofradía de las Alubias*, puts on a festival and cooking competition every November to celebrate their little purple-black wonders. A few years ago I was in Basque Country with my friend Wylie Dufresne, chef and owner of the celebrated restaurant WD-50 in New York. We found our way to the bean festival in Tolosa. It was a cold, rainy November evening. In a huge open shed, nearly a hundred Basque cooks were stirring huge earthenware pots of bean soup and grilling massive steaks over dried grapevines.

There is an orthodoxy that surrounds the preparation of *alubias de Tolosa*, the preferred method being in large earthenware pots with just water and onion, perhaps a bay leaf or two. Surprise, surprise, I like to deviate a little from tradition and make the beans slightly more dynamic. But still, this soup reminds me of the smells of that rainy evening in Tolosa.

Serves 4–6

- 2 **tablespoons fruity olive oil, plus plenty more for serving**
- 2 ***morcillas* (Spanish blood sausages), cut into 1-inch slices**
- 1 **large dried chorizo, cut into 2-inch chunks**
- 1 **onion, quartered**
- 1 **carrot, cut into large chunks**
- 2 **cloves garlic, sliced**
  Sherry vinegar
- 2 **cups dried Tolosa beans, soaked overnight and drained**
- 2 **bay leaves**
- 1 **green cabbage, roughly chopped**
  Salt
  Freshly ground black pepper

Heat the 2 tablespoons olive oil in a pressure cooker over medium-high heat and carefully brown the *morcillas* on all sides, then remove to a plate. Add the chorizo and quickly brown as well to release some of its spicy oil, then remove to another plate. Add the onion, carrot, and garlic to the pot and quickly sauté them, then deglaze with a drizzle of sherry vinegar. Add the beans and bay leaves and cover with about 6 cups of cold water.

Fit the pressure cooker with the lid and raise the temperature to high until it starts to whistle. Reduce to the lowest setting and cook for 25 minutes. Carefully remove the lid and add the chorizo. Cover again and cook for another 10 minutes, or until the beans are cooked through. Alternately, put all the ingredients in a large heavy-bottomed pot, bring to a boil, and immediately reduce to a simmer. Cook, covered, until the beans are tender and creamy, about 2 hours.

Once the beans are tender but still have their skins on (they should be a glossy, deep purple-black color), add the *morcillas* and cabbage. Simmer, uncovered, until the cabbage is nicely wilted. This shouldn't take more than 10 minutes. Adjust the seasoning with salt and pepper. The consistency should be a just little soupy. Discard the bay leaves. Ladle the beans into warm bowls and top with a generous splash of olive oil.

A NOTE ON...BLACK BEANS

If you can't get your hands on the elusive Tolosa beans, small black turtle beans are a good substitute. Traditionally the beans aren't even soaked, they're just simmered for hours. I prefer the texture that soaking delivers. I'm hoping the Brotherhood of the Bean won't come after me for that suggestion!

Cazuela of Mongetes and Cockles

IN CATALUNYA, it's very common to find a bit of pork mixed in with seafood in a distinct "surf 'n' turf" combo called *mar i muntanya* ("sea and mountain"). A little bacon is thrown into the pressure cooker with beans to add a depth of flavor that goes so well with shellfish. *Mongetes* are white beans similar to cannellinis. If you can't find them, other small white beans will work well. For white wine, I like txakoli, a bright, effervescent Basque wine that brings out the cockels' natural sweetness. If you can't find cockles, substitute small clams.

Serves 4

FOR THE BEANS

- 2   cups dried *mongetes*, soaked overnight and drained
- 1   nice chunk slab bacon, about ¼ pound
- 1   whole large carrot, halved
- 1   onion, quartered
- 1   head garlic, cut in half horizontally
- 2   *guindilla* peppers, or 2 pieces ancho chile
- 1   fresh bay leaf
- 2   cups Caldo del Día (page 128) or chicken stock

Combine all the ingredients in the pressure cooker and bring to a boil. Reduce to the lowest setting and cook until the beans are tender; this will take 25 to 30 minutes. Remove from the heat and let the beans cool in the cooking liquid. Drain the beans, reserving the cooking liquid and discarding the aromatics. Alternately, cook all the ingredients in a large, heavy-bottomed pot, covered, for about 1½ hours, or until the beans are tender. Discard the bay leaf.

FOR THE FINAL DISH

- 2   tablespoons olive oil, preferably Arbequina, plus more for drizzling
- 1   large shallot, finely minced
- 2   cloves garlic, thinly sliced
- 4   sprigs fresh thyme
- 1   pound artichokes, prepared as for Crispy Fried Artichokes (page 27), in lemon juice
- 1   cup white wine
     Salt
     Freshly ground black pepper
- 2   dozen cockles, soaked in cold water for 30 minutes to purge sand
- 1   small handful coarsely chopped fresh parsley

Heat the 2 tablespoons olive oil in a large heavy-bottomed pot over medium-low heat and add the shallots, garlic, and thyme. Sweat until translucent, about 3 minutes, then add the artichokes and white wine. Cook until the artichokes start to get tender, about 8 minutes.

Add 2 cups cooked *mongetes* to the pot and season to taste with salt and pepper. Continue cooking, uncovered, for a few more minutes so that all the flavors come together.

Add the cockles and a bit of the cooking liquid from the beans (if needed). Cover to steam until the cockles open, about 4 minutes. Remove the pot from the heat. Cockles that don't open might need some help from a butter knife. Just make sure they smell sweet when opened, otherwise discard them.

Discard the thyme sprigs. Transfer the cockless, artichokes, and beans to a large serving bowl. Finish with a generous drizzle of good extra-virgin olive oil and a scattering of parsley.

Truffled Lentils and Eggs

LENTILS ARE INCREDIBLY VERSATILE BEANS. They can be puréed, stewed, or formed into cakes and fried. And, unlike other dried beans, they need no soaking and cook quickly. Like so many other things I love to cook, I fell for lentils in Spain. It all started with a simple lentil soup in Burgos where I was spending my senior year of high school. That soup had chunks of ham and a healthy dose of vinegar. Now I always add a splash of good-quality vinegar to my lentils. This dish is an updated version of that lentil soup I remember so well. To really control the cooking, I prepare the beans in two stages, first with simple aromatics, then with another set of ingredients.

A note on decadence: everyone knows how expensive truffles are, and pretty much anyone who's been to Spain has fallen for Ibérico ham (page 43). The pungent aroma of truffles can be overbearing if overused, but fresh or even preserved truffles used with a judicious hand, can add an incomparable earthiness to many dishes.

Serves 4

FOR THE LENTILS

- 2 cups dried Pardina lentils or French green lentils
- 1 carrot, halved
- 1 rib celery, halved
- 2 cloves garlic, peeled
- 1 nice large chunk slab bacon, about ¼ pound
- 2 cups Caldo del Día (page 128) or chicken stock
- 2 sprigs fresh thyme
- 2 fresh bay leaves

Give the lentils a quick rinse and make sure there are no little pebbles. (When I was working in a restaurant in San Sebastián, I bit down on a stone in some lentils from family meal and shattered a molar, so I know the importance of checking).

Combine the rinsed lentils with the rest of the ingredients in a large heavy-bottomed pot and bring to a simmer. Cook at medium-low heat, uncovered, until the lentils are very tender, about 45 minutes. Drain the lentils (reserving some liquid) and discard the aromatics. Makes 4 cups.

I like my lentils creamy and cooked through; but if you prefer lentils that retain the shape of the bean, bring them to a rolling boil first in water and cook for 1 minute, then strain, refill the pot with water, boil 1 minute and drain again. Now they can be cooked. This helps to set the beans' shape and keep their skins from bursting.

FOR THE FINAL DISH

- 1 teaspoon olive oil
- ¼ cup cubed slab bacon
- 1 shallot, finely minced
- 1 clove garlic, finely minced
- 1 teaspoon sherry vinegar
  Salt
  Freshly ground black pepper
- ¼ cup finely grated Idiazábal or Manchego cheese
- 4 eggs poached in olive oil (page 22)
- 1 tablespoon truffle paste, or a fresh black truffle
- 1 teaspoon unsalted butter
- 4 thin slices Ibérico ham

Heat the olive oil in a saucepan over medium-high heat and add the bacon, browning evenly. Once the bacon is nicely browned, add the shallots and garlic and sauté briefly until translucent. Then add the vinegar to deglaze all the bits of bacon goodness stuck to the pan.

Reduce the heat to medium low, add the cooked lentils, and season conservatively with salt and pepper. With a rubber spatula, gently fold in the cheese until completely melted. The lentils should have a creamy texture: not too dry but not soupy either. Add some lentil cooking liquid as necessary to adjust the texture.

Meanwhile, poach the eggs in olive oil and keep warm. If you're using truffle paste, fold it into the lentils now; otherwise, for fresh truffles, wait and shave as much as you can afford directly over the finished dish.

Remove the pot from the heat and fold in the butter. Divide the lentils among 4 bowls, top with a poached egg a fold of Ibérico ham.

A NOTE ON... IBÉRICO HAM

Ibérico ham is one of the world's greatest delicacies and justifiably costly. The black-footed Ibérico pig has rooted around in the shady acorn groves, or *dehesa*, since the time of the Phoenicians. Ibérico ham is D.O., a certified product in Spain. Because of the pigs' natural acorn diet, these 18- to 36-month-old hams have a unique nutty flavor and sit proudly at the top of the kingdom of ham. They're priced accordingly. Some can fetch up to $300 a pound. Just as there are different grades of olive oil, there are different grades of Ibérico ham, the most prized being *bellota* ("acorn") ham, from pigs with an all-natural diet of acorns, apples, and anything they can forage in the wild.

Nutritionally, however, you can almost justify the cost. Not only does the Spanish government require that these pigs be raised naturally, they are hormone- and antibiotic-free and require a significant amount of acreage to roam. Their *dehesa* diet leads to a high level of oleic acid (a monounsaturated fat) in the ham, which may help lower cholesterol levels.

Flageolets with Autumn Greens and Fresh Bacon

I LOVE FLAGEOLETS, the immature kidney beans that the French have been cultivating since the 1800s. They come in a variety of colors; I prefer the green ones, which are slightly firmer than a kidney bean, because they have a wonderful flavor and are really elegant in salads and stews. A little fresh bacon goes a long way toward making these beans remarkable. Curing it for a few hours in salt and sugar helps the bacon retain its flavor in the cooking process. For the greens, I like to use kale and mustard greens, but this dish is wonderful with any hearty green like dandelion greens or even cabbage. The pressure cooker helps to cook the beans easily and imparts all the wonderful porky-ness of the bacon.

Serves 6

¼	**pound fresh bacon**
2	**cups kosher salt mixed with 2 cups sugar**
2	**cups dried flageolet beans, soaked overnight and drained**
1	**carrot, halved**
1	**onion, quartered**
1	**whole head garlic, halved widthwise**
¼	**cup dried apricots, roughly chopped**
2	**bay leaves**
1	**dried ancho chile**
	About 2 tablespoons fino sherry vinegar
	Salt
	Freshly ground black pepper
	A few leaves Tuscan kale
	A few leaves black kale
	A few leaves mustard greens
	Good olive oil for drizzling

Pack the fresh bacon in the salt and sugar mixture, cover, and refrigerate for up to 4 hours. Rinse and pat dry, then cut into ½-inch cubes.

Combine the bacon, beans, carrot, onion, garlic, apricots, bay leaves, and chile in a pressure cooker and add cold water to come an inch above the beans. Fit the pressure cooker with the lid and raise the temperature to high until it starts to whistle. Reduce to the lowest setting and cook until the beans are creamy and cooked through, roughly 25 minutes. Remove the lid and adjust the seasoning with vinegar, salt, and pepper. Alternately, bring the ingredients to a boil in a large, heavy-bottomed pot and immediately reduce the heat to a simmer. Cook, covered, until the beans are thoroughly cooked through and creamy, roughly 1¾ hours.

Remove the large aromatic vegetables, garlic, chile, and bay leaves from the pot and discard. They've done their flavoring job. Coarsely chop the greens or tear with your hands, then fold them into the beans. Simmer for another 5 minutes, or until the greens are tender.

Serve with warm crusty bread and a healthy dose of olive oil.

chapter three

ALMONDS

CRUNCHY

✳ ✳ ✳

VERSATILE

✳ ✳ ✳

NUTRITIOUS

I WAS 30 AND COOKING AT MUGARITZ, THE GREAT restaurant in the Spanish Basque Country before I ever took almonds seriously. The chef, Andoni Luis Aduriz, greatly affected the way I think about food. Andoni's cooking is very Basque in the sense that he tries to evoke his immediate surroundings in his food. Foraging was crucial to his cuisine. Every morning, cooks from Mugaritz would go out into the woods and fields that surrounded the restaurant and hunt mushrooms, wild carrots and leeks, wild herbs, field strawberries, and other edible plants. One morning Andoni took me out to collect green almonds. I'd eaten almonds all my life, but it never occurred to me to visualize the way they grew. We picked large, fuzzy pods from the delicate branches of graceful trees. Andoni cracked a pod to show me the soft seed of the almond inside, just like the seed of plums and other stone fruit cousins.

It was a revelation: I had never experienced the almond raw, its refined shape, its distinctive flavor. We're so used to the processed version of things, it was wonderful to discover an almond in its natural state. I tasted one and instead of the toasted saltiness of the almonds I knew, it was sweet and soft and completely unlike any almond I'd ever met.

We gathered several bucketfuls of green almonds, took them back to the kitchen, and removed the delicate white almonds from their pods one by one. They were served with fresh, line-caught squid, about 2 or 3 inches long. When I touched the squid their skin would radiate different colors, changing from green to blue. We cleaned them still alive, then seared them on a hot grill with a bit of cold-pressed almond oil and served them with a little salad of raw almonds and some wild herbs. For me, caramelized squid has forever the sweet nutty taste I associate with almonds.

Thus began my love affair with almonds. A year later, living in Barcelona, I discovered the dream almond shop. At Casa Gispert,

"Almonds can be a paste, a thickener, a flour. They can be the star of the show, even a dessert. In this book, the almond's a superhero."

they have been roasting almonds and hazelnuts in the same wood-fired oven in the back of the shop since 1851. Little about the place has changed since. It's still a jumble of burlap bags full of nuts, baskets of dried fruit, the air rich with the aromas of roasting nuts and coffee. You can buy almonds and other nuts by the paper-bagful, sometimes still warm from the oven.

Most American almonds come from California, where they were planted in monastaries in the 18th century by Spanish Franciscan monks. In other words, they're Spanish! However most of the almonds we find in stores, still in their brown papery skins, sit around too long on grocery shelves where they lose freshness. Older almonds in the skin are just not as flavorful as the blanched almonds I call for in these recipes.

Almonds are not only a great protein food, but also a high-fat food. The great news, however, is that this high-fat food is *good* for you. We need fat at the cellular level for the structure of those cells. It's the *kind* of fat (and amount) that matters.

Almonds are high in monounsaturated fats, which are understood to be *healthier* fats, as they work to help lower bad cholesterol and help raise good cholesterol when they replace solid fats. Almonds also have more calcium and more fat-soluble vitamin E, a powerful antioxidant, than the same amount of any other nut. In order to absorb fat-soluble vitamins, the body needs fat; the fat in almonds is an efficient vehicle for vitamin absorption.

I think of antioxidants like vitamin E as cleansing agents that help my body do away with toxic byproducts and free up my immune system to do its job. There is growing consensus in the scientific community that vitamin E, as a part of our healthy eating pattern, can help delay or prevent the onset of chronic illnesses linked to environmentally produced toxins. Consider how wonderfully versatile almonds are as an ingredient—they can be a snack, be ground into flour, or become a thickener or a paste for other flavors. They can be the star of the show, and even a dessert. In this book the almond is not just a Hero, it's a *superhero*.

Ajo Blanco with Sardine Confit

AJO BLANCO LITERALLY MEANS "white garlic," but this soup is not as garlicky as it sounds. *Ajo blanco* is a classic chilled almond soup made with bread that's soaked overnight in sherry vinegar, and garlic. I add shallots and sherry, too, for their pleasing sweetness. Traditionally, *ajo blanco* is served as a chilled soup in Southern Spain, but I like to use it as a component in other dishes as well.

   This recipe combines the creamy *ajo blanco* with the silky texture of lightly cooked sardines. While this soup is deceptively simple, it is, however, very important to macerate the ingredients for at least a few hours in the refrigerator, and preferably overnight. I prefer Arbequina olive oil here for its low residual bitterness—especially since almonds can be a touch bitter, too. Almonds are so rich in protein; coupled with sardines, with their high concentrations of omega-3s, they make *ajo blanco* a Heroic dish.

Serves 4

FOR THE AJO BLANCO
- 1 cup cubed sourdough country bread, crusts removed
- 10 ounces blanched almonds
- 2 shallots, finely diced
- 4 cloves garlic, finely diced
- ¼ cup amontillado sherry, alcohol cooked off
- ¼ cup sherry vinegar
- 1 cup Arbequina or other good extra-virgin olive oil
  Salt
  Freshly ground black pepper

FOR THE SARDINE CONFIT

1	cup Smoked Olive Oil (TECHNIQUE, page 22)
4	sardines, fresh as possible, scaled, gutted, and filleted
	Salt
	Freshly ground black pepper
½	cup seedless grapes
¼	cup toasted Marcona almonds, roughly chopped
	Dried Aleppo pepper

To make the *ajo blanco,* combine the bread, blanched almonds, shallots, garlic, sherry, and sherry vinegar with 3½ cups water. Cover and refrigerate overnight. The next day, place in a Vitamix blender or a food processor and process on high until creamy. Lower the speed and drizzle in the olive oil until fully incorporated. Adjust the seasoning with salt and pepper. Set aside to chill in the refrigerator.

Meanwhile, for the sardine confit, heat the smoked olive oil in a small pan until it registers 130° on a candy thermometer. Season the sardine fillets with salt and pepper and cook gently for 3–4 minutes, until opaque and cooked through.

Evenly distribute the *ajo blanco* among 4 bowls. Make a small nest in the center of each bowl with the grapes and Marcona almonds. Place one sardine fillet on each nest and garnish with a pinch of Aleppo pepper.

Pork and Almond Stew

I LOVE TO USE ALMONDS in a classic paste called *picada* to thicken sauces and stews. *Picada* is said to date to the Roman occupation of Spain in the 2nd century BC; some believe the Arabs brought the idea of an almond paste even earlier. The saffron and dried apricots give the stew a beautiful, golden color. I like to prepare it a day ahead, let it sit overnight, then gently reheat it.
Serves 6–8

FOR THE PICADA

	Small pinch saffron, lightly toasted in a dry pan
	Splash dry sherry (fino or manzanilla)
¼	cup olive oil
2	cloves garlic, peeled
1	cup Marcona almonds, preferably unsalted and raw
1	cup pine nuts
1	cup cubed day-old bread
	Splash sherry vinegar
3	*ñora* peppers, soaked and cleaned
	Small handful coarsely chopped fresh parsley
	Salt
	Freshly ground black pepper

FOR THE STEW

3	tablespoons olive oil
3	pounds boneless pork shoulder, cut into 2-inch pieces
	Salt
	Freshly ground black pepper
1	cup whole shitake mushrooms, stems trimmed
1½	cups white wine
½	cup dried apricots
3	cups Caldo del Día (page 128) or chicken stock
1	small bunch mustard greens, stems removed
	Sherry vinegar

For the *picada*, combine the saffron and a splash of sherry in a small bowl and allow to steep while you're preparing the other ingredients.

Heat the olive oil over medium-high heat in a large skillet and shallow-fry the garlic cloves until golden brown, about 3 minutes. Take care not to burn them. Carefully remove the garlic with a slotted spoon and set aside. Repeat the process with the Marcona almonds. (If you can only find roasted almonds, skip this step.) Repeat with the pine nuts, then the cubed bread.

In a large mortar and pestle, combine the garlic, almonds, pine nuts, and bread, a splash of sherry vinegar, and 2 tablespoons of the olive oil from the skillet. Work all the ingredients into a rough paste. There will still be small chunks of almond and bread, but this is a rustic preparation that's not meant to be perfectly smooth.

Add the sherry/saffron mixture, the cleaned *ñora* peppers, and the parsley to the mortar and fully incorporate. If the *picada* is too dry and lumpy, add a bit more olive oil until you achieve the consistency of a wet paste. Remember this will be used to thicken and flavor your stew. Season with salt and pepper. (If you don't have a mortar and pestle, use a food processor; just be sure to slowly pulse the ingredients so you do not overprocess them.) Makes about 3 cups.

For the stew, preheat the oven to 325°. Heat the olive oil in a large, heavy-bottomed pot over medium-high heat. Season the pork with salt and pepper and brown on all sides. Remove the pork from the pot and set aside.

Add the shitake mushrooms to the pot, season with salt and pepper, and sauté until they start to take on color. Deglaze the pan with the white wine, scraping up any brown bits, until the alcohol has evaporated and the liquid has reduced by a third. Add the apricots and caldo, then whisk in 1 cup of the *picada* to thicken the sauce. Return the browned pork to the pot, cover tightly with aluminum foil, and braise in the oven until the pork is tender, about 2 hours.

Just before serving, heat the stew on the stove over medium heat and stir in the mustard greens. Cook until they are just wilted but still vibrantly green, about 3 minutes. Taste and adjust the seasoning with salt, pepper, and sherry vinegar.

From our Barcelona room with this view of Plaça Catalunya and its tiny kitchen, we cooked and photographed the food for the first chapters of *Hero Food*.

Grilled Asparagus and Leeks with Romesco Sauce

IN CATALUNYA, spring is welcomed with a *calçotada,* a festival where bushels and bushels of *calçots,* a sort-of wild leek, are grilled over hot coals and eaten outdoors with Romesco or *Salbitxada* (page 56). When I was growing up in Vermont, ramps—a wild, edible plant in the garlic family—and asparagus were similar harbingers of spring. This recipe brings together these two memories in one dish. Romesco (opposite) is a very versatile sauce that is delicious with grilled meats, eggs, and roasted and steamed vegetables.

Serves 4–6 as an appetizer

2   bunches baby leeks, about 10
    Zest of 1 lemon
1   clove garlic, finely grated
2   tablespoons olive oil
1   tablespoon sherry vinegar
    Salt
    Freshly ground black pepper
1   bunch asparagus
    Romesco Sauce (TECHNIQUE, opposite)

Wash the leek greens under cold running water to remove any residual sand. Set aside to dry. In a large mixing bowl, combine the lemon zest, garlic, olive oil, vinegar, and salt and pepper. Toss with the asparagus and leeks to coat evenly.

On a hot grill, grill the leeks until charred and completely black on the outside. On a cooler part of the grill, grill the asparagus until tender. Carefully peel away the charred exterior of the leeks. Serve the tender leek hearts and grilled asparagus with the Romesco Sauce.

Making Romesco Sauce

Makes about 2 cups

3	red bell peppers
2	tomatoes
1	onion, quartered, skin on
1	head garlic
1	cup cubed bread
¼	cup blanched Marcona almonds
2	dried *ñora* peppers
¼	cup olive oil
	Splash sherry vinegar
	Pimentón
	Salt
	Freshly ground black pepper

IDEALLY, THE VEGETABLES for Romesco are cooked over a hot grill and charred until their skins are black. If you're grilling the vegetables, grill over high heat until thoroughly blackened. Alternatively, roast the vegetables in a 450° oven for 45 minutes, until very dark.

Remove the vegetables from the heat and wrap in newspaper (preferably *El País*) to cool. Once the vegetables have cooled, carefully peel away and discard the charred skins.

In a deep skillet over medium heat, toast the bread and almonds until nicely browned. Transfer to a food processor or mortar and pestle, add the roasted vegetables and dried peppers, and work into a paste. Add the olive oil and a splash of sherry vinegar and adjust seasoning with pimentón, salt, and pepper.

Salbitxada

PRONOUNCED "SAHL-BEE-CHA-DAH", *salbitxada* is the most traditional sauce, served with grilled spring vegetables in Spain. I love the depth of flavor the hazelnuts and smoky pimentón give the sauce. In addition to accompanying grilled vegetables, *salbitxada* is wonderful with grilled meats; thinned out with chicken stock, it makes a succulent base for braised chicken. Or add a bit of water, vinegar, and olive oil and you have a complex, delicious vinaigrette for crispy lettuce.

Makes about ¾ cup

1	head garlic, unpeeled
¼	cup dry sherry (fino or manzanilla)
¼	cup olive oil
¼	cup hazelnuts
¼	cup Marcona almonds
1	tomato, grated on a cheese grater, skin discarded (TECHNIQUE, page 64)
2	*guindilla* peppers, or 2 pieces ancho chiles, finely ground in a spice mill
	Handful fresh parsley, coarsely chopped
2	teaspoons sherry vinegar
1	teaspoon pimentón
	Salt
	Freshly ground black pepper

Preheat the oven to 350°. Place the garlic head in a small pan and roast for 30 minutes, until soft. When cool enough to handle, remove the soft pulp from the skins. Reduce the sherry in a small saucepan over medium heat until you have about 2 tablespoons.

Heat the olive oil in a small skillet over medium heat. Add the hazelnuts and almonds and toast, stirring, until golden brown.

In a mortar and pestle or a food processor, combine the garlic pulp, reduced sherry, toasted nuts, tomato, dried peppers, parsley, sherry vinegar, and pimentón. Work together all the ingredients until fully incorporated. Drizzle in the olive oil from the toasted nuts. Adjust seasoning with salt and pepper.

10 THINGS TO DO WITH ALMONDS

1. Toast a handful of blanched almonds in a pan with olive oil (or almond oil if you have it), then coarsely chop and toss into a salad.

2. Sauté slivered almonds with garlic and dandelion greens and a drizzle of lemon juice.

3. Fry Marcona almonds in olive oil and then season with sea salt, ground coriander, and cayenne for a healthful snack.

4. Mix coarsely chopped salted Marcona almonds with fresh cream, spring strawberries, and mint for a quick sweet and salty dessert.

5. Sprinkle a handful of whole Largueta almonds over sliced roasted beets.

6. Grind equal parts bread crumbs and blanched almonds with fresh herbs to crust a rack of lamb.

7. Toast a handful of blanched almonds in a dry pan, then finely chop and mix with almond oil and sherry vinegar to make a nutty vinaigrette.

8. Soak 1 cup of blanched almonds in water overnight, then blend with banana, ginger, and kale for a healthy smoothie.

9. Add a handful of almonds to a slow-cooked stew for a delicious unexpected and surprise.

10. Make almond ice cream by infusing the cream base with toasted blanched almonds pulsed in a food processor, ½ cup ground almonds for each cup of liquid. Strain the cream and proceed with your ice cream maker's directions.

A branch of Marcona almonds and their green fuzzy pods shows clearly how almonds are pits and related to stone fruit.

Almond Sablé

I FIRST MADE THIS ALMOND PASTRY working at Abac restaurant in Barcelona. I've never been in a restaurant where almonds are so generously used—it seemed like every other dish had almonds in it. This pastry is really versatile: it can be the shell of a tart filled with some fresh berries, or cut into circles to make cookies, or baked on a cookie sheet and crumbled over ice cream. Rather than buying almond flour, I prefer to begin with fresh Marcona almonds and grind them myself in the food processor. The resulting flour has a richer, more complex flavor.

Makes one 10–12-inch tart shell or 10 small cookies

- 1 cup roasted Marcona almonds, or ¾ cup almond flour
- 1 cup (2 sticks) chilled unsalted butter, cut into cubes
- ¾ cup powdered sugar
- 2 eggs, beaten
- 2¼ cups all-purpose flour, sifted

In a food processor, grind the almonds to a fine powder. Combine the ground almonds (or almond flour), butter, and sugar in a standing mixer fitted with a paddle. Cream on medium-low speed until thoroughly incorporated, about 3 minutes. With the mixer running, slowly add the eggs to incorporate. Add the flour, a little bit at a time, stopping the mixer periodically to scrape down the bowl.

Shape the dough into a ball and place between 2 pieces of parchment paper or plastic wrap. Refrigerate for at least 1 hour.

Preheat the oven to 350°. Roll the dough on a lightly floured surface and cut out shapes for cookies, or make a tart shell. Bake until golden, about 15 minutes.

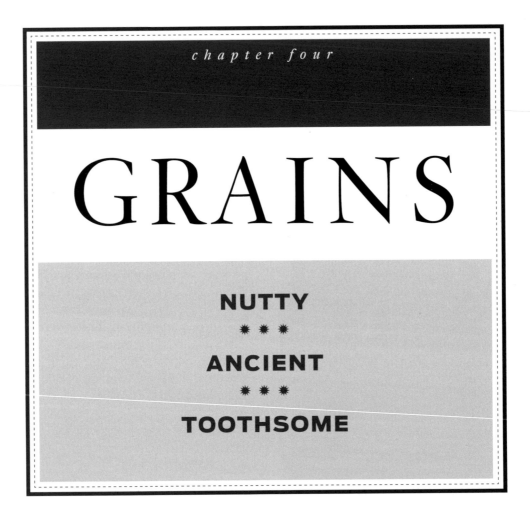

chapter four

GRAINS

NUTTY

✳ ✳ ✳

ANCIENT

✳ ✳ ✳

TOOTHSOME

MY FATHER HAS BAKED BREAD ever since I was an infant. His early hippie-dippie attempts were dry and amorphous and only resembled bread until the moment the loaf was introduced to the knife, then quickly became a pile of crumbs. Over the years his efforts improved and now, some 30 years later, he is a very accomplished baker and a true advocate of whole grains. I baked a lot of bread early in my career, but since I've

"Why not take a supplement instead of worrying so much about whole grains? I believe in eating the right foods, not pills from a bottle."

become more interested in cooking with grains, I've decided to leave the baking to the masters!

There are so many wonderful grains to cook with, from the ancient spelt, a nutritious pre-hybrid variety of wheat, to farro (which is often confused with spelt, but is actually a very old grain called emmer wheat), to wheat berries, the true whole wheat grain, as well all the hand-harvested varietals of rice with their bran and germ intact. Much as with dried beans, the success or failure of a grain-based dish depends mostly upon the character of the flavors you choose to cook into them.

Here's something you should know about me: I hate hot cereal. Cream of Wheat? Oatmeal? Porridge for breakfast? Gag. Strange, right? I only have two food phobias and hot cereal is one of them. (The other is artificial watermelon flavor, like Hubba Bubba gum or Jolly Rancher candy, but that's another story.) Surely something in my childhood didn't go just right—most likely all those gloppy hot breakfasts in elementary school.

Because I dislike hot cereal so much, I completely wrote off most grains, just like that. Then, about eight years ago, I had a grain revelation. I was at Heston Blumenthal's acclaimed restaurant, The Fat Duck, in Bray outside of London. Snail Porridge was on the menu and, though I was skeptical, the name sounded enticing enough for me to order it. Snail Porridge turned out to be boiled oats cooked in a rich snail stock with delicious braised snails and Jabugo ham, all folded together with parsley butter. And not a trace of maple syrup! I was floored. Suddenly I began to consider the savory possibilities of grains.

And since that minor epiphany, I've come to love cooking with grains and have integrated them into my menus in many unexpected ways. I'd never experienced wheat berries, for example, and it was like opening up a new and interesting door. These whole grains add so much more variety and depth to the grains repertoire. Rather than thinking of whole grains as just an alternative to rice, I found I could treat them like rice, but then expect something

In addition, whole grains (like farro, whole barley, brown rice, buckwheat, bulgur, and oats) are packed with B vitamins, antioxidants like vitamin E and selenium and other important minerals. Whole grains matter because unlike refined grains that leave only part of the grain, the whole grain retains the bran and the germ. These two are the source of the majority of grain's fiber as well as much of its vitamins and minerals.

So, you might ask, why not take supplements instead of worrying so much about whole grains? Well, that's what this book is about: understanding and loving the foods that can help us by consuming the right delicious whole foods and not eating pills from a bottle. I firmly believe that joy is a crucial part of well-being. And what's more joyful than eating these good foods—foods that are good for you—with your friends and family?

quite different from their texture and flavor.

The fiber benefits of whole grains—including that they help move food through the digestive tract—are well understood.

Grating Tomatoes

IN SPAIN, A BOX GRATER is not just for cheese (the Spanish rarely use grated cheese). Instead, the box grater is for grating tomato into a fresh tomato pulp that's used in sauces and stocks, or simply spooned over toasted bread with olive oil, often for breakfast, below. Until quite recently, Spain was such a poor country that many techniques and dishes that were born of necessity have become emblematic of the cuisine (like bread soup, gazpacho, and *migas,* fried bread crumbs with an egg). In the same way, a bit of grated tomato on several pieces of toast could effectively feed a whole family.

To grate a tomato, slice it in half horizontally. With the box grater over a bowl, rub the cut side of the tomato over the coarse side of the grater until all that's left is the skin. Discard the skin and repeat. This coarse tomato pulp is the base for *sofrito,* opposite.

Making Sofrito

SOFRITO IS THE FLAVOR BASE for soups and stews, and almost always the first step in making any rice dish.
Makes 5–6 cups

2   dried *ñora* peppers, or 1 ancho chile
¼   cup olive oil
8   Spanish or Vidalia onions, finely diced
2   red bell peppers, finely diced
4   vine-ripe tomatoes, grated
     (TECHNIQUE, opposite)
4   cloves garlic, finely minced
2   tablespoons white wine vinegar
     Salt
     Freshly ground black pepper

Bring 2 cups water to a boil in a small saucepan. Remove from the heat, add the dried peppers, and soak until soft, about 10 minutes. With a small knife, cut the peppers in half and remove and discard the seeds. Carefully scrape the flesh away from the skin and discard the skins. Set aside the flesh.

In a large heavy-bottomed pot, heat the olive oil over medium-high heat. Add the onions and sweat until translucent, about 5 minutes. Add the flesh from the dried peppers, bell peppers, grated tomatoes, garlic, vinegar, and salt and pepper. Lower the heat and simmer, stirring periodically, for at least 2 hours. It takes that long to develop the sugars and bring out the sweetness of the vegetables, which is so important to the characteristic rich flavor of *sofrito*.

You can freeze leftovers in small batches to defrost and use as needed. Even for a quick rice or pasta dish, a bit of *sofrito* makes all the difference in flavor.

Risotto of Irish Oats

RISOTTO OF IRISH OATS? Well, I'm (sort of) Irish and Irish oats are (sort of) Irish. For enhanced Irishness, I like to use Irish Cheddar and good Irish butter like Kerrygold to finish the risotto. I suppose if you really wanted to be authentic, you could use Irish whiskey instead of the white wine, but that might be a bit much.

Whole oats are the whole grain, but they are simply not digestible as is. All oats must have the hard outer hull removed; this, however, does not strip away the source of their nutrients.

Once hulled, there are three ways to render the oats more pleasant to eat: With steel-cut or Irish oats, the oat is cut into smaller pieces with steel blades. Since they are the least processed of oats, and still contain the whole grain including the bran, they are the most nutritious oats. With old-fashioned or rolled oats, the oat is steamed, rolled flat into flakes and sometimes steamed again, then dried. Usually the bran is removed. Rolled oats are good for making granola or oatmeal porridge. They cook faster and aren't as chewy as Irish oats. Don't even think about using the third option, instant oats, because most of the nutrients that reside in the bran are removed in the very processing that makes them quick cooking. What remains is cooked into oat oblivion.

Serves 4

1	teaspoon olive oil
½	cup diced double-smoked bacon
1	shallot, finely diced
½	pound mixed wild mushrooms
1	teaspoon good white wine vinegar
¼	cup white wine
2	cups steel-cut Irish oats
4	cups Caldo del Día (page 128) or chicken stock, heated
½	cup finely grated Irish Cheddar cheese
2	tablespoons Irish butter
2	tablespoons coarsely chopped fresh parsley
	Salt
	Freshly ground black pepper

Warm the olive oil in a large heavy-bottomed pot over medium heat and add the bacon. Sauté until golden brown. Add the shallots and mushrooms and sauté until the shallots are translucent, about 2 minutes. Add the vinegar, cook for 30 seconds, and add the white wine. Cook until the alcohol has evaporated, about 2 minutes. The mushrooms should be moist and there should still be a little liquid in the bottom of the pot.

Toss in the oats, then a ladleful of the caldo and stir with a rubber spatula. As the oats absorb the liquid, add in a bit more just as you would to make a risotto, stirring the whole time. Stirring helps the starch in the oats come together and lends a nice creamy texture to the risotto.

Once the oats are fully cooked through, about 15 minutes, fold in the cheese and then the butter. Adjust the seasoning as needed. Serve with a fried egg, if you like, and a sprinkling of parsley. Think of this as a main course that's perfect paired with a salad.

Eggs are everywhere in Spain, even in murals like this one in an old Barcelona neighborhood.

Farro Salad with Preserved Tuna

FARRO, ALSO KNOWN AS EMMER WHEAT, is one of the oldest cultivated grains, dating all the way back to biblical times. I love its nutty flavor with our Preserved Tuna. Look for unprocessed whole grain farro with bran and germ intact. It is loaded with fiber which can help lower cholesterol levels in the blood as well as keep things moving to promote healthy digestion. Farro has a higher level of protein than most other grains. If it was good enough for Moses, it's good enough for me!

Serves 4

2	**cups farro**
1	**carrot, peeled and cut into large pieces**
1	**onion, peeled and quartered**
4	**cloves garlic, peeled**
2	***guindilla* peppers, or 2 pieces ancho chile**
1	**bay leaf**
	Kosher salt
2	**large organic eggs**
½	**cup Preserved Tuna (page 224), or good quality canned tuna in olive oil**
¼	**cup Pickled Mushrooms (page 265)**
2	**tablespoons finely minced Quick-Cured Lemons (page 18)**
	Handful arugula
	Healthy splash My Favorite Vinaigrette (page 21)
	Salt
	Freshly ground black pepper

Thoroughly rinse the farro in a large colander under running water. Transfer to a large heavy-bottomed pot and add the carrots, onions, garlic, peppers, bay leaf, and 4 cups water. Add enough kosher salt so the water tastes like sea water.

Cover, place over high heat, and bring to a boil. Reduce the heat and simmer for 20–25 minutes, until the grain is soft and cooked through. Drain the farro (discarding the aromatics) and set aside to cool.

Soft-boil the eggs in a small saucepan: Bring 3–4 cups water to a boil and add the eggs. Reduce the heat and simmer for 5–6 minutes. Run the eggs under cold water, then peel and quarter them. The yolks should be golden and creamy.

Combine the preserved tuna, mushrooms, lemons, and arugula in a large serving bowl, then add the cooled farro and dress with the vinaigrette. Season with salt and pepper and garnish the salad with the soft-cooked eggs.

Creamy Grits with Slow-Cooked Pork Loin

REMEMBER MY DISDAIN for sweet hot cereal? Well grits are the perfect antidote! They're made by grinding dried corn kernels. Their natural sweetness with the saltiness of pork loin, or even the runny yolk of a fried egg, are much more interesting to me than a bowl of Cream of Wheat. I prefer organic, stone ground grits, and never, ever use instant. Yellow corn meal is a good source of folic acid and magnesium, both of which may have anti-inflammatory benefits. Brining the meat ads more flavor than just sprinkling it with seasoning. For brining other meats, see page 297.

Serves 4

1	**2-pound boneless pork loin**

FOR THE BRINE

½	**cup salt**
½	**cup sugar**
2	**bay leaves**
1	**orange, quartered**
1	**large carrot, peeled and cut into chunks**
1	**onion, peeled and quartered**
	Freshly ground black pepper
	Salt
	Freshly ground black pepper
2	**tablespoons olive oil**
¼	**cup diced double-smoked bacon**
2	**shallots, finely minced**
1	**tablespoon sherry vinegar**
4½	**cups Caldo del Día (page 128) or chicken stock**
1½	**cups organic stone ground grits, yellow or white**
½	**cup finely grated Cheddar cheese**

Make a brine using all the ingredients at left (see TECHNIQUE, page 297). Add the pork, cover, and refrigerate overnight. Remove the pork, pat dry, and refrigerate, uncovered, for at least 1 hour.

Preheat the oven to 325°. Remove the pork loin from the refrigerator and season thoroughly with salt and pepper.

In a roasting pan, heat 1 tablespoon of the olive oil over medium-high heat and evenly brown the pork loin on all sides. Slide the pan in the oven and roast until the center of the loin registers 145° on a meat thermometer, about 20–25 minutes. Remove the pork from the oven and set aside to rest for 10 minutes.

While the pork is roasting, heat the remaining tablespoon of olive oil in a large saucepan over medium-high heat. Add the bacon and sauté until golden brown. Add the shallots and cook for another minute, until translucent. Deglaze the pan with the sherry vinegar and reduce for 2 minutes, until the shallots and bacon are nicely coated with vinegar. With a rubber spatula, remove the shallots and bacon to a plate.

Add the caldo to the saucepan and bring to a boil. Pour in the grits and reduce the heat to a simmer. Once the grits have absorbed most of the liquid, about 15 minutes, fold the bacon and shallot mixture back in and adjust the seasoning with salt and pepper. Cook for another 10 minutes, until the grits are cooked through. Remove the pan from the heat and fold in the grated cheese.

Transfer the grits to a serving dish. Thinly slice the pork and serve it over the grits.

		PEIX	
Pan Tostado	1'40	CALAM. ROM.	6'00
BOMBA	1'6U	ARENGUE	2'50
Morcillas	3'30	SARDINAS	4'50
XAMPINYONS	3'00	BARAT	4'50
BACON	1'80	CALAMAR	6'8
HABAS	2'10	PULPO	3'20
BUTIFARRA	3'50	RECORTES PULPO	3'20
CHORIZO	3'30	BACALAO	5'50
Cap i Pota	3'50	ESCABECHE	4'50
AMANIDA	2'10	ESQUEIXADA	5'50
Judias	2'00	GAMBES	10'80
GARBANZOS	2'00	ESCAMARLANS	10'00
ENSALADILLA	2'80	BUNYOLS BAC.	3'60

The daily menu in one of my favorite restaurants, La Cova Fumada, in Barcelona's port district, la Barceloneta. It specializes in the simple unfussy seafood I love like fried sardines and grilled squid.

Cleaning Squid

SQUID IS A CEPHALOPOD, in the same family as cuttlefish and octopus. When prepared properly, squid has a firm, meaty texture and a delicious, sweet flavor. At first it may seem a little daunting to clean these creatures, but once you get the hang of it, it's really quite easy. (Of course you can buy them cleaned, but that's cheating!)

A common confusion is that the tentacles form the tail of the squid, when in reality they surround the head. In the center of the head, there's a large, hard beak that must be removed. First, pull the head with your fingers, and, under cold running water, squeeze the beak out and discard.

Then, still under running water, slip your finger inside the body of the squid and remove and discard the intestines. Rinse thoroughly. Along the top of the body, you'll feel a hard transparent quill that runs the length of the body and looks almost like a thin strip of plastic. Slip it out and discard. At this point you can either peel the skin off and get rid of it (for a milder flavor), or keep it on (it will turn purplish when you cook it, and will lend a rich seafood flavor to the dish). Either way, the squid is now cleaned and ready to cook.

A NOTE ON...BOMBA RICE

There are a few acceptable options for rice when it comes to paella, and while they're all fine, none truly compares to the Bomba varietal. Rice is the seed of a grass, cultivated in flooded plains. Essentially the grass grows up from the water, then goes to seed and the seed is harvested, hulled, polished, dried, cooked, and eaten! Bomba is an unusual rice in that it has the ability to absorb three times its volume in liquid. Since most of the flavor from a rice dish comes from the cooking liquid, it follows that the more liquid the rice can absorb, the tastier the rice. Unfortunately there's a downside to our friend Bomba. It's rather persnickety to grow and doesn't go to seed until the grass is quite tall, which means it has a penchant for falling over in the wind, getting soaked, and spoiling. It takes a tremendous amount of care to grow Bomba and hence it is more expensive than other short-grained options. And because Bomba (and all short-grain paella rice) is a processed white grain (its bran layer is removed), it is obviously not as nutritionally powerful as a whole grain brown rice with its hull intact. Everything's a trade-off, however, and in this case, for me tradition trumps nutrition.

Rice with Squid and Green Beans

I LOVE TO COOK WITH FIRE. There is something nostalgic about it that takes me straight back to Spain. The grill is a great place to prepare an outdoor summer meal of paella (for more on paella, see pages 132–135). In Valencia, paellas are traditionally cooked over an open flame and whenever I have the option of preparing my rice dishes this way, I always do it.

This recipe combines so many things that I love: the slightly smoky and sweet dried pepper from Catalunya called *ñora*, and *sofrito*, the flavor foundation of any good rice dish. There are a good many steps to this recipe, but the components can be prepared ahead of time and the effort is well worth it once you taste the rice.

Serves 6–8

FOR THE STOCK

  2 **tablespoons olive oil**
  4 **onions, thinly sliced**
  1 **pound cleaned fresh or frozen squid with the skin on, roughly chopped**
  2 **tomatoes, roughly chopped**
  2 **cloves garlic, peeled**
  1 **bay leaf**
  1 **dried *ñora* pepper, or 1 piece ancho chile**
  1 **cup dry white wine**

FOR THE RICE

  2 **tablespoons olive oil**
  3 **pounds large squid, cleaned and skinned, (TECHNIQUE, page 73)**
     Salt
     Freshly ground black pepper
  2 **cups *sofrito* (TECHNIQUE, page 65)**
  1 **cup fresh runner beans, cut into 1½-inch lengths**
2½ **cups Bomba or other short-grain rice (such as Arborio)**
  2 **teaspoons squid ink**
     Lemon wedges for serving
     All i Oli (page 21) for serving
  3 **cups squid stock, recipe follows**

For the stock, in a large heavy-bottomed pot, heat the olive oil over medium heat and gently brown the onions, stirring frequently, until caramelized, about 35 minutes.

Raise the heat to medium high and add the squid, tomatoes, garlic, bay leaf, and peppers. Cook down for 20 minutes, until the ingredients come together nicely and give off a sweet, seafood aroma. Add the white wine and simmer for an additional 10 minutes, until the alcohol has cooked off. (If you take a deep breath over the pot and can still feel a slight burning in your nose, you'll know there's still some alcohol left.)

Once the alcohol has cooked off, add 8 cups water and simmer, uncovered, for 2 hours. Strain the stock into a bowl. It should have a lovely amber hue and a delicate, sweet flavor. If it tastes a little weak, once it's strained you can return it to the stove and reduce it to concentrate the flavor.

For the rice, preheat the oven to 450°. Bring 3 cups of the squid stock to a simmer in a large saucepan and keep warm.

In a perfect world, I'd cook the rice in a paella pan over a wood-fired grill, but if you don't have a paella pan or a grill handy, a large, shallow, ovenproof pan on a conventional stovetop will suffice. Heat the olive oil in the pan over medium-high heat. While the olive oil is heating up, slice the skinned squid into ½-inch rings and season with salt and pepper. Add the squid to the pan and sauté vigorously for 2 minutes, then remove to a plate lined with paper towels.

Add the *sofrito* to the pan, then the runner beans and 2 ladlefuls of stock. Stir well to incorporate and bring to a rolling boil. Add the rice and squid ink, season with salt and pepper, and gently shake the pan to evenly distribute the rice. Reduce the heat to a simmer, and add stock periodically until the rice is almost fully cooked, 18–20 minutes. The rice should still be a bit toothy, but not chalky at all.

Add enough stock so that the rice mixture is just a little wet and transfer the pan to the oven for 5–8 minutes. The rice pan should have a little crispy crust around the sides and the surface should be glossy and unctuous.

Remove from the oven and set aside to rest for 5–10 minutes before serving. Serve with fresh lemon wedges and a drizzle of *all i oli*.

chapter five

ANCHOVIES

BRINY

✳ ✳ ✳

SHINY

✳ ✳ ✳

ESSENTIAL

ANCHOVIES ARE ONE OF THOSE POLARIZING INGREDIENTS that can make friends—or enemies—quickly. I truly believe that if more people could taste the anchovies I've had in Getaria, a small town in Basque Country in northern Spain about 15 miles from San Sebastían, there wouldn't be a single anchovy detractor left on earth! These incredible fish are packed with goodness and flavor; anchovies are the secret weapon in

so many dishes, deliver-
ing the experience of such
deep, mellow flavor that
you never even suspect
their presence. In Getaria,
small Basque boats go out
in the early morning, net
the anchovies, then sort
them into baskets and bring
them in immediately for processing. Traditionally the husbands were the fishermen
and their wives sold the fish in the markets
or had the job of packing them. It's extremely important to process anchovies quickly
and delicately or they will spoil. Each little
fish must be filleted and packed by hand.
When I'm lucky enough to find fresh ancho-

vies, I will fry some up right
away and then set aside the
rest to preserve. This is so
much easier that it sounds as
I show in complete step-by-
step directions—with pictures
(page 81).

The canned anchovies of
northern Spain are one of the
true delicacies of Spanish gastronomy.
Fisheries on the banks of the Cantabrian
Sea are home to the *anchoas del Cantábrico*,
lovely, thick, cold-water anchovies that,
when preserved in oil, are among my most
favorite things to eat. Every respectable
cannery in the Basque Country processes its
fish by hand, carefully cleaning and packing

"Anchovies are a polarizing ingredient that can make friends or enemies quickly. Inferior canned anchovies give the fish a bad rap."

them in salt to cure for three to four months, then canning them in olive oil. When choosing anchovies, I suggest sticking with a Spanish or Italian product such as Ortiz or Nardin, both available in specialty stores and online. They have none of that oily fishiness that we associate with those supermarket anchovies whose less-than-careful processors have given the anchovy its bad rap. The difference in quality between a can that costs $3 and one that costs $9 is so significant that it's worth the few extra dollars. And remember, you don't need to use a whole lot of anchovies to achieve a whole lot of flavor.

Anchovies really are wonder fish. In my life, their nutritional benefits vie with flavor for supremacy. They're high in protein, vitamins D and E, and because you eat the bones, calcium. But probably the best news for me that they're so rich in the polyunsaturated fatty acids called omega-3s. Anchovies contain about as much omega-3s as the same-size serving of salmon.

The consensus in the nutrition community is that foods rich in omega-3 fatty acids are good for us for many reasons, among them is that they may help reduce inflammation. For rheumatoid arthritis sufferers specifically, omega-3s may help relieve the joint tenderness and stiffness that inflammation causes. It's tough to cook without using your hands but I don't have much choice other than to soldier through the discomfort. Anything that I can do to help minimize that pain means a great deal to me. So those delicious little fishies, especially anchovies (and sardines, too), form a small but critical part of my diet.

Anchovies happen to be a good source of an important trace mineral, selenium, an antioxidant that helps our bodies lessen the oxidative damage caused by free radicals (what one doctor likened to exhaust fumes in our bodies. The kind you need to get rid of.)

In a world of diminishing fish stocks, it is good to know that anchovies are plentiful and fished responsibly. For me, they are a remarkable ingredient to work with. They help me feel better *and* they go a long way toward helping my food taste better.

TECHNIQUE

Cleaning Anchovies

YOU'LL WANT TO PERFORM this operation in the sink, with a drizzle of cold water running from the tap and a colander to catch all the bits you don't want. Or work on a table covered with Spanish newspapers!

If you're right-handed, hold a fish in your left hand, with the head up and the belly to the right. With your left thumb and forefinger, pop the head off the little fish. With your right hand, gently run your index finger behind the spine, removing the entrails and vertebrae as you go. inevitably there will be a few sloppy ones at first, but you'll get the hang of it and become qualified to work at the canning factory in Getaria in no time!

The idea is to butterfly the little fish, so that the two fillets are joined at the tail and along the back by a thin flap of skin. The cleaned anchovies are now ready to fry, grill, or cure and preserve in olive oil with garlic, herbs, and spices (opposite).

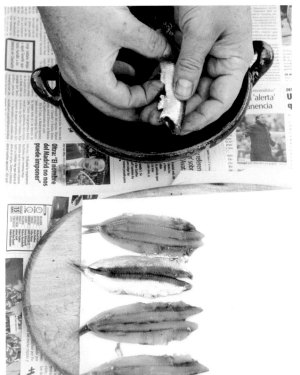

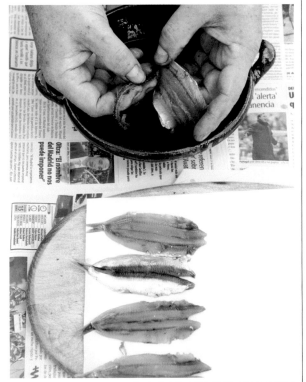

Homemade Potted Anchovies

IF YOU'RE LUCKY ENOUGH to find fresh anchovies, here's a simple way to prepare them so they'll keep for a few weeks.

Makes 8 jars

1	pound salt
1	pound sugar
5	pounds fresh anchovies, cleaned and butterflied (TECHNIQUE, page 81)
4	cups good olive oil
6	cloves garlic
1	tablespoon *guindilla* peppers
	Peel of 2 lemons, cut with a vegetable peeler
2	branches fresh thyme or oregano
2	bay leaves

Mix the salt and sugar together. Spread a thin layer in the bottom of a baking dish. Layer the butterflied anchovies neatly on the salt/sugar mixture, skin side up, covering them with additional mixture as you go. Once you've managed to prepare them all, take a deep breath, have a glass of wine, and get ready to witness the magical transformative power of salt! Cover the anchovies and refrigerate for 4 days.

Sterilize 8 canning jars by boiling for 1 minute, then set aside to cool.

Remove the anchovies from the salt/sugar mixture and rinse carefully under cold running water. It's very important that the water be cold, as bacteria can't multiply in cold water and the flesh of the fish will also stay much firmer.

In a large bowl, combine the olive oil, garlic, pepper, lemon peel, herbs, and bay leaves. Layer the anchovies into the jars as carefully as possible, top each jar with the oil mixture, and evenly distribute the herbs and garlic.

Seal the jars, refrigerate, and enjoy. They'll keep a month or more in the refrigerator.

A NOTE ON... PRESERVING ANCHOVIES

If you want to use the fresh anchovies right away and you don't feel like waiting 4 days for them to cure in salt and sugar, as in Homemade Potted Anchovies, then just pack them in the curing mixture and refrigerate for a few hours. Remove the anchovies from the salt, rinse them, and carefully pat dry. Slip them into a bowl of olive oil, bay leaves, basil, lemon peel, peppercorns, and thyme (page 80). Anchovies preserved like this will last 3 or 4 days in the refrigerator and are a great addition to potato salad and fresh pasta. Or just serve them on garlic-rubbed toast with a squeeze of lemon juice.

Anchoas y Escalivada, or Anchovies and Charred Vegetables

TOASTS TOPPED WITH THESE LITTLE GUYS are delicious flavor-bombs with the intense, smoky taste of the open fire, and the bright anchovy, balanced by the cooling labne. Each toast is one perfect, big bite. *Escalivada* literally refers to vegetables that have been charred. Labne is yogurt that has been hung in muslin to remove the watery whey, leaving it with a consistency closer to fresh cheese. Feel free to substitute strained plain yogurt or even fresh ricotta.

Serves 4 as an appetizer

FOR THE ESCALIVADA

- 2 **red bell peppers**
- 2 **bulbs fennel, fronds removed and reserved**
- 1 **sweet onion, skin left on**
- 2 **Italian eggplants (I love the white and purple Rosa Biancas)**
  Healthy drizzle good olive oil
  Splash sherry vinegar
  Handful fresh parsley and fennel fronds, coarsely chopped
  Salt
  Freshly ground black pepper

- ¼ **cup labne or yogurt**
- 4 **smallish slices toast (I like sourdough country bread)**
- 8 **fillets best-quality salted anchovies or Homemade Potted Anchovies (page 82)**
  Small handful fresh parsley and fennel fronds, coarsely chopped

For the *escalivada,* preheat an outdoor grill. Or, use a heavy cast iron skillet on the stove, making sure that it's very hot before grilling. Grill the red bell peppers, fennel bulbs, sweet onion, and eggplants until they are thoroughly charred. Use a sharp knife to check that the inside of all the vegetables are soft and cooked through. The fennel and onion will take a little longer than the pepper and eggplant.

Remove the vegetables from the heat and wrap in newspaper (preferably *El País*—I have always found that *escalivada* tastes better when the vegetables are wrapped in Spanish newspapers). Once thoroughly cooled, carefully peel away and discard the charred skin of all the vegetables, discard the pepper seeds, and slice the vegetables into thin strips.

Place the sliced vegetables in a large mixing bowl and carefully fold together with the olive oil, sherry vinegar, chopped parsley and fennel fronds, and salt and pepper. Makes about 4 cups *escalivada*.

To serve: Spread a little bit of labne on each piece of toast. Top each with a dollop of *escalivada* and 2 anchovy fillets. Garnish with parsley and fennel fronds.

Lightly Smoked Sardines on Toast

MY FATHER'S FATHER WAS SWEDISH and he was obsessed with cans of little fish. He loved anchovies, mackerel, and especially smoked kippers (or herring) on toast. He used to spread a thick layer of butter on sourdough toast and top it off with half a dozen fillets of smoked kippers. I like kippers too (probably not as much as my grandfather), but I *really* like smoked sardines.

Serves 4–6 as a side dish

1	cup kosher salt
1	cup sugar
4	freshest sardines, cleaned and filleted
1	cup Smoked Olive Oil (TECHNIQUE, page22)
4	slices rustic country bread
1	clove garlic, peeled and cut in half
1	fresh tomato, cut in half horizontally
	Flaky sea salt
	A few leaves fresh basil and parsley, coarsely chopped

Combine the kosher salt and sugar in a plastic container, bury the sardine fillets in the mixture, and refrigerate for 1 hour. Remove, rinse the fillets thoroughly under cold running water, and pat dry. In a small skillet, heat the smoked olive oil over low heat until it registers 130° on a candy thermometer.

Toast or grill the bread, then rub with the clove of garlic and the cut tomato. With a pastry brush, paint the toast liberally with some of the warm smoked olive oil. Sprinkle each slice of toast with good sea salt.

Slip the sardine fillets into the pan with the smoked olive oil and cook gently for 3–5 minutes, until the fish is slightly opaque and just cooked through. The sardines shouldn't be raw, but not quite cooked either. With a slotted spoon, transfer two fillets to each piece of toast, sprinkle with the herbs, and enjoy.

Fish shopping with my friend, the late Albert Asín of the famous Bar Pinotxo in the Boqueria market.

A NOTE ON... SMOKING SARDINES

The only thing I don't like about most smoked sardines is that they become so overcooked that they taste more of smoke than they do of fish. A few years ago in the restaurant we were playing around with cooking in olive oil at a low temperature and it dawned on me that we could infuse the olive oil with different flavors and subtly affect the flavor of whatever we were cooking. I liked the idea of a smoked fish that had the consistency of a delicately poached fish. After a lot of experimenting, we came up with the idea of first smoking the olive oil (page 22) and then gently cooking the sardines in that smoked olive oil. In essence we ended up with a warm, juicy, succulent sardine that had the delicate smoky flavor I love. Problem solved!

Caramelized Cauliflower with Anchovies

YEARS AGO, when I was working with Chef Floyd Cardoz at Tabla in New York, he made a dish with salt-cured anchovies and pickled cauliflower with Indian spices. I loved the salty and sour contrast, but what really stuck with me was how brilliantly anchovies and cauliflower work together. Cauliflower is a great foil for salted ingredients—cauliflower cream and caviar is delicious! This dish combines the lovely nuttiness of Romesco with the punch of anchovies and the subtleness of cauliflower.

Serves 4–6 as a side dish

1 cup Romesco Sauce (TECHNIQUE, page 55)
2 tablespoons butter
1 head cauliflower, cut into florets and blanched (see Note, page 139)
¼ cup best-quality salted anchovies or Homemade Potted Anchovies (page 82), coarsely chopped

Small handful coarsely chopped fresh parsley
1 lemon, cut into wedges
A pinch of Aleppo pepper

Warm the Romesco in a small pot. In a large skillet, heat the butter over medium-high heat until the foam subsides and the butter turns brown and gives off a nutty aroma. Add the cauliflower and sauté for 5–7 minutes, until golden brown. Toss in the anchovies and sauté for another minute.

Remove the skillet from the heat and transfer the cauliflower to a platter. Top with the warm Romesco, and finish with the parsley, a squeeze of lemon juice, and a pinch of Aleppo pepper.

Ensalada of Preserved Anchovies

IN CATALUNYA there's a classic salad called *xató* (its name is believed to derive from the French *chateau*, or castle) that combines frisée, salt cod, anchovies, and olives. I like *xató* and, in fact, give you my favorite recipe (page 276). But all those preserved ingredients can be quite salty. This is an updated version with some creamy fingerling potatoes for substance and cured lemons for a dynamic contrast.

Makes 4 small salads

10	small fingerling potatoes
2	bay leaves
2	cloves garlic
1	sprig fresh thyme
2	*guindilla* peppers or 2 pieces ancho chile
2	medium organic eggs
8	fillets best-quality salted anchovies or Homemade Potted Anchovies (page 82)
2	heads frisée, green leaves only
6	slices Quick-Cured Lemons (page 18)
¼	cup Castelvetrano olives or other fresh green olives, pitted and coarsely chopped
¼	cup toasted pine nuts
	Salt
	Freshly ground black pepper
	Healthy shot My Favorite Vinaigrette (page 21)

Combine the whole, unpeeled potatoes, bay leaves, garlic, thyme, and peppers in a small saucepan with well-salted water. Bring to a boil, reduce to a simmer, and cook for 15–20 minutes, until the potatoes are cooked through. Drain and discard the aromatics.

Meanwhile, place the eggs in a small sauce-pan, cover with cold water, and bring to a boil. Reduce the heat to low and cook for 5–6 minutes. Run the eggs under cold water, peel, and quarter. The eggs should have golden, creamy yolks, a bit softer than traditional hard-boiled eggs.

Combine the eggs, potatoes, anchovies, frisée, cured lemon slices, olives, and pine nuts in a salad bowl. Season with salt, pepper, and vinaigrette.

Flash-Fried Anchovies with Crispy Lemons and Sage

UNFORTUNATELY, MANY PEOPLE associate anchovies with the strong flavors of cheap, less-than-fresh canned anchovies. A truly fresh anchovy has none of that "fishiness" and is delicious quickly fried up in olive oil. When we opened Boqueria, many of our guests were initially skeptical of our fried anchovy and sardine dishes, but with a little coaxing and encouragement from our staff, these little fishes gained a popular following. This is one of the original specialties from our opening menu and it's still one of my favorite ways to prepare anchovies.

Serves 4 as an appetizer

2	cups olive oil for frying
½	pound cleaned fresh anchovies
	Salt
2	lemons, sliced into paper-thin rounds
	Leaves from 1 bunch fresh sage
½	cup rice flour mixed with ½ cup garbanzo flour or fine cornmeal, which adds a nice texture to fried anchovies
	Pimentón
1	lemon, cut into wedges

In a large, heavy-bottomed pot, heat the olive oil over medium-high heat until it registers 325° on a candy thermometer.

Spread the anchovies on a plate lined with paper towels, pat dry, and season with salt. Carefully dust the anchovies, lemon slices, and sage with the garbanzo/rice flour mixture.

Line a large platter with newspaper (ideally *El País*). Quickly fry the fish, lemon slices, and sage in small batches in the olive oil until crispy and golden, roughly 2 minutes per batch. With a slotted spoon, remove the lovely fryables from the oil to the newspaper. Repeat until all the ingredients have been fried. Season with a dusting of pimentón and serve immediately with fresh lemon wedges.

Two Kinds of Anchovies, One Kind of Flatbread

THIS MARRIAGE OF SALTED AND PICKLED anchovies has just the right mix of acidity and saltiness that combine in an anchovy-ness that I love. In Spain there is a very similar dish called *coca de matrimonio*—because the anchovies are white and black, just like the bride and groom in a wedding! A little fresh ricotta helps temper the flavors and a drizzle of *saba* gives it a nice sweet finish. Piled onto flatbreads and cut into little pieces, it's perfect finger food that is great for entertaining.

Serves 4 as an appetizer

8	fresh Italian plum tomatoes
¼	cup olive oil
	Splash sherry vinegar
2	cloves garlic, grated
	Leaves from 4 sprigs fresh thyme
	Leaves from 2 branches fresh basil, plus more for serving
	Salt
	Freshly ground black pepper
	Grilled Flatbreads (recipe follows)
2	cups sheep's milk ricotta
8	fillets best-quality salted anchovies or Homemade Potted Anchovies (page 82)
8	fillets *boquerones* (pickled white anchovies from Spain)
	Saba

To prepare the tomatoes, preheat the oven to 325°. Slice the tomatoes in half lengthwise and combine in a large mixing bowl with the olive oil, sherry vinegar, garlic, thyme, and basil; season with salt and pepper. Place the tomatoes cut side down on a large baking sheet and gently roast in the oven for 1½ hours. Carefully remove and discard the skins—they should slip off easily—and set aside to cool.

To assemble each flatbread, once you've grilled both sides, with the flatbread still on the grill top or griddle, evenly distribute the ricotta cheese, tomato halves, and both kinds of anchovies. Finish with a drizzle of *saba* and some torn leaves of basil.

GRILLED FLATBREADS
Makes 4 flatbreads

2	teaspoons active dry yeast
⅓	cup olive oil, plus more for brushing
1	egg, lightly beaten
1	teaspoon salt
1	teaspoon cold butter
1½	cups all-purpose flour, plus more for kneading

In a large bowl, dissolve the yeast in ⅓ cup lukewarm water and let stand 5 minutes. Once foamy, add the olive oil, egg, and salt. Meanwhile, in a small bowl, work the cold butter with your fingers into ¼ cup of the flour until well incorporated but clumpy.

Put the yeast/egg mixture in a standing mixer with a dough hook or in a food processor fitted with a plastic dough blade and mix at low speed. Gradually add the butter mixture and the rest of the flour until the dough is smooth and elastic. Remove to a well-floured surface and knead by hand for 5 minutes. Transfer the dough to a lightly oiled bowl, cover with plastic wrap, and let rise for 30 minutes in a warm place.

Preheat the grill. If you don't have a grill, you can also use a heavy cast iron skillet on the stovetop, just make sure that it's very hot before grilling the flatbread.

Divide the dough evenly into 4 balls and roll into ovals as thin as possible, about 3 by 10 inches. Brush with olive oil and place on oiled upside-down cookie sheets.

Carefully turn the flatbreads, two at a time, onto the hot grill and grill for about 4 minutes each side, until cooked through and nicely charred. Or cook one at a time in the hot cast iron skillet on the stove.

ON MY ROOFTOP

CH. 6: Good Eggs FRESH ✳ SUNNY ✳ VITAL

CH. 7: Good Birds TASTY ✳ WHOLESOME ✳ SUCCULENT

CH. 8: Sweet Peas BRIGHT ✳ GREEN ✳ CRISPY

CH. 9: Parsley POTENT ✳ LEAFY ✳ BENEFICIAL

CH. 10: Berries RIPE ✳ SWEET ✳ SEASONAL

93

Nothing says spring like the first paella on my rooftop with my chef friends. Shelling fava beans, left, which will be added at the last minute, just after the littleneck and razor clams and mussels. Lobster, right, is sauteed first, added later. Below, cooking with Zak Pelaccio, chef of Fatty Crab and Fatty 'Cue, and Marco Canora of Hearth and the Terroir Wine Bars.

Amanda Freitag, above, my dear friend and fellow competitor on *The Next Iron Chef*. Making paella is easy fun compared with what we've been through together! Offering my fiancée, Lynn Juang, right, a first taste of the paella rice.

SPRING

A large propane-fueled burner, above, is the next best thing, if you don't happen to be near a vineyard to make a fire of dry grapevines to cook your paella. I add stock by the ladleful as the rice absorbs the liquid. For the step-by-step recipe, see page 134. Pickled raisins are a punchy addition to Duck Liver Toasts (page 122), right.

Lobster and shellfish provide a vibrant color contrast, top left. They are added to the paella pan at the last minute so they don't get overcooked and rubbery. My red-headed cook friend Tyler Viggiano joins my merry rooftop table, below left.

The finished paella pan is our table's own centerpiece, left, and it's a delicious pleasure to serve up such bountiful plates. Chef Akhtar Nawab and his daughter, Ela, below, add so much fun to our group. Paella is great for kids, especially Amanda and Marco, right.

SPRING

chapter six

GOOD EGGS

FRESH

* * *

SUNNY

* * *

VITAL

WHEN I LEFT HOME IN RURAL VERMONT for boarding school at age 15, it was a shock in more ways than one. I was prepared for many things, but garbage food wasn't one of them. I took good eggs for granted; they were what our own hens laid, period. Their yolks were vibrantly orange or saffron depending on the time of year, the whites were thick and substantial, and the shells were strong and hard to break. My first semester in

"A few minutes of research will pay off big time. Discover where good eggs are sold near you and work that place into your routine."

boarding school I had a job for two hours a day working in the kitchen, exposed to the sad reality of Chef Wiggins's institutional cooking (we used to say today's barbecued beef was tomorrow's Tex-Mex strata). The first time I picked up an egg in her kitchen, the shell was so frail that I was afraid that if I looked at it the wrong way it'd break. Where I come from, you had to rap an egg pretty hard against the counter to crack the shell.

There is serious difference between a factory-farmed egg and a real farm egg. Put simply, good eggs come from happy, healthy chickens: chickens with space to run around, spread their wings, and stretch their legs; chickens with soil to scratch in and bugs and worms to eat. This is a natural life, free from hormones and antibiotics, and free, too, from the poor nutrition inferior feed provides (yes, even organic feed). Makes sense that the eggs from those happy chickens will be far superior to eggs from a crowded factory operation.

Eggs from pasture-raised chickens (as compared to caged and grainfed supermarket eggs) are said to produce eggs with less saturated fat. They have more vitamins A and E, more of those beneficial mono- and polyunsaturated fats, and more betacarotene. These may be the results of just a few studies, but they sure make sense to me.

Obviously in cooking we have to make compromises about our ingredients. But the questionable conditions in which factory hens are raised make it difficult for me to even consider those eggs as good food. For the sake of clarity, in recipes where I call for eggs, I ask that you try to find free-range eggs (from chickens given the opportunity to hunt for their own food). Room to run around and a varied diet are more important than organic feed, though that matters too, of course. When hens are caged, the whole food chain misses an opportunity.

Choosing the right eggs may seem to be a lot of work, but a few minutes of research to find your local sources will pay off big time. It's too easy to be misled by clever labeling on those supermarket boxes. I'm lucky enough to live a few blocks away from a wonderful farmers market. Three times a

Eggs have all the essential amino acids that our bodies require and the highest quality protein of any food. The significant levels of dietary cholesterol in eggs used to make them seem like a no-no, but the USDA has updated its nutrient database, noting that today's eggs (all of them) have somewhat less cholesterol; even the American Heart Association no longer recommends a limit to egg consumption as long as cholesterol is limited to no more than 300 mg a day.

Typically we think of eggs as breakfast food, but not so in the rest of the world. In this book, you'll find that I frequently build lunches and dinners, too, around lovely eggs. Adding a fried duck, hen, or quail egg to almost any dish instantly elevates it. I like to use pullet eggs, those smaller eggs from young hens just beginning to lay. Scrambled, pullet eggs are a rich sunshiny yellow. And since pullet eggs are so small, when you cook them they tend to stay together.

week, I can buy eggs direct from the folks who raise them. Discover where good eggs are sold in your community and work that place into your shopping routine.

A solid information source is provided by the Cornucopia Institute. Use their Organic Egg Scorecard (cornucopia.org/organic-egg-scorecard) to find out where the good eggs are available near you.

Gently Scrambled Eggs with Wild Vegetables

THIS DISH IS, FOR ME, the epitome of spring. Wild vegetables just folded together with fresh herbs, spring eggs, and crème fraîche. As a child, I spent a lot of time foraging for morel mushrooms, fiddlehead ferns, and wild ramps with my mother. She would scramble our harvest with our own farm eggs in a dish not so different from this one. Come spring, this is a regular feature on our lunch menu and it sells out every time.

Serves 4 as an appetizer or 2 for breakfast

6   eggs
    Salt
    Freshly ground black pepper
2   tablespoons soft butter
1   tablespoon crème fraîche
    Stems of 2 garlic scapes, finely minced
    A few leaves fresh basil
    A few leaves fresh marjoram
    A few leaves fresh savory
    A few pieces fresh chives
¼   cup fresh fava beans, blanched and peeled
2   ramps, bulbs cut in half, leaves minced
    Small handful fiddlehead ferns
    Small handful fresh morel mushrooms
1   teaspoon sweet sherry vinegar
    Slices of good country bread, toasted
    Drizzle of Arbequina or other good olive oil

Crack the eggs into a large mixing bowl and gently whisk together. Season with salt and pepper. Stir in 1 tablespoon of the butter, the crème fraîche, garlic scapes, and all the herbs; set aside.

Meanwhile, in a medium-size skillet, heat the remaining 1 tablespoon butter over medium-high heat until foamy. Add the fava beans, ramps (greens and bulbs), fiddlehead ferns, and morel mushrooms and sauté for 2 minutes. Deglaze the pan with the vinegar and cook for 1 more minute, until all the moisture has evaporated.

Reduce the heat to medium low, add the egg mixture, and with a rubber spatula gently stir as the eggs come together. It should take 3–4 minutes to cook, and the resulting eggs should be fluffy and creamy. Serve with toasted country bread and a drizzle of olive oil.

Deviled Eggs

I CAN'T RESIST DEVILED EGGS, they're one of my favorite snacks. The addition of homemade preserved tuna takes them over the top.

Makes 12 halves

6	eggs
¼	cup Preserved Tuna (TECHNIQUE, page 224) or highest quality canned tuna, finely minced
	Zest and juice of 1 lemon
1	tablespoon Dijon mustard
1	tablespoon finely minced cornichons
1	teaspoon finely minced shallot
1	teaspoon capers, finely minced
½	clove garlic, grated
	Salt
	Freshly ground black pepper
	Pinch pimentón

Bring 8 cups of water to a boil. Lower in the eggs, reduce the heat, and simmer for about 6 minutes. Remove from the heat, run under cold water, and carefully peel. Cut the eggs in half with a sharp knife and remove the yolks.

In a small mixing bowl with a fork, fold together the yolks, tuna, lemon juice, mustard, cornichons, shallots, capers, garlic, and salt and pepper.

Spoon the yolk mixture back into the egg halves, then finish with a scattering of lemon zest and a sprinkle of pimentón.

Five-Minute Eggs with Romesco

WHEN I WAS GROWING UP, my English grand-mother would make me soft-boiled eggs with toast "soldiers" for a treat. A great thing about being a grown-up is that now I can make them whenever I want! How simple: boil some eggs, make a batch of Romesco, and *voilà*—a lovely lunch or indulgent breakfast. If you're especially careful not to cook them too long, you'll have eggs with yummy, unctuous yolks. These eggs are fine warm or cold and make an easy snack or first course with leftover Romesco. Feel free to get creative and add a strip of cured ham, some crispy bacon, or even smoked salmon.

Makes 6 halves

3	pullet eggs
1	cup Romesco Sauce (TECHNIQUE, page 55)
1	tablespoon Arbequina or other good olive oil
	Flaky sea salt
	A few sprigs fresh parsley

Make the Five-Minute Eggs: In a small saucepan, bring 4 cups of water to a boil. Add the eggs, reduce the heat, and simmer for 5–6 minutes, depending on the size of the eggs. Run the eggs under cold water, peel, and halve; the eggs should have nice golden, creamy yolks.

On a large plate, spoon dollops of Romesco Sauce, then nestle in the egg halves. Finish with a dab of Romesco, a drizzle of olive oil, a sprinkle of sea salt, and a parsley leaf or two.

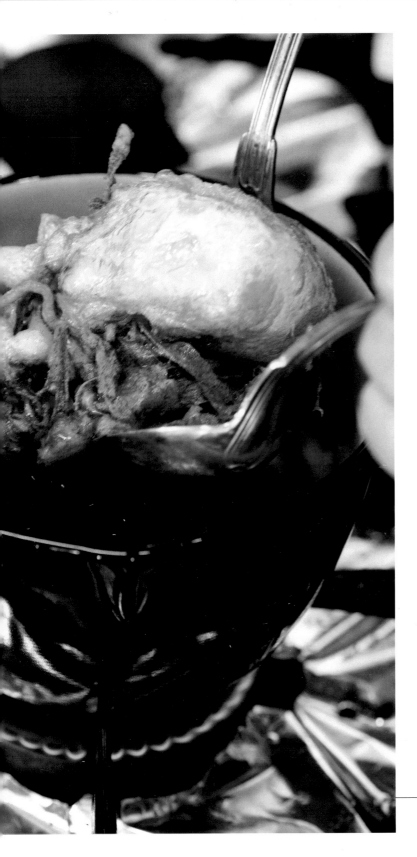

Deep-Frying an Egg in Olive Oil

IT'S OBVIOUS THAT I LOVE EGGS. When I was 16 on my first trip to Spain, my host-mother would prepare fried eggs for me every morning. But these were different from any fried eggs I'd ever had. She would heat up a generous amount of olive oil in a skillet and literally shallow-fry the egg in the oil. The white of the egg would bubble up, turn crispy, and form what she called *puntillas,* Spanish for lace. But I like to take it a step further and actually deep-fry the egg in olive oil. The result is a sphere with a crispy white on the outside that protects the gooey yolk inside.

Here's how you do it: In a small, deep saucepan, heat 2 cups olive oil to 300°. (Use any inexpensive olive oil suitable for frying.) Crack a large hen's egg or duck egg into a small coffee cup (I like duck eggs because they're bigger).

Carefully pour the egg into the hot oil. The white will immediately foam up and form large bubbles. Using two large metal spoons, fold the whites together to help the egg form a sphere and gently turn the egg in the oil so it browns nicely on all sides. With a slotted spoon, transfer the egg to a plate lined with paper towels to drain. Repeat to fry more eggs. Then plop the crispy eggs on top of some steamed greens or nestle them into some fork-mashed potatoes.

Fork-Crushed Sweet Potatoes with Sobrassada and a Fried Egg

JORDI VILÀ TAUGHT ME how to deep-fry eggs in olive oil when I worked for him at Alkimia restaurant in Barcelona. He was also the first person to turn me on to duck eggs. Not surprisingly, this dish always reminds me of Jordi. I love the rich flavor of the duck eggs with the spicy *sobrassada* and sweetness of quince paste.
Serves 4

3   tablespoons Arbequina or other good olive oil
2   sweet potatoes baked in salt
     (TECHNIQUE, page 182), cooled and peeled
     Salt
     Freshly ground black pepper
4   slices *sobrassada*
2   tablespoons quince paste, diced
4   duck (or chicken) eggs, deep-fried in olive oil
     (TECHNIQUE, page 107)
     Leaves from a small handful fresh parsley,
     coarsely chopped

Bake the sweet potatoes in the oven or use the salt-baked method on page 182. Heat the olive oil in a medium-sized skillet over medium heat. Mash the baked sweet potatoes with a fork into the olive oil to incorporate and heat through. Season with salt and pepper and keep warm.

Heat another medium-sized skillet over medium heat. Add the *sobrassada* and fry on both sides until golden brown.

Divide the sweet potatoes among 4 plates. Top with the *sobrassada* and evenly distribute the quince paste on top. Place a fried egg on top of each serving and sprinkle some chopped parsley over the plate.

A NOTE ON...SOBRASSADA

Sobrassada is a lightly cured pork sausage from the Balearic islands of Spain. It's typically made with finely minced pork loin, belly, and shoulder mixed with salt, pimentón, and sometimes even cayenne pepper for a little heat. It's hung to cure for a few weeks, but it's not a hard sausage. It can then be spread directly on bread, or cooked. I prefer to cook it. It's a great addition to stews, and when cut into little knobs is so tasty on flatbreads and pizzas. You can find *sobrassada,* quince paste and *boquerones* in Spanish groceries or at latienda.com.

Soft-Cooked Gribiche with Pickled Anchovies on Toast

GRIBICHE IS LIKE A MAYONNAISE made with hard-boiled eggs, and these delicious little toasts are a great way to turn your friends on to anchovies. The rich flavor of the egg perfectly tames the acidic punch of pickled anchovies. Feel free to finish with a drizzle of olive oil.
Serves 4 as an appetizer

2   Five-Minute Eggs (page 104), coarsely chopped
1   teaspoon grainy Dijon mustard
1   shallot, finely minced
¼   teaspoon turmeric
2   slices Quick-Cured Lemon (page 18),
     finely chopped
     Salt
     Freshly ground black pepper
2   slices country sourdough toast, cut into rectangles
4   *boquerones* (pickled white anchovies)
     Sprinkle of pimentón

Fold the eggs together with the mustard, shallots, turmeric, lemon, salt, and pepper and spread on the toast, face up. Top each toast with an anchovy and a sprinkle of pimentón.

Tortilla Española

THIS CREAMY POTATO OMELET is one of the great classics of the Spanish kitchen and there are as many versions as there are grandmothers. Whatever the recipe, one thing is key: abundant olive oil. Unlike its French cousin, this omelet isn't folded but rather flipped in the pan and served flat. Typically a *tortilla* is eaten in the late afternoon, with a beer or a glass of wine, but if you'd like to have it for breakfast or lunch, I won't tell.

Serves 6–8

8	eggs
	Salt
2	cups olive oil
1	Vidalia onion, thinly sliced
1	clove garlic, slightly crushed
3	large Yukon Gold potatoes, peeled and sliced into ¼-inch rounds

Lightly beat the eggs, season with a generous sprinkle of salt, and set aside.

In a large skillet, heat the olive oil over medium-low heat. Add the onions and garlic and gently cook until translucent, about 15 minutes. Add the potatoes and continue to cook for about 20 minutes, or until the potatoes have completely fallen apart. Take care to keep the heat low enough that the potatoes and onions don't take on any color.

Drain the onions and potatoes through a colander, reserving the olive oil for cooking the *tortilla*. (You'll only need a couple tablespoons; save the remaining oil for the next time you make a *tortilla*. If you continue to use this same oil, each time you make the *tortilla* the flavor will improve.)

Season the potato and onion mixture with salt and mix with the beaten eggs; it should be roughly equal parts potatoes and eggs, as you want the mixture to be just barely held together with the eggs.

Heat a 10-inch nonstick skillet over medium-low heat and add 1 tablespoon of the cooking oil from the potatoes and onions. Pour the potato and egg mixture into the pan and leave it alone for 2 minutes, until the bottom starts to set up. Gently shake the pan to release the eggs from the bottom of the pan; using a rubber spatula, gently pull the eggs away from the edge to make sure they're not sticking at all. Cook for 5 minutes or so, until the bottom is set but the top is very wet.

Place a large, flat plate on top of the skillet, hold it tightly, and in one quick motion (it's probably best to perform this over the sink the first few times) flip over the pan and the *tortilla*.

Wipe out the pan with a paper towel and return it to the heat. Add another tablespoon of the cooking oil and carefully slip the *tortilla* back into the pan. Using a rubber spatula, carefully tuck the edges of the *tortilla* into the pan and cook for another 3 minutes. Once the bottom is set up, you're going to repeat the flipping process 1 or 2 times to get a perfectly rounded edge. If at any time the *tortilla* starts to swell, just poke it with a fork to deflate. When done, the *tortilla* should be nice and golden on the outside and creamy and gooey on the inside. It can be served hot or room temperature.

Lamb Tartare with Spring Pullet Eggs

WHEN MY FRIEND, the very talented chef Zak Pelaccio, and I were in Vermont at my mother's place butchering autumn lambs a few years ago, we beheld the freshest lamb meat we'd ever seen. On the spot, we invented this lamb tartare. If you can't find really fresh lamb loin, use top round; just avoid any cut with a lot of sinew, like leg or shoulder.

Serves 4 as an appetizer

1	lamb loin, about ½ pound
6	Cerignola olives, pitted and finely minced
	Zest and juice of 1 lemon
2	tablespoons Arbequina or other good olive oil
	Yolks of 2 pullet eggs
½	teaspoon Dijon mustard
1	teaspoon minced, seeded red or green jalapeño
	Leaves from 1 sprig fresh rosemary, finely minced
1	clove garlic, finely minced
	Salt
	Freshly ground black pepper
	Toast for serving

Carefully clean and remove any silverskin or fat from the lamb loin and pat dry. With a sharp knife, finely mince the meat. Set the meat in a metal bowl on top of another bowl filled with ice, cover, and place in the refrigerator to chill.

Once the meat is thoroughly chilled through, about 20 minutes, fold in the olives, lemon zest and juice, olive oil, egg yolks, mustard, jalapeño, rosemary, and garlic. Season to your liking with salt and pepper and serve with toast.

chapter seven

GOOD BIRDS

TASTY

✳ ✳ ✳

WHOLESOME

✳ ✳ ✳

SUCCULENT

FOR ME, IT'S AN ETHICAL QUESTION: IF ANIMALS (including birds), are raised in a humane way, given plenty of space to move around and access to the out of doors—in other words, if they are less crowded and less stressed—doesn't it follow that the meat from those animals will be healthier to eat? We have all but forgotten the succulent flavor of a properly raised chicken. Most of the birds in our markets are produced in such

"Birds are tasty and can bring us joy, and most poultry has lower fat, higher protein benefits. But what matters is the *good* in birds."

crowded conditions that illness, for which they have to be routinely medicated, is inevitable. And these are the birds we eat. As a practice, I take antibiotics only if I'm really sick; I ask myself how can eating birds or other meat treated with them be good for me?

Good birds are tasty and can bring us joy; most poultry has lower fat, higher protein benefits. As the late David Servan-Schreiber, a doctor and scientist wrote in *Anticancer: A New Way of Life*: "The lesson is simple, when we respect the needs and bodies of the animals that feed us, our own bodies are better balanced."

I grew up with good birds. We had close to a hundred chickens roaming around our pastures, all different colors and sizes. When I was quite young I remember going to a big, commercial chicken farm in a nearby Vermont town. A long building was filled with thousands and thousands of birds, cages stacked to the ceiling. Not to put too fine a point on it, but it was clear that the birds on the top sent their droppings streaming down to the layers of birds below. I recall a stack that was about 20 cages high. Even to the eyes of a seven-year-old, something was clearly amiss, and the manure smell was foul. When I contracted salmonella in high school I remembered that factory farm; the outbreak was traced to tainted birds. That episode was enough to turn me into a vegetarian for a few years. Not until I went to Spain and tasted really good meat did I began to eat it again.

Finding good birds may take a little extra effort and time, but that's just fine. The discovery of a good source is reason to celebrate, even though they're not always easy to find. Say you can get great farm-raised birds only once a week at your local farmers market. That's not a bad thing. We should celebrate birds and other meat and eat it a lot less frequently.

Good birds like guinea hen, pheasant, pigeon, woodcock, quail, and partridge are common in the markets in Spain, which is where I learned to cook them. I consider wild game the healthiest—birds that are raised that close to nature are better for us.

Wild game is illegal to sell in the United States, though more farm-raised game birds are available as our appetite for them increases. And birds from those game farms are generally healthier; producers are smaller and don't raise their birds in factory conditions.

What I love about cooking good birds is that each has its own special flavor and response to cooking techniques. A delicately pickled quail in *escabeche* (page 127) couldn't be more different than a crisp roasted guinea hen (page 131), yet both are memorable.

A NOTE ON... CHICKEN STOCK

I'm not a fan of the idea of stock-pot as the proverbial garbage can, a place where any old scrap is thrown, but I also don't believe that stock should be a reverential science project, fretted and obsessed over. I like to think of the soup pot more as a well-curated recycling bin. What do I do when I have a bit of dried ham left over? Into the pot. The remains of a roast chicken? Ditto. One thing I always include is a healthy portion of dried garbanzo beans, which round out the flavor and make it less like a meaty stock and more of an aromatic broth. See recipes for "our daily broth," Caldo del Día, and Sopa de Enfermos, both on page 128).

Poached Long Island Duck Breasts with Farro

TRADITIONALLY WE POACH DUCK LEGS in duck fat then store them in the fat to make confit. But here I poach the breasts in oil. This is a rather unorthodox way cooking duck breast, but I've discovered it's the best way. Duck breast is so juicy and rosy because (and this is admittedly my theory!) ducks use those muscles to control their wings. Chickens are flightless, hence the light color of the meat in their breasts, whereas ducks fly and so have much more developed breast muscles. Duck meat has a lot of myoglobin, a protein loaded with iron. I believe that when it's overcooked, duck meat can take on that nasty, metallic flavor I associate with awful diner plates of liver and onions.

It occurred to me that if I cook the breast gently, controlling the temperature, I can maintain that rosy color, keep the breast juicy and delectable, and make sure it's properly cooked. To do this, it's important that the flesh side of the breast never directly touch the hot pan. I transfer the duck from the skin side in the hot pan directly into the infused olive oil.

Serves 4

FOR THE FARRO
- 2 cups farro
- 1 carrot, peeled and cut into large pieces
- 1 onion, quartered
- 4 cloves garlic, peeled and lightly crushed
- 2 *guindilla* peppers, or 2 pieces ancho chile
- 1 bay leaf
- Kosher salt
- ½ cup fontina cheese cut into small pieces
- 1 tablespoon butter
- 1 head radicchio, cut into small bits
- Salt
- Freshly ground black pepper

FOR THE DUCK
- 2 duck breasts, each cut in half lengthwise
- 2½ cups olive oil
- Peel of 1 orange
- 2 *guindilla* peppers, or 2 pieces ancho chile
- 2 branches fresh thyme
- 1 clove garlic, peeled and lightly crushed
- Salt
- Freshly ground black pepper

For the farro, thoroughly rinse it in a large colander under running water. Transfer to a large heavy-bottomed pot and add the carrots, onions, garlic, peppers, bay leaf, and 4 cups of water. Add enough kosher salt so the water tastes like sea water. Cover, place over high heat, and bring to a boil. Reduce the heat and simmer for 20–25 minutes, until the grain is soft and cooked through. Once the farro is fully cooked, drain, and discard the aromatics.

Fold the fontina cheese, butter, and radicchio into the cooked farro. Season with salt and pepper. Set aside.

For the duck, in a skillet large enough to fit all four pieces of the duck breasts, combine the olive oil, orange peel, peppers, thyme, and garlic clove. Place the skillet on the burner on the lowest heat you can manage and gently heat the oil until it registers 150° on a meat thermometer. If you have trouble setting your stove low enough, use a cast iron trivet or heat diffuser. I like to leave the thermometer in the oil so I can regulate the heat as necessary and maintain 150°. When you add the duck, the temperature will drop a bit, so you may need to increase the heat slightly.

Score the skin of the duck breasts and season thoroughly with salt and pepper. Heat up another skillet (roughly the same size) over medium-low heat and sear the duck breasts, skin-side down, without moving them at all, until they are crispy and golden brown, 5–7 minutes. Once the skin is golden brown, remove from the pan and now place skin-side up in the 150° olive oil. Poach the duck breasts in the olive oil for 7–10 minutes, until the breasts are firm, medium rare, and just cooked through. Remove from the heat, slice, and serve with the farro.

 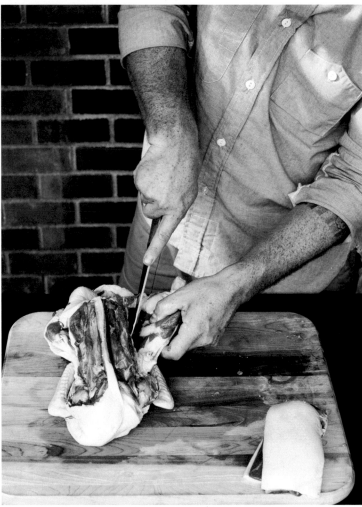

Cutting Up a Duck

THERE ARE SO MANY delicious benefits to buying a whole duck and cutting it yourself, the liver being an obvious one (see Duck Liver Toasts, page 122).

1 duck
1 sharp knife
2 hands

First, thoroughly scrub your hands. Place the duck, breast-side up, on a cutting board.

With your non-cutting hand, run your fingers down the center of the duck; you'll feel a slight indentation that separates the two breast muscles. If you're right-handed, you'll want to start with the breast that's on the left side. Carefully run your knife in one single cutting motion following that line. Then gently peel open the incision and repeat the same motion, taking care to keep the tip of your knife as close to the breast plate as you can; the idea is to leave as little meat as possible on the bone. A good technique is to peel the meat back and use the tip of your

knife to make a little feather-cutting motion and gently pull the meat away from the bone.

Keep doing this until the breast opens up off the bone like a book; the breast muscle should be completely detached from the bone except for where it's connected by the skin at the side of the bird. Run your knife along the skin and completely remove the breast. The breast shape should be roughly rectangular.

Rotate the bird 180º and repeat the procedure on the other breast. To remove the legs, press down on one of the legs to open it as much as

possible from the carcass, and insert the tip of your knife until you find the leg joint. Insert the tip of the blade into the socket of the hip joint to separate the leg bone from the hip joint. Press down on it with your non-cutting hand. You'll hear a slight pop, and the leg will mostly detach from the carcass. With the tip of your knife, repeat the feather-cutting action along the bone until you've completely removed the leg.

The legs and breasts are ready for their next culinary act. The carcass can be used to make a delicious duck soup or duck stock.

Duck Liver Toasts and Pickled Raisins

LIVER PÂTÉ NEEDN'T BE FOIE GRAS to be decadently delicious. Duck liver is really yummy and this recipe makes a silky, sweet, rich mousse that is always one of the top sellers at the restaurant. A spicy sachet adds layers of flavor and perfumes the pâté with sweet star anise and allspice that pair so well with the liver.

Serves 8 as an appetizer

½   **pound duck livers**
4   **cups milk mixed with ½ cup kosher salt**
6   **tablespoons butter**
3   **slices bacon, coarsely chopped**
2   **shallots, coarsely chopped**
½   **clove garlic, coarsely chopped**
2   **bay leaves, 2 sprigs fresh thyme, 2 teaspoons pink peppercorns, 2 teaspoons** *guindilla* **pepper, 2 teaspoons allspice, and 2 teaspoons star anise, tied into cheesecloth to make a sachet**
⅓   **cup Pedro Ximenez sherry or other sweet sherry Kosher salt**
1   **egg white**
1   **tablespon olive oil**
½   **cup golden raisins**
1   **cup Vegetable Pickling Liquid (page 185) Crusty bread, toasted**

Soak the livers in the salted milk for at least 2 hours. Clarify the butter by heating it over medium-low heat in a small saucepan until the solids separate from the fat. With a small slotted spoon, remove and discard the solids that float to the top. After 7–10 minutes you should have clear butter with a golden, amber hue. Set the clarified butter aside.

Heat a medium-sized skillet over medium-low heat and gently sauté the bacon to render the fat, about 5 minutes. Add the shallots and garlic and the sachet and cook slowly for 7–10 minutes, until the shallots are translucent. Deglaze the pan with the sherry and reduce slowly for a few minutes until the sherry has a syrupy consistency and the bacon and shallots are thoroughly glazed.

Drain the livers, rinse them gently under cold running water, and pat dry. Season liberally with kosher salt. Heat the olive oil in a separate pan, ideally cast iron, over high heat, and sear the livers to medium rare, about 2 minutes on each side. Remove from the pan to cool.

Remove the sachet from the shallot mixture. Mix the shallot mixture, livers, and egg white in a Vitamix or food processor and puree. Increase the speed and slowly drizzle in the clarified butter until the mousse is smooth and creamy.

With a rubber spatula, divide the liver mousse among several small ramekins or one larger one, and set in the refrigerator to chill.

Put the raisins in a bowl. Bring the pickling liquid to a boil, pour over the raisins, and cover with plastic wrap. Let cool in the refrigerator for 1 hour, then drain.

Serve the duck liver with crusty toast and the pickled raisins on the side.

Homemade Duck Sausage

SAUSAGE IS FUN TO MAKE. Especially if you've got a friend (like chef Amanda Freitag, above) to help you do it. Homemade sausage is also very, very rewarding. If you're like me, once you start making sausage, you won't want to stop and you'll make all kinds of sausage and every nook and cranny of your fridge will be draped with links. This is good. Sausage makes friends fast. Heading to meet your girlfriend's parents for the first time? Woo them with some homemade duck or pork sausage. A little late dropping off the rent check? A lamb sausage or two and your landlord might just lower your rent.

Sausage making is not just fun. It can be healthier if you control *all* the ingredients. Even many of the best commercial sausages have preservatives and who knows what else.

The KitchenAid has a great grinder and stuffing adapter, but once you get really serious about making sausage, you'll want to spring for a hand-cranked stuffer. This recipe makes a delicious duck sausage that is equally at home on a Sunday morning with some fried duck eggs as it is thrown on a grill and all dressed up with a nice bowl of beans on a Saturday night.

Makes about 4 pounds of sausage

3	pounds duck meat, preferably legs and thighs, ground
1	pound double-smoked bacon, ground
3	tablespoons kosher salt
1	clove garlic, ground to a paste with a mortar and pestle
	Zest of 1 orange
1	tablespoon coarsely ground black pepper
1	tablespoon ground star anise
1	tablespoon ground coriander
1	teaspoon ground cinnamon
1	cup red wine, reduced to ½ cup and chilled
½	cup ice water
8–10 feet hog casing, soaked for 1 hour in warm water	

In a large bowl, combine the ground duck, ground bacon, salt, garlic, orange zest, and all of the spices. Mix thoroughly, spread out on a baking sheet, and place in the freezer for 20 minutes, until very cold but not quite frozen.

Meanwhile, set up a standing mixer with a paddle attachment. Once the meat is thoroughly chilled, add it and mix at medium speed, drizzling in the wine and water to emulsify, about 1 minute. Transfer to the sausage stuffer and process according to the manufacturer's instructions.

Now it's time for the hog casing (which you'll get salted or frozen from your butcher). Remove the casing from the soaking water. Find the end, and fit it onto the spigot of your water faucet and run some cold water through it. This will open it up and make it easier to slip onto the sausage stuffer. Make sure to tie a double square knot in the end. Carefully stuff the casing, poking the casing periodically with the tip of a sharp knife to release any air bubbles that form. Once you've filled the casing with the sausage mixture, taking care not to fill it too tightly, tie another double square knot at the end. Every 7 inches along the casing, carefully twist it a few times in opposite directions to form sausage links.

Set the string of links aside on a baking sheet fitted with a cooling rack and refrigerate overnight to dry the sausage.

To cook, heat up a grill with a hot fire on one side, leaving the other side cooler. Grill for 2 minutes over high heat, then move to the cooler side of the grill and heat until the sausage is cooked through and a meat thermometer registers 165° when inserted in the center.

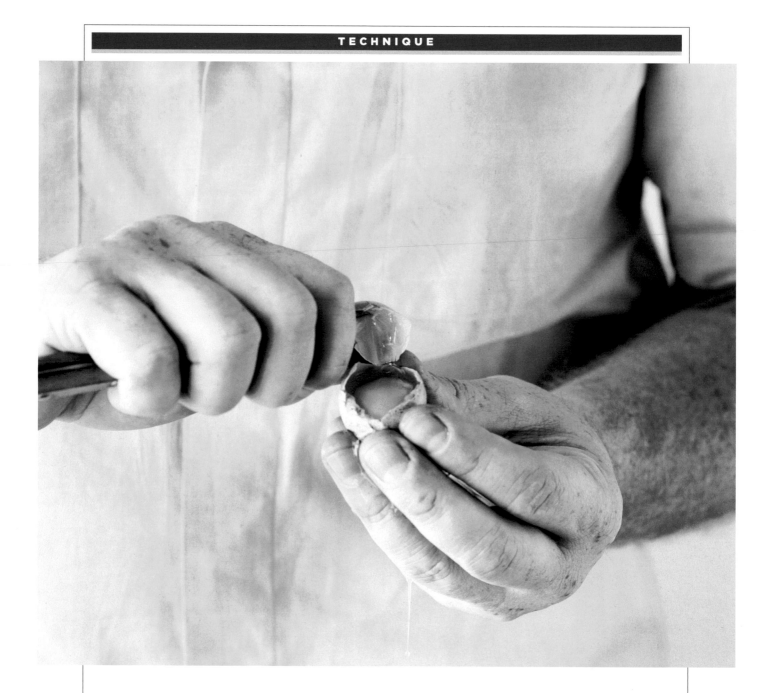

Cutting a Quail Egg

IT MAY SEEM SOMEWHAT DAUNTING to open a tiny little quail egg without destroying its delicate yolk, and certainly if you crack it on the counter, as you would a chicken egg, you won't succeed. However, there's a simple trick. You'll notice the egg has a pointed side and a fatter, rounded side.

Hold the egg in one hand with the fatter side up, insert just the tip of a small sharp paring knife gingerly into the eggshell, and cut in a circle until you've removed the top of the shell like a lid. Pour the yolk and the white into a small cup or directly into a hot pan to fry.

Quail en Escabeche with Fried Quail Eggs

PREPARING THINGS IN *escabeche*, or "in a pickle," is an age-old way of preserving meats and fish. Though it's no longer a necessity, this gentle pickling adds a unique and delicious flavor to so many foods. This recipe is typically used for quail, although it can also be successful with chicken, partridge, and even squab.

Serves 4

2	tablespoons olive oil, plus more to taste
4	quail, quartered
	Salt
	Freshly ground black pepper
2	cups *escabeche* (right)
4	quail eggs
	Small handful frisée

In a medium-sized skillet, heat the olive oil over medium-high heat. Season the quail with salt and pepper. Gently sear the quail, skin-side down, until their skins are golden, about 2 minutes. Turn the quail over, add the *escabeche* liquid to the pan, and reduce the heat to very low. Simmer for 5–7 minutes, until the meat is tender. Set the pan aside and let the quail cool in the liquid.

Meanwhile, heat a well-seasoned cast iron pan over medium-high heat. Drizzle a couple drops of olive oil into the hot pan and then wipe with a paper towel so the pan is shiny but there's no residual olive oil. Cut open the quail egg carefully (TECHNIQUE, left); slide the quail eggs into the pan and cook sunnyside up.

Remove the quail from the *escabeche* liquid and pat dry. In a large mixing bowl, combine the frisée and quail with a few tablespoons of the *escabeche* cooking liquid and a generous drizzle of olive oil. Season with salt and pepper. Divide evenly among 4 plates and top each serving with a fried quail egg.

TECHNIQUE

Escabeche for Pickling Poultry or Fish

ESCABECHE SOUNDS LIKE ceviche. When the Spanish arrived in Peru in the sixteenth century, the natives were curing seafood with lime juice to preserve it. This ceviche reminded them of the *escabeche* of their homeland, just another way of preserving meat and fish before refrigeration.

But refrigeration often sacrificed flavor for efficiency. Preservation techniques are universal: salt curing, air drying, and pickling have a transformative effect on the flavor of food, changing often for the better. Think of the potted herring of Scandinavia, the pickled anchovy *boquerones* of Northern Spain, or simply a crispy half-sour pickle. Pickling fish lets us taste it a new way. For fish like mackerel (page 266), I sear the skin side first; for poultry like quail, left, I brown it first, skin on, then add the *escabeche* liquid to the skillet and gently poach it.

Makes 2½ cups

2	cups good olive oil
¼	cup white wine vinegar
¼	cup sugar
1	carrot, peeled and thinly sliced
1	stalk celery, thinly sliced
1	onion, thinly sliced
2	cloves garlic, peeled
2	bay leaves
	Zest of 1 lemon
2	sprigs fresh thyme
2	sprigs fresh dill
1	tablespoon each black peppercorns, coriander, and fennel seeds
2	tablespoons pimentón

Bring all the ingredients to a boil in a medium saucepan. Reduce the heat and gently simmer for 30 minutes.

Caldo del Día

HERE'S WHAT YOU DO TO MAKE the really lovely broth that is at the heart of so many dishes in this book. It literally means "our daily broth" and is not unlike the Italian *brodo*. Caldo is an old Spanish word that refers to the vessel as well as the soup that's made in it. This is not a precise recipe. How could it be—people have been making it for hundreds of years with whatever they have on hand.

What can make this broth special is the cured ham bone we always have at the restaurant. We go through two hams a week and we save and freeze all those bones for our caldo. If the guy behind the counter at the gourmet deli in your neighborhood is worth his salt, he'll know that the bone in the center of the cured ham he's selling is pure flavor. Try to talk him out of it. It'll give your caldo a rich, incomparable quality.

Makes about 8 cups

- 1 large stewing chicken
- 4 large carrots, peeled and cut into chunks
- 4 large onions, cut into quarters
- 2 stalks celery, coarsely chopped
- 2 cloves garlic, lightly crushed with the back of a knife
- 2 slices bacon, or 1 small chunk dried ham like prosciutto or serrano, or cured ham bone
- 1 pound dried garbanzo beans

In a very large, heavy-bottomed pot, combine all the ingredients, add 3 gallons water, and bring to a boil. Reduce the heat and simmer for 3 hours. While the stock is simmering, it's important to skim the impurities and here's an easy way to do it: Move the pot off center on the burner which will create a hot spot on the edge of the pot, forcing the detritus to the cooler surface and making it easier to skim. When skimming, dip your skimmer into the stock just below the surface over the hot spot and skim away from the heat. This will prevent you from mixing the impurities back into the stock.

Strain the broth, and chill if you do not intend to use it immediately. Seasoning depends upon the way you intend to use the broth.

Sopa de Enfermos

THE FIRST TIME I HAD "SICK MAN'S SOUP" I was about 19 and on a hunting trip in Extremadura, in rugged southwestern Spain. We spent the night in the mountains and made this soup over a campfire with the partridge we'd shot. Nobody remembered the salt. The romantic in me would like to report it was incredible, but it was pretty awful. Remember the salt and you'll have the soup I crave when I'm not feeling tip-top.

Serves 4

- 6 cups Caldo del Día (left) or good chicken stock
- 1 carrot, peeled and cut into large pieces
- 1 onion, quartered
- 1 cup small dried garbanzo beans, soaked overnight
- 1 bay leaf
    Salt
- 1 tablespoon olive oil
- 1 pound chicken drumsticks and thighs, rinsed and and patted dry
- 1 cup *picada* (page 52)
- 1 small bunch sorrel or watercress
    Freshly ground black pepper

Combine the caldo, carrot, onion, garbanzo beans, bay leaf, and salt in a pressure cooker. Close the lid and heat over high heat until it whistles. Reduce the heat to medium-low and simmer for 25 minutes. Release the pressure and remove the lid. Or cook the ingredients in a large pot, covered, over low heat for an hour.

In a medium skillet over medium-high heat, heat the olive oil. Add the chicken pieces and sear until the skin is golden brown, 5 minutes.

Add the browned chicken to the pressure cooker, cover, and and increase the pressure. Reduce to simmer and cook for 10 minutes; the chicken should be flaking off the bone. Release the pressure and remove the lid. Or cook the seared chicken in a covered pot over low heat until cooked through. Stir in the *picada* and sorrel and season well with salt and pepper.

Sunday Roast Chicken

THERE'S NOTHING QUITE LIKE a roast chicken to end the weekend and begin the week. Leftover leg meat, pulled apart and folded into some *all i oli*, makes delicious chicken salad and the carcass can be turned into an easy, satisfying stock. The main problem with cooking birds is the classic cooking conundrum: the breasts and the legs require completely different cooking times. Otherwise you wind up with perfectly cooked breast and raw legs, or succulent legs and leathery breast.

Fear not! Science prevails! Here's a terrifically simple way to ensure a juicy bird that's perfectly cooked on all four corners. By roasting it at two temperatures the legs cook slowly, breaking down all the connective tissue that makes the meat tougher, and the breast isn't overexposed to high heat. At the very end, you crank up the temperature for a nice golden, crispy skin. Serve the roast with a crispy and succulent bread salad.

Serves 4 or more

1	3–5-pound roasting chicken, brined overnight and air-dried in the refrigerator (TECHNIQUE, page 297)
	Salt
	Freshly ground black pepper
2	lemons, cut into quarters
1	head garlic, 1 clove set aside and the rest peeled and lightly crushed
	Handful each fresh basil and tarragon
7	tablespoons olive oil
½	loaf country bread, cut into 1-inch cubes
1	shallot, sliced paper thin on a mandoline
1	quart mixed heirloom tomatoes, cut into rustic chunks
	Healthy shot sweet sherry vinegar such as Pedro Ximenez

Preheat the oven to 300°. Season the chicken inside and out with salt and pepper. Stuff the cavity with the lemon quarters, lightly crushed garlic, and basil and tarragon, setting aside a few leaves of the herbs for the bread salad.

Place the chicken in a large roasting pan, breast side up with the wings tucked under its back, and tie the legs together to close the cavity. Roast at 300° for 1 hour, until both the thigh and the breast read 150° on a meat thermometer. Thoroughly brush the chicken with 2 tablespoons olive oil. Increase the oven temperature to 400°. Return the chicken to the oven and roast until crispy and golden brown, 10–15 minutes. Set aside to rest while you prepare the bread salad.

Heat 1 tablespoon olive oil in a large skillet over medium-high heat and add the bread. Sauté until crispy and golden. Once it's golden, grate the remaining clove of garlic and toss with the bread over the heat for 20 seconds more. Remove to a large bowl. Add the shallots and tomatoes to the bread in the bowl; drizzle with 4 tablespoons olive oil, the sherry vinegar, and torn leaves of the basil and tarragon; toss and set aside.

When you're ready to serve, arrange the bread salad around the chicken in the roasting pan or on a platter.

Crispy Guinea Hen

GUINEA HENS CAN BE REALLY NASTY birds. I remember the guinea hens we had on the farm growing up; they'd chase me and my brother all over the place. On more than one occasion they actually caught us. When my brother was three, a guinea rooster jumped on his head and started pecking at him. He can show you the scars! I've been exacting my delicious revenge on those birds ever since.

Becasue guinea hens spend a lot of time running around and hunting for grubs and bugs, they have really strong muscles, loaded with myoglobin so that the meat is really rosy. Guinea hen meat is always a little pink: and that is the color you're going for. The whole grains of wheat berries complement the rosy meat.

Serves 4

1½   cups dried wheat berries
     Salt
1   onion, quartered
1   carrot, peeled
1   bay leaf
1   dried *ñora* pepper
1   guinea hen, brined overnight and air-dried
     in the refrigerator (TECHNIQUE, page 297)
     Freshly ground black pepper
4   tablespoons olive oil
2   tablespoons butter
3   branches fresh thyme
1   branch fresh rosemary
1   clove garlic, lightly crushed
1   cup oyster mushrooms
1   shallot, finely minced
½   cup diced unpeeled English cucumber
5   leaves fresh mint, torn
1   tablespoon My Favorite Vinaigrette (page 21)

SPECIAL EQUIPMENT: 2 bricks wrapped in aluminum foil, or a medium-sized heavy cast iron pan

Preheat the oven to 400°. To make the wheat berries, combine them with 3 cups water, 1½ tablespoons salt, the onion, carrot, bay leaf, and *ñora* pepper in a pressure cooker. Close the lid and heat over high heat until it starts to whistle. Reduce the heat to medium-low and simmer for 45 minutes. Or simmer all the ingredients, covered, in a large pot for about 1½ hours.

Cut up the guinea hen just as you would cut a duck (TECHNIQUE, page 120). Season thoroughly with salt and pepper. Heat 3 tablespoons of the olive oil in a large cast iron skillet over medium-high heat. Place the guinea hen pieces in the pan, skin-side down, and weight down with the bricks or the pan. Sear for 6–7 minutes, until the skin is golden and crispy.

Remove the weights and turn the pieces over. Add the butter, thyme, rosemary, and garlic to the pan. Roast in the oven for 15 minutes, until a meat thermometer inserted in the center registers 150°. Set aside to rest.

While the guinea hen is roasting, heat the remaining 1 tablespoon olive oil in a medium saucepan over medium-high heat. Add the mushrooms and sauté for 3 minutes, until golden. Add the shallots and cucumber and sauté for another 2 minutes. Season with salt and pepper. Reserve.

Once the wheat berries are cooked through and tender, turn off the heat, open the valve to release the steam, and remove the lid. Discard the carrot, onion, bay leaf, and pepper. Fold the sautéed mushroom mixture, torn mint leaves, and vinaigrette into the wheat berries. Season well with salt and pepper.

Spoon the wheat berries onto a large serving platter and top with the roasted guinea hen.

A NOTE ON...PAELLA

Paella comes from the Latin word *patella,* meaning "pan." Paella is one of the oldest dishes in the repertoire of classic Spanish cooking. Its origin is in the rice fields of Valencia on the Mediterranean coast, where nearly all the rice in Spain is grown.

There are as many recipes for paella as there are paella cooks, but there are a few hard and fast rules liable to change according to whomever you ask. The only rule that seems universal is: *just leave it alone!* Unlike risotto and many other rice dishes, you stir your paella rice as little as possible, letting the violent boil of the stock tumble the grains and release the starch so that the grains just barely stick together without losing their form. The best paella is made with Bomba rice (page 73), an ancient varietal that has the ability to absorb up to three times its volume in liquid. The more liquid rice absorbs, the more flavor your paella will have. You can certainly make paella with another short-grained rice like Arborio.

There are many secrets to making good paella, but perhaps the most important thing I can pass along is to slowly build layers of flavors. The *sofrito* of slow-cooked onions and tomato in olive oil (page 65)\ is the first layer of flavor and it becomes the foundation of the dish. Always make a bit more *sofrito* than you need; freeze the extra and it will find a happy home in any number of dishes.

Whenever I have the chance, I try to make paella outside. Traditionally, it's cooked over an open fire on the beach with fresh seafood. In the summer I love to have friends over on the weekend to cook paella on my roof (page 134). It's one of my favorite things to cook.

Chicken and Seafood Paella

Serves 4–6

FOR THE LOBSTER STOCK

2	lobsters
2	tablespoons olive oil
2	tablespoons tomato paste
¼	cup brandy
1	large onion, peeled and quartered
2	large carrots, halved and cut into big chunks
1	tomato, quartered
1	fennel bulb, quartered
2	cloves garlic
1	bunch fresh basil
	Pinch of saffron

Bring a large pot of water to a boil and boil the lobsters for 5 minutes. Remove the lobsters, reserving the water. Separate the tails and the claws from the bodies and set aside for the paella. Place the bodies with the legs facing up and cut in half and then into quarters with a large heavy knife or cleaver.

In a large saucepan, heat the olive oil over medium-high heat and add the lobster bodies. Stir with a wooden spoon for 5–7 minutes, until the lobsters give off an intense aroma. Add the tomato paste and stir to thoroughly coat the lobster bodies. Deglaze the pan with the brandy and cook off the alcohol, about 1 minute. Add the onions, carrots, tomato, fennel, garlic, and basil and sauté for 3–5 minutes, until the vegetables begin to take on color. Add 6 cups of the reserved lobster water, reduce the heat to medium low, and simmer for 2–3 hours.

Strain the stock, or if you want more flavor run the whole darn thing through a food mill; this will extract all the delicious juices from the lobster bodies and give you a rich stock. Remove about a cup of the stock and steep a small pinch of saffron in the liquid for 3 or 4 minutes, then return the saffron-infused broth to the stockpot. (Steeping saffron in a bit of liquid maximizes the spice's flavor and color.)
Makes about 5 cups

FOR THE PAELLA

	Tails and claws of 2 lobsters, reserved from the lobster stock recipe
¼	cup olive oil
2	pounds chicken drumsticks and thighs
6	jumbo shrimp

Salt

Freshly ground black pepper

½   cup diced chorizo

1   cup *sofrito* (page 65)

5   cups lobster stock (left)

2   cups Bomba rice

½   pound mussels

½   pound Manila clams

Paella pan, about 18 inches in diameter; for a smaller paella pan, cut the recipe in half

Cut each lobster tail crosswise into 3 pieces with a sharp knife, leaving the shell on. Set the tails and claws aside.

In a large paella pan over an outdoor grill or on a stovetop, heat the olive oil over medium-high heat. If you're doing the paella on the stovetop, you can use two burners if your pan is large. Season the chicken parts and shrimp with salt and pepper and sear in the paella pan. Once they've turned nicely golden, remove the shrimp and set aside. Add the chorizo to the pan with the chicken and cook to slightly render the oil, about 2 minutes.

Add the *sofrito* (or make it as pictured below) and about two-thirds of the stock and bring to a rolling boil. Add all the rice and gently stir until evenly mixed. It's important that the stock be boiling when you add the rice so the grains release their starch and create the slightly creamy texture that binds the grains of rice together. Season with salt and move to the cooler side of the grill or reduce the temperature to medium. You want the stock to be gently bubbling over the rice. Throughout the remainder of the preparation, add the remaining hot stock little by little as the rice absorbs the liquid until you've used all the stock.

After the rice has simmered for 10 minutes, bury the mussels and clams in the rice. Cook for 4 minutes, then evenly distribute the lobster tails and claws and the shrimp and cook for another 4 minutes. At this point the rice should have absorbed all of the stock and the grains should be plump and moist with a slight tooth but no chalky starch. Discard any unopened mussels or clams. Remove the paella from the heat and let rest for 5 minutes before serving.

chapter eight

SWEET PEAS

BRIGHT

✳ ✳ ✳

GREEN

✳ ✳ ✳

CRISPY

GREEN IS MY FAVORITE COLOR and I love green food—not in a *Green Eggs and Ham* kind of way, but I'm crazy about springy green peas. I think of them as the greenest of green food—they even taste healthy—and I've been devoted to them all my life. For some reason peas seem to be popular with kids. My niece and nephew are pretty good eaters, they'll eat their broccoli, but they *love* their peas. Maybe it runs in the family?

"For Andoni, luxury didn't mean foie gras and caviar, it meant simple things like the first sweet peas of the season, no bigger than fish eggs."

There are so many different, delicious ways to cook peas (or even eat them raw); they're as versatile a vegetable as any. There's a rich variety of sweet peas, from plump sugar snaps to tender snow peas to sweet shelling peas and their pea shoots. I love them all. Even frozen peas can be appealing. I believe that they are, in fact, a far better choice than those drab and dismal so-called fresh peas in the shell probably shipped from halfway around the world to your supermarket, particularly in winter.

There are few rules about cooking peas, but here is the only one you need to know: make sure not to overcook them. So many of the tasty good things in peas can be lost in the cooking. How long is too long? When your peas start to change color from vibrant green to dullish green, you've gone too far. Better to err on the side of undercooking.

When I worked at Mugaritz in San Sebastián, Andoni was always making a case for what he called *comida lujosa,* luxury food. For him luxury didn't mean lobster and foie gras, but rather the simpler things,

like the first sweet peas of the season, so tiny they were no bigger than fish eggs. Andoni called them green caviar and had us prepare a small pile of these minute peas in the bottom of a shallow bowl and cover them with what he called a "veil" of ginger gelee. The bowl was lightly warmed under the broiler and then finished with sweet pea flowers. Perfection.

Just looking at a big bowl of peas it's not hard to imagine how good they are for us. I think of them as bright green pills filled with nutrients such as vitamins A, C, and K, and some B complex vitamins, plus some zinc, manganese and dietary fiber.

Then there are the plant-based phyto-nutrients with names like coumestrol and saponin, that offer health benefits beyond the basics. Not as obsessively researched or as highly touted as their legume cousins The Beans, sweet peas are for me the unsung healthy heroes.

A NOTE ON...BLANCHING

Blanching is the process of briefly plunging vegetables (or fruit) in boiling water to partially cook them and intensify their color and flavor. When blanching vegetables, it's important to have a large bowl of ice water ready for dunking the vegetables to stop the cooking process. I've observed that most home cooks don't use nearly enough ice. Remember, when you add the hot vegetables to the ice water a lot of that ice will melt. We want the ice to cool the vegetables, not the vegetables to melt the ice. So when I say a lot of ice, I'm talking at least two trays' worth, and preferably twice that.

I always like to blanch vegetables with abundant water in the largest pot I have, to avoid overcrowding. A crowded pot will lower the water temperature and screw up the blanching process. I add a handful of salt to the water before I toss in the vegetables. Always taste your blanching water; it should be as salty as the Dead Sea, or maybe just the Mediterranean.

Timing is really a matter of choice. If I still want the veggies to have a fresh snap and just take the raw edge off, I'll blanch them briefly, say 30 seconds. If I'm making a salad and I want some summer squash that's not quite raw but not quite cooked, I'll blanch them for 45 seconds or so before shocking them in the ice bath. Other things like tiny root vegetables need to be blanched until they're cooked all the way through. In the summer it's nice to keep the colors bright, if you blanch veggies too long, they'll lose their vibrancy.

Pea Tendrils a la Catalana

THE CLASSIC CATALAN DISH, *Espinacas a la Catalana*, with pine nuts and golden raisins, is a near-perfect balance of sweet and salty. The original dish uses spinach, but this version takes the idea one step further with pea shoots and creamy garbanzo beans. Dim sum in Chinatown is our Sunday morning ritual and one of my favorite things to have there is sautéed pea shoots. One day it occurred to me that fresh pea shoots would be brilliant *a la Catalana;* they are!

Serves 2

¼	cup pine nuts
2	tablespoons olive oil
2	cloves garlic, thinly sliced
½	cup cooked garbanzo beans (TECHNIQUE, right)
½	pound pea tendrils
¼	cup golden raisins
	Salt
	Freshly ground black pepper
	Juice of 1 lemon

Place a large skillet over medium-high heat and add the pine nuts to the dry pan. As the pine nuts begin to toast and turn golden brown, shake the pan to make sure they don't burn. Once they're browned and giving off a nutty aroma, about 3 minutes, add the olive oil, garlic, and garbanzo beans and sauté until the garlic starts to take on color. Toss the pea tendrils into the pan, add the raisins, and swiftly sauté to just wilt the tendrils, about 2 minutes. Season with salt and pepper, drizzle with lemon juice, and serve.

TECHNIQUE

Cooking Garbanzo Beans

A PERFECTLY COOKED, CREAMY garbanzo bean is a very satisfying thing and though technically not a sweet pea, the two are related and combine beautifully. Unless you are truly in a pinch, I urge you to avoid canned beans. Quality dried beans from a reliable source are always preferable, and if by chance you find green garbanzos in the pod, snap them up, blanch them quickly, and toss in a salad. I do recommend soaking uncooked dried beans, overnight.

Most garbanzos available here are from Mexico or India (but *garbanzo* is the Spanish word for chickpea!). In Spain there are three varieties: the tiny, smooth *pedrosillanos* are my favorite; *Castillanos* are medium-sized; and the largest are *blanco lechosos*.

To cook garbanzos, soak 2 cups of beans overnight, then drain and combine in a pressure cooker or a large heavy-bottomed pot with 4 cups of water, 1 bay leaf, 1 carrot, 1 onion, and 4 slices of bacon (the bacon is optional). Place over high heat until the pressure cooker starts to whistle, then reduce the temperature to low and cook for 30–45 minutes, depending on the size of the beans. (Cooking in a conventional pot will take about twice the time.) Release the steam, and taste. The beans should be softened, yet still maintain their shape. Discard the aromatics and proceed with the recipe.

Simply Sweet Peas

SOMETIMES YOU JUST WANT the fresh green taste of sweet peas. Right now. Here's a quick way to get your pea fix.

Serves 2

1	tablespoon fruity olive oil
2	cups shelled sweet peas, about 2 pounds peas in the shell
1	teaspoon unsalted butter
	Salt
	Freshly ground black pepper
	A few torn leaves fresh mint and basil
	Parmigiano for shaving
	Salt
	Freshly ground black pepper

Heat the olive oil in a medium skillet over medium heat. Add the peas and sauté vigorously. When the peas turn a vibrant green and are just cooked through, about 3 minutes, add the butter, season with salt and pepper, toss in the torn herbs, and roll it all together in the pan.

With a rubber spatula, scrape the peas into a large serving bowl, making sure to get all the juicy bits left in the pan. With a sharp vegetable peeler, shave a few thin slices of Parmigiano over the peas and serve.

Sugar Snap Pea Salad

AS SOON AS SUGAR SNAPS show up at the farmers market, I'm instantly happy. Sweet, crisp, snappy, and sugary! This salad is all about the sugar snaps, with a pinch of Aleppo pepper for heat, some fresh ricotta cheese for richness and texture, and edible flowers for color. It comes together easily, looks gorgeous, and is oh so easy to love.

Serves 4

1	pound fresh sugar snap peas
1	bunch radishes
½	cup fresh ricotta cheese
	A few leaves fresh peppermint
	Salt
	Freshly ground black pepper
	Juice of 1 lemon
	Olive oil to taste
	Pinch Aleppo pepper or red pepper flakes
	Handful of edible flowers, such as pea blossoms or nasturtiums

With a sharp knife, trim the tips of the sugar snap peas on both ends, remove the strings if they bother you, and cut some in half lengthwise. Blanch the sugar snaps quickly, just about 30 seconds and shock in ice water (see Note, page 139). Slice the radishes thinly into coin shapes or half-moons. Combine the peas, radishes, cheese, and peppermint in a large bowl. Season with salt and pepper and toss with the lemon juice and olive oil. Serve with a sprinkle of Aleppo pepper and garnish of edible flowers.

Squid with Baby Favas, Mint, and Basil

THIS DISH SWIMS SOMEWHERE in the brackish waters between salad course and appetizer. It's really lovely on a hot day with a refreshing glass of crisp white wine. There are two options with cooking squid: barely cook it very quickly at a high temperature, or cook it for a longer time at a lower temperature. Anything in between and your squid will come out rubbery.

Here the squid are delicately braised. If the squid you find are any bigger than your index finger, cut them into smaller pieces. Some people like to peel the purple skin off the squid; but

particularly with small squid, I like to leave it on because it adds texture and flavor.

Serves 4 as an appetizer

- 2   tablespoons olive oil
- 1   shallot, finely diced
- 1   tablespoon white wine vinegar
- ½   pound cleaned baby squid, smallest available
     Salt
     Freshly ground black pepper
- 1   cup shelled sweet peas

1 cup baby fava beans, unpeeled
1 small bunch asparagus, shaved into
   thin ribbons with a vegetable peeler
6 slices Quick-Cured Lemons (page 18), halved
1 tablespoon pine nuts, toasted
5 leaves fresh basil
5 leaves fresh mint

Heat the olive oil in a large saucepan over medium-high heat. Add the shallots and sweat until translucent. Add the vinegar and reduce for 2 minutes. Reduce the heat to medium low. Season the squid with salt and pepper and add to the olive oil. Stir and gently braise for 15 minutes.

Add the peas, fava beans, and asparagus. Cook for another 3 minutes, until the vegetables are tender. Adjust the seasoning with salt and pepper. Toss in the cured lemon, pine nuts, basil, and mint and serve on a platter.

Whole Black Sea Bass with Pea and Butter Sauce

IN NEW YORK CITY we're very lucky to be so close to the rich waters of Long Island and all its incredible seafood. Black sea bass is, in the humble opinion of this cook, one of the finest eating fish in the sea. Its meat is firm and sweet, its numbers are plentiful, and it is easy to prepare.

I have a soft-spot for these little guys too—they spend their entire lives trying to escape from the wildly aggressive striped bass. A few years ago I was fishing in my friend Sy's boat off Montauk Point at the end of Long Island. It was getting late and we were nearly out of bait. On one of my last casts, I hooked a nice 2-pound black sea bass. As I reeled it in alongside the boat and Sy reached for the net, a huge striper swam up and engulfed my handsome little black bass. I yanked my line. Sy swung his net and we landed a tremendous two-for-one bass special.

Serves 4

1   2–3-pound black sea bass, head and tail on, cleaned and scaled
    Salt
    Freshly ground black pepper
1   lemon, halved
    Bunches of fresh basil, tarragon, and thyme, handfuls of basil and tarragon reserved and torn into pieces
2   tablespoons olive oil
1   shallot, finely diced
½   cup txakoli
4   cups shelled sweet peas, about 4 pounds peas in the shell
    Zest of 2 lemons
2   tablespoons butter

Preheat the oven to 350°. Season the black bass with salt and pepper both inside the cavity and outside. Thinly slice one half of the lemon. Score the bass skin and place a few lemon slices in the slits and follow with a few sprigs of thyme. Stuff

146

A NOTE ON...TXAKOLI

I often like to use txakoli, an effervescent white wine from the Basque region of Spain, to make the sauce (then I'll throw the bottle in a bucket of ice water to drink with the dish). Txakoli has a little spritz to it. Traditionally it's poured from high above the shoulder into a glass held beneath the waist, and besides the obvious theatrics, this does help aerate the wine. If you're lucky enough to come upon rosé txakoli, buy it all. Every last bottle. You won't regret it.

the cavity of the fish with the bunches of basil, tarragon, and thyme.

Place the fish in a large roasting pan and roast for 25–30 minutes. To check to see if the fish is done, insert the tip of a sharp knife into the thickest part of the fillet. Pull it out and touch it to your lip. It should be hot, but not enough to burn you. If the knife is just warm, return the fish to the oven for another 5 or 10 minutes. Once the fish is done, transfer it to a serving platter.

Heat the olive oil in a large saucepan over medium-high heat. Add the shallots and sweat until translucent. Add the txakoli and reduce for 2 minutes. Add the peas and lemon zest, season with salt and pepper, and cook until the peas are tender, 3–5 minutes. Add the butter, a generous handful of torn basil and tarragon, and swirl around the pan until the butter is melted. Spoon the peas over the fish and serve immediately.

Chilled Sweet Pea Soup

NOTHING SAYS SPRING like a fresh pea soup. This is the antithesis of the gummy, chalky, pale, Army-green pea soup of our childhoods.

Serves 4 as an appetizer

- 2 cups shelled sweet peas, about 2 pounds peas in the shell
- 6 tablespoons olive oil
- 1 shallot, finely minced
- 1 clove garlic, finely minced
- 2 tablespoons good, sweet cider vinegar (or Champagne vinegar or white balsamic vinegar)
- 1 slice country white bread, crust removed, bread torn
- 6 whole fresh basil leaves
  Salt
  Freshly ground black pepper
  Zest of 1 lemon
- 4 tablespoons plain yogurt

Fill a big pot with well-salted water and bring to a boil. Blanch the peas for 3 minutes and shock in an ice water bath (see Note, page 139).

In a small skillet, heat 2 tablespoons of the olive oil and sweat the shallots and garlic until translucent, about 3 minutes. Add the vinegar and reduce by half.

Combine the shallot/garlic mixture with the blanched peas in a blender with 2 cups water and purée on high until completely smooth. Add the bread and basil leaves and process until smooth. Reduce the speed of the blender and drizzle in the remaining 4 tablespoons of the olive oil until fully incorporated.

Season with salt, pepper, and lemon zest and divide among 4 chilled bowls. Finish each bowl with a dollop of yogurt.

Lightly Cured Wild Salmon with Pea Salad

CURING YOUR OWN SALMON might seem a little daunting at first, but it's really quite simple and the results are truly rewarding. I love having control over the herbs that I choose to put into my curing mixture; adding citrus zest makes the final product so much more flavorful.

Serves 4–6

FOR THE CURED SALMON
- 1 **pound salt**
- 1 **pound sugar**
- 2 **cloves garlic, crushed to a paste in a mortar and pestle**
- **Zest of 1 lemon**
- 1 **healthy bunch dill, coarsely chopped, 1 tablespoon reserved for the salad**
- 1 **tablespoon whole peppercorns**
- 1 **fillet wild salmon, skin on, about 2 pounds**

FOR THE PEA SALAD
- 4 **cups fresh shelled sweet peas, about 4 pounds in the shell**
- 1 **crisp apple, such as Macoun or Winesap**
- 1 **bulb fennel, fronds chopped and reserved**
- **Small handful fresh basil leaves, torn**
- **Salt**
- **Freshly ground black pepper**

FOR THE KEFIR VINAIGRETTE
- 1 **clove garlic**
- **Zest of 1 lemon**
- ¼ **cup plain kefir or yogurt**
- ¼ **cup olive oil**
- **Aleppo pepper to taste**

For the salmon, in a large bowl, combine the salt, sugar, garlic paste, zest, dill, and peppercorns. Line a baking sheet large enough to hold the salmon fillet with plastic wrap twice the length of the sheet. Spread a thin layer of the mixture on the wrap and place the fillet, skin-side up, on top. Pour the remainder of the salt mixture over the salmon to cover. Wrap well in the plastic wrap and refrigerate for 36 hours.

Rinse the fish thoroughly under cold running water and pat dry.

For the salad, bring a large pot of well-salted water to a rolling boil and blanch the peas for 1 minute; immediately shock in an ice bath (see Note, page 139).

Cut the apple in quarters, remove the core, and slice into paper-thin slices. Repeat with the fennel bulb. You should have a healthy pile of shaved apple and fennel. Toss the peas with the apple and fennel. Add the torn basil, chopped fennel fronds, and the reserved 1 tablespoon chopped dill, and season with salt and pepper.

For the kefir vinaigrette, grate the garlic and whisk together with the zest, kefir (or yogurt), and olive oil in a small bowl.

Place the salmon skin-side down on a cutting board. With a sharp knife, slice into thin, delicate ribbons as if you were slicing smoked salmon, without slicing the skin. Discard the skin.

To serve, pile the pea salad in a bowl or platter and drizzle with the vinaigrette. Top with the thinly sliced salmon and sprinkle with Aleppo pepper.

A NOTE ON...TORN HERBS

One of the secrets of this dish is torn herbs. I almost always try to tear my fresh herbs instead of chopping them. Herbs are delicate little things and too much brutality can bruise them and wreck their flavor. A leaf of basil, right, torn at the last minute, will perfume your dish with its essential oils and make it sing.

chapter nine

PARSLEY

POTENT

✳ ✳ ✳

LEAFY

✳ ✳ ✳

BENEFICIAL

I REMEMBER JUST WHEN I FELL FOR PARSLEY. I was in college in Kalamazoo, Michigan, cooking at a little restaurant called the International Café, which turned out to be neither, but I didn't know that then.

Kiki Babeluc was the first real chef I ever worked for. Wrinkled, rough, brash, and lovely, she grew up in Marseilles in the 1940s and spent the decades after traveling the world, cooking at such places as a hunting

lodge in South Africa and a grandiose hotel in Patagonia. To this day, I have no idea how she wound up in Kalamazoo. She would never tell me. She was left-handed and her hand was curled into a club from arthritis and years of gripping a knife. Whenever I screwed up in the kitchen, that club would come out of nowhere and box me on the side of the head. Despite many, many mistakes, I could never anticipate it.

Even though I frustrated her, Kiki was fond of me and we had unforgettable adventures together. Once, as we were closing the restaurant at 11 PM, she told me to be back there at 4 in the morning, and to bring rubber boots. At the appointed hour,

we loaded flashlights, nets, buckets, and Scotch into my tiny rusted Toyota (one of Kiki's idiosyncrasies was that despite traveling the world, she didn't drive) and she directed me out of town into the woods to a small lake. Between chugs of Scotch and cigarettes Kiki and I scooped fat Michigan bullfrogs into our nets as she explained in detail how we'd prepare them for a special that night. Needless to say, *les cuisses de grenouilles* were not a big hit in western Michigan and we ended up eating them all ourselves. But Kiki was happy to have shown me "real French cooking."

So when Kiki led me to her herb garden in a little plot behind the restaurant, and with great pride showed me the rows and rows of

"Even if only a fraction of the health claims are accurate, parsley is a wonder herb. And it's just plain wonderful to cook with."

parsley she grew, I was inclined to believe she was onto something. It surprised me the way she managed to infuse her cooking with fresh parsley—folded into mashed potatoes, sprinkled over roasted eggplant, pureed and used to brighten salads.

We didn't get much seafood in Kalamazoo, but just like me, Kiki was in love with anchovies. Every morning she'd mash up some anchovy with a clove of garlic, a handful of parsley, a squeeze of lemon, and finely grated Parmigiano cheese and spread it on toast for breakfast.

Even with Kiki's cred, at first I looked down my nose at this curly business that seemed, well, pretty ordinary and more at home lining the edges of the breakfast buffet at the local Friendly's. But once I really got to know parsley the way Kiki did, I fell into total appreciation. Kiki was right (as she was about so many things). And now that I know more, I recognize parsley as the Hero it is.

If you dive into the research on parsley, and even if only a fraction of the health claims are accurate, you'll come up believing it's a miracle herb. I try to have parsley juice or a green smoothie every day (see page 155). I have experienced parsley's benefits first-hand. Literally. When I'm having a lot of pain in my finger joints, which unfortunately happens quite frequently, I believe that parsley helps me. Perhaps it's the folate in parsley, combined with the fact that the herb is a natural diuretic, that helps reduce the uric acid in my blood. Loaded with vitamins A and C and flavonoids (plant pigments with antioxidant properties), parsley is also an important source of potassium, which I like to think of as the muscle mineral. Given the many ways parsley seems to help me, it can't be bad for the rest of you, either.

Parsley is one of the most widely cultivated herbs in the world. And unlike so many precious and obscure ingredients, it is accessible and affordable. But no matter how beneficial it can be, when I look at parsley today, I think of Kiki and remember how just plain wonderful it is to cook with.

Salsa Verde

THIS POTENT AND VERSATILE green sauce is excellent drizzled over grilled steak, pork chops, and steamed fish, or even folded into a risotto at the last minute for a vibrant hit of flavor. When I'm steaming clams in white wine, I love to throw in a couple spoonfuls at the end.

Makes 1 good cup

	Good handful fresh parsley, stems and all
	Small handful fresh mint
½	**cup olive oil**
1	**clove garlic**
	Zest of 1 lemon
1	**shallot**
1	**small dried chile**

Either toss all the ingredients in a blender and pulse quickly or work together with a mortar and pestle into a coarse blend.

Parsley Juice

THIS IS NOT A JUICE IN THE TRUE SENSE of the word, it has more texture. Parsley juice is pretty strong to drink straight, hence the apple and other ingredients. I prefer to use a Vitamix or a blender to make green drinks instead of a juicer. Unlike juicers that extract just the juice and discard the fiber, the Vitamix doesn't break down food into nutrients and fiber, it lets our digestive juices do that good work.

Makes 1 small glass

1	**bunch fresh parsley, stems and all**
1	**apple**
	Juice of 1 lemon
2	**tablespoons honey**
1	**teaspoon grated peeled fresh ginger**

Rinse the parsley thoroughly. Core the apple and cut into quarters. Combine the parsley, apple, lemon juice, honey, and ginger in a Vitamix or blender with ¼ cup of water and a couple of ice cubes. Process until liquid and serve.

A Real Smoothie

THIS SMOOTHIE, which is very easy to make, digests easily and seems to make me feel good in general. It's a light way to make sure you're getting enough dietary fiber and is actually quite filling. Feel free to improvise with ingredients, like using organic peaches instead of berries.
If I'm feeling a bit under the weather, I'll add a nice chunk of ginger. But I never omit the greens, or the banana to keep it smooth.

Makes 1 tall glass

	Small handful fresh parsley, stems and all
4	**leaves kale**
1	**cup frozen organic berries, like strawberries or raspberries**
1	**banana**
1	**teaspoon ground flaxseed**

Combine all the ingredients in a blender jar, add 1 cup water, and blend until smooth. If the drink seems a little thick, add more water.

TECHNIQUE

Pickled Shallots

BY NOW YOU'VE FIGURED out that I really like pickled things. These shallots are a really simple way to add a flavor pop to salads and appetizers.

Makes 1 cup

3   shallots
1   cup Vegetable Pickling Liquid
    (page 185)

Slice the shallots paper-thin on a mandoline. In a small skillet, combine the shallots and pickling liquid and bring to a simmer. Simmer for 2 minutes, then remove from the heat and let steep for 10 minutes. Refrigerate in the pickling liquid, covered, for up to a week.

Salad of Marble Potatoes

THE FIRST TINY POTATOES of the season are really my favorites, especially the creamy French variety called La Ratte. A really good potato doesn't need much help to be delicious, but there is one trick to cooking potatoes that I swear by: seasoning the cooking water. I like to add a few cloves of garlic, some *guindilla* chiles, a handful of kosher salt, and herbs. Potatoes are like flavor sponges; you'll be amazed at how much intensity they'll pick up. Cover the potatoes and aromatics with cold water, bring to a boil, and then reduce to a gentle simmer until the potatoes are soft and buttery. I generally like to leave the skins on potatoes when I cook them, I think they taste better and, of course, many nutrients are in the skins.

Serves 4

1   pound new potatoes, smallest available
2   *guindilla* peppers, or 2 dried chile peppers
    Branch fresh thyme
1   bay leaf
    Salt
    Leaves from 1 large bunch fresh parsley, washed, dried, and coarsely chopped
4   slices Quick-Cured Lemons (page 18), diced
2   tablespoons pickled shallots (TECHNIQUE, left)
¼   cup good olive oil
    Juice of 2 lemons
1   teaspoon ras el hanout, or a blend of coriander, cumin, cayenne, clove, cardamom, ginger, and fennel seeds, all spices toasted and ground

In a medium saucepan, combine the potatoes, *guindilla* peppers, thyme, and bay leaf with enough cold water to cover the potatoes. Season the water generously with salt; it should taste like seawater. Bring the water to a boil and reduce to a simmer. Cook until the potatoes are fork tender, 20–30 minutes, depending on the size. Drain the potatoes, discard the aromatics, and set aside to cool.

Combine the potatoes, parsley, cured lemons, shallots, olive oil, and lemon juice in a large serving bowl. Season with the ras el hanout and toss together.

White Bean Salad with Preserved Tuna and Parsley Vinaigrette

I LOVE BEAN SALADS with parsley. Parsley Vinaigrette makes this simple salad of marinated white beans and tuna come to life. Crisp, tasty, and light, the salad makes a wonderful lunch salad or a small tapas sharing dish. If you want to really flex your cooking muscles, throw in some Quick-Cured Lemons (page 18) and you'll be amazed at how this salad sings.

Serves 4 as an appetizer

1 cup dried cannellini beans, soaked overnight
1 large carrot, peeled and roughly chopped
2 stalks celery
1 onion, quartered
2 bay leaves
1 cup Preserved Tuna (TECHNIQUE, page 224) or good quality canned tuna
1 head radicchio, finely chopped
Salt
Freshly ground black pepper
Parsley Vinaigrette (right)

Combine the beans, carrot, 1 celery stalk, the onion, and bay leaves in the pressure cooker. Add 4 cups water, close, and heat over high heat until it starts to whistle. Reduce the heat and simmer for 45 minutes, until the beans are tender. Alternatively, cook in a covered heavy-bottomed pot for 2 hours over medium-low heat. Once the beans are tender and cooked through, drain and discard the veggies. Set the beans aside to cool.

Thinly slice the remaining stalk of celery on the bias. Flake the tuna into a bowl and combine with the celery, beans, and radicchio. Season with salt and pepper and toss with the Parsley Vinaigrette. This salad can be eaten right way, but the flavor is even better if you let it sit in the fridge for a few hours.

Parsley Vinaigrette

A PARSLEY VINAIGRETTE is a terrifically versatile thing, perfect with all sorts of salads, like potato salad and bean salad. But I also use it to spark up a sautéed piece of fish or grilled meat and vegetables. All hail Lady Parsley.

Makes ½ cup

Handful fresh parsley leaves and stems
1 clove garlic
Juice of 1 lemon
½ tablespoon Champagne vinegar
¼ cup Arbequina or other good olive oil
Salt
Freshly ground black pepper

Combine the parsley, garlic, lemon juice, and vinegar in a Vitamix or blender. Process until smooth and bright green; remove to a bowl and whisk in the olive oil. Adjust the seasoning with salt and pepper.

Cooking Octopus

1 3–5-pound octopus
1 large carrot
1 onion
2 bay leaves
4 cloves garlic
3 cups red wine, alcohol cooked off

Combine all the ingredients in a pressure cooker. Seal the lid and bring to a boil over high heat until it whistles. Reduce the heat and simmer for 25–30 minutes, until the octopus is tender. Or combine the ingredients in a heavy-bottomed pot and cook, covered, for about an hour. Drain, discard the aromatics, and set aside to cool. The cooking liquid can be frozen and re-used for future octopus. Each time you use it, it gets more flavorful.

With a sharp knife, remove the tentacles from the octopus and dice the body into bite-sized chunks.

Heat a large cast iron skillet over high heat and rub thoroughly with a little bit of olive oil on a paper towel. Sear the octopus tentacles until golden brown on all sides. Set aside. Repeat with the diced octopus.

Octopus and Parsley Salad

A LITTLE CHARRED OCTOPUS, some bright lemon, a few potatoes, a handful of other lovely things. But to me, it's really the parsley that's the star of this show. I love this salad with a chilled rosé.
Serves 4

1 pound new potatoes, smallest available, cooked as for Salad of Marble Potatoes (page 156) and cooled
1 octopus, cooked and charred (TECHNIQUE, left)
1 stalk celery, sliced
1 Persian cucumber, cut into bite-size chunks
½ cup fresh green olives, such as Castelvetrano or Cerignola, pitted and coarsely chopped
¼ cup walnuts, toasted and coarsely chopped
   Leaves from a generous handful fresh parsley, washed and dried
1 small shallot, halved and thinly sliced
¼ cup olive oil
   Juice of 2 lemons
2 teaspoons za'atar
   Salt
   Freshly ground black pepper

In a large mixing bowl, combine the cooked potatoes, diced octopus (reserve the tentacles for serving), celery, cucumber, olives, walnuts, parsley, and shallots. Season with the olive oil, lemon juice, za'atar, salt, and pepper and toss.

Divide equally among 4 small plates; top each serving with two crispy octopus tentacles.

chapter ten

BERRIES

RIPE

✳ ✳ ✳

SWEET

✳ ✳ ✳

SEASONAL

BERRIES IS WHERE MANY OF THE SO-CALLED "SUPER FOODS" books begin. I can't possibly deny how wonderful berries are, nor would I want to. Their antioxidant properties and vitamin and mineral benefits are so well-documented. But my question is this: If I'm going to get these health benefits with blueberries, just how much of them must I eat? And how many of those berries are sprayed with toxic pesticides, picked

"I'd rather pick my berries at the height of their flavor, or wait until berry season comes around again. Which it always seems to do."

unripe, treated with preservative gases, then shipped from halfway around the world to our markets out of season in the dead of winter? And don't even get me started on the flavor of those berries—or lack thereof.

So here's my very opinionated take on berries. I'm no scientist, but it just does not seem logical to me that all the negatives of out-of-season berries can be outweighed by the positives, if in fact any remain after the fruit has been subjected to such treatment. And I haven't even gotten to genetically modified fruit. I've read about the prospect of putting fish genes in strawberries so that they can resist frost and have a longer growing season. Is this a good idea? I don't think so. I'd rather pick my berries at the height of their flavor and enjoy them on the spot or quickly freeze them. Or I'll just do without and wait until strawberry season comes around again. Which it always seems to do.

A few years ago, my friend Franca Tantillo, introduced me to the Tristar strawberry that she grows on her farm, Berried Treasures in upstate New York. Tristar is a deep red, glossy, firm, day-neutral straw-berry, which means it produces multiple harvests in a single season and tastes sweeter and richer than any ordinary strawberry. To me Tristars actually taste more like Vermont wild strawberries. Those obese, cottony strawberries in plastic clamshells that I see in supermarkets have nothing to do with real strawberries like these.

I was practically born in a berry patch. Gooseberries, blackberries, raspberries, currants, strawberries, blueberries; on our farm we grew, picked, and processed all of these. The first sign of summer in Vermont was the ripening of the little red wild straw-berries that grew in our fields. As soon as the wild strawberries began to flower, we'd have to move the sheep to a more wooded area or they'd gobble them up. I have distinct memories of using my pocket knife to cut an opening in a plastic milk jug, threading my belt through the hole and setting off for the fields for hours to pick those wild strawberries. My brother Nils was much more disciplined than I and always returned with twice as many berries, and inevitably my shirt would be more stained. Wild black-

berries were a bit more challenging; as small kids we were sent in to crawl beneath the high brambles. We used to pretend we were characters in *Hogan's Heroes,* sneaking under the razor wire of a POW camp.

The only problem with picking blackberries is that just when you're ready to pack it in and go home, you always come upon one more bush laden with fat berries that are almost out of reach. In my family, to return without scratched arms or eyes stinging from summer sweat means you never really went blackberry picking.

I'm not really a big sweets person, but one thing that really excites me is any dessert involving fresh berries. The dessert shouldn't be complex; when it is the berries lose their charm as well as their identity.

Mutti's Blueberry Boy Bait

THIS CAKE IS A FAMILY CLASSIC that my grand-mother has been making for me since I was a little guy, and I still love it. It's a very simple cake, and for me the very best way to end a meal. My grandmother remembers this recipe from a Fannie Farmer cookbook, but Blueberry Boy Bait actually turns out to be the creation of a 15-year-old girl competing in the junior division of a Pillsbury baking contest in the 1950s.

Serves 8

½	cup butter
1	cup sugar, plus a bit more for sprinkling
2	eggs, separated
1	teaspoon vanilla
¼	teaspoon salt
1½	cups plus 1 tablespoon all-purpose flour
1	teaspoon baking powder
½	cup milk
1½	cups blueberries

Preheat the oven to 350°. Butter a round 9-inch springform pan, line with a round of parchment paper, and butter the paper.

In a standing mixer, cream together the butter and ¾ cup of the sugar. Add the egg yolks, vanilla, and salt and mix until creamy.

Sift the 1½ cups flour and the baking powder together. Add the sifted flour and the milk to the butter mixture and gently combine.

In another large bowl, beat the egg whites with the remaining ¼ cup sugar until they make stiff peaks. Fold the whites into the batter. Coat the berries with the remaining 1 tablespoon flour and add to the batter.

Pour the batter into the prepared pan and sprinkle the top with sugar. Bake for 50 minutes, or until a knife comes out clean. Serve with a whole lot of love, and maybe a dollop of whipped cream.

Strawberry Ice Cream

THIS ICE CREAM IS DELICIOUS with fresh strawberries, but it's also really great with frozen ones. When the farmers market is overflowing with berries, I buy flats of the more beaten up ones and freeze them. Basically I take a plastic freezer bag, fill it with berries, suck the air out of it, and twist the bag closed. You can also do this with a Ziploc bag, but it's a bit harder to get all the air out. That way I can make berry ice cream year round. A scattering of wild strawberries and a drizzle of aged balsamic vinegar are perfect complements to strawberry ice cream.

Makes about 1 quart

1½	cups sugar
3	cups fresh strawberries
1	cup heavy cream
1	cup fresh wild strawberries
	Drizzle of *saba* or aged balsamic vinegar

Bring the sugar, 3 cups strawberries, and ½ cup water to a simmer. Puree in the Vitamix or blender, pour into a bowl, and whisk in the cream. Set aside to cool.

Once it has cooled, process in an ice cream maker following the manufacturer's instructions.

Serve with fresh wild strawberries and a drizzle of *saba* or aged balsamic vinegar.

Raspberries and Yogurt with Buttermilk Crêpes

MOST PEOPLE THINK OF CRÊPES as breakfast food, but I prefer a savory breakfast. The tart yogurt filling and the buttermilk in the batter balance really well with the sweet raspberries.

Serves 4

1	cup all-purpose flour
1	tablespoon granulated sugar
¼	teaspoon salt
2	eggs
1¼	cups milk
¼	cup buttermilk
4	tablespoons clarified butter
	Zest of 3 lemons
1½	cups plain unsweetened yogurt
2	tablespoons honey
	Freshly ground black pepper
1	cup fresh raspberries
	Sprinkle of confectioners' sugar

Mix together the flour, granulated sugar, and salt. In another bowl, whisk together the eggs, milk, buttermilk, 3 tablespoons of the clarified butter, and the zest of 1 lemon. Slowly add the dry ingredients to the wet ingredients and whisk into a nice, thin batter. If the batter seems too thick, add a bit more buttermilk.

Heat a crêpe pan or 10-inch nonstick skillet over medium-high heat. Brush the pan with butter. Add about 2 tablespoons batter, lift the pan and roll the batter around to create a thin, even layer. Once the crêpe starts to form little holes, bubble a bit, and begins to turn golden brown, it's ready to turn. With a spatula, carefully flip the crêpe over and cook another 30 seconds. Remove the crêpe to a large plate and repeat until you've used all the batter, making about 10 crêpes.

In a small bowl mix together the remaining zest, yogurt, honey, and pepper. Place one crêpe on a large plate, smear on a thin layer of yogurt, and top with another crêpe. Repeat until you've layered all the crêpes into a beautiful cake. Top with raspberries and confectioners' sugar.

Blackberry and Almond Crumble

PLUMP, TART BLACKBERRIES are one of my favorite things about summer. When I buy them in the morning at the farmers market, I usually devour them all before I make it home. On the rare occasions that I manage to save a few, I like to make this crumble. I like my desserts to be simple (mostly because I'm not much of a pastry chef and they've got to be simple or I'll screw them up). This one is about as easy as they come. Chopped almonds (I like to use Marconas) give the topping a great little twist.

Serves 4

1	cup rolled oats
¾	cup sugar
1	cup almond flour
¼	teaspoon baking soda
	Couple pinches salt
3	tablespoons butter
½	cup almonds, preferably Marcona, chopped
3	cups fresh blackberries
	Zest of ½ orange
	Juice of 1 orange
½	teaspoon ground cinnamon

Preheat the oven to 375°. Combine the oats, ¼ cup of the sugar, the almond flour, baking soda, and a pinch of salt in a food processor and pulse. Add the butter and pulse until combined. Remove to a bowl and mix in the chopped almonds.

Mix the remaining ½ cup sugar, the blackberries, orange zest, orange juice, cinnamon, and a pinch of salt and arrange in a baking dish.

Spread the crumble mixture on top of the berries. Bake for 35–40 minutes, until golden and bubbly. Serve alone, or with vanilla ice cream… or better yet, almond ice cream (see 10 Things to Do with Almonds, page 58).

Currant Glaze for Pork

CURRANTS ARE BRILLIANT with pork and game; this currant glaze will turn a nice roast pork into something really divine. Even smeared on a pork loin, the glaze is awesome. If you're feeling adventurous and want to try your hand at venison or wild boar, currant glaze is a perfect accompaniment. Just spread it on the meat before putting it into the oven and you'll have made an ordinary dish special.

Makes 2 cups glaze

1¾	pounds red currants
1	teaspoon grated fresh ginger
¾	cup sugar
1	teaspoon apple cider vinegar

Combine the currants, ginger, and ½ cup water in a medium saucepan and bring to a simmer over medium-high heat. Reduce the heat and simmer for 3–4 minutes, until the currants are soft. Mix together the sugar and vinegar, then stir into the pot. Raise the heat and bring to a boil, then cook until the fruit syrup begins to thicken, about 8–10 minutes more. Transfer the glaze to a sterilized canning jar. It'll keep for months in the refrigerator and is wonderful on morning toast.

SEASON

III

SUMMER

172

ON THE FARM

CH. 11: Carrots SUGARY ✳ SNAPPY ✳ VIVID

CH. 12: Corn SUMMERY ✳ JOYFUL ✳ DELICIOUS

CH. 13: Stone Fruit LUSCIOUS ✳ COLORFUL ✳ RADIANT

CH. 14: Good Fish SCARCE ✳ SUSTAINABLE ✳ SATISFYING

173

I really believe in getting to know the people who grow the produce I buy, and nothing pleases me more than spending time on their farms. I've found that most farmers have one thing in common: They do what they do for love, not money. Patty Gentry, far right, is a remarkable young woman with a small organic farm in East Moriches, on Eastern Long Island.

Before she became a farmer, Patty was a chef, so she knows just what to grow to please her restaurant clients and to sell at the weekend stand at her Early Girl Farm, left. Many of the herbs and vegetables we used throughout this book come from Patty's farm, such as Kyoto red carrots, right, sweet potatoes, and tomatoes in many wonderful shapes and colors, above.

Patty works tirelessly planting (and planning and scheming about what to plant), plus weeding, pruning, picking, and preparing her produce for chef clients—and lucky locals, too.

SUMMER

REALLY REALLY FRIGGIN! HOT PEPPER PLANTS 2.00

From the small farmstand, above left, Patty sells just-picked vegetables and herbs, like cilantro, left, from simple wooden shelves. An old refrigerator keeps greens garden fresh. The root vegetables, right, that I've baked in seasoned salt (page 182) were in the ground at Early Girl Farm just minutes before.

Shallots
$3/lb

cippolini
$3/lb

Eggplant
$2/lb

Zucchini
Squash
$2/lb

Slicing peaches on a mandoline, left, to serve with pistachios, ricotta, and honey (page 211). Patty, right, harvests and dries a rainbow of red, yellow, and white onions, garlic, and shallots in an airy shed.

SUMMER

Digging sweet potatoes with Patty, right, turns work into pure pleasure. I love to use sweet potatoes (an unsung Hero) instead of white potatoes in so many dishes, like Fork-Crushed Sweet Potatoes with Sobrassada (page 108) and fried into chips (page 28). It's lovely how the sunlight falls onto well-worn tools in Early Girl's shed, left.

chapter eleven

CARROTS

SUGARY

✳ ✳ ✳

SNAPPY

✳ ✳ ✳

VIVID

WHY DOES THE ORDINARY CARROT take on heroic stature in this book? Quite simply, carrots are the foundation of so much of my cooking: if I'm making a soup or a stock, or braising meat, carrots are in there. But I like to think of carrots as more than just workhorses in the kitchen. I love to make a pot of beans and throw carrots in at the end—creamy beans and snappy carrots. I like to use a vegetable peeler to shave carrots into ribbons that I toss into the pasta water at the last minute, the carrots lending color and crunch to the pasta. I bake carrots in salt and gently rub the skins off. I slice them into thin coins on a mandoline and dunk them briefly in ice water to crisp them up, then add them to a salad. Pickled carrots are my go-to condiment to serve with cured meat, or just as an hors d'oeuvre. In my kitchen, carrots are the everyday miracle.

One of my favorite times of the year is when the first early carrots arrive at the Greenmarket in Union Square; it's the first sign of the summer season. By mid-June the market is packed with carrots of every shape and color: knobby little Thumbelina carrots are a favorite for roasting, gorgeous Kyoto red carrots are vibrant and sweet in a salad. I'm crazy about the palest yellow carrots, white, and even carrot-colored carrots.

When I think of baby carrots, I imagine something as big as my index finger, a small, slim little thing just pulled from the ground and eaten right there with a bit of dirt still clinging to the root, its tops a tender green. Those fresh-pulled carrots with their rich, sweet, mineral-y flavor have *nothing* in common with the so-called baby carrots you find ready-packed in plastic in the produce aisle

"Carrots are the first sign of summer. By mid-June the market is packed with Thumbelinas, red Kyotos, and even carrot-colored carrots."

of your supermarket. While they might have begun life as an actual carrot, they're sort of the Benjamin Button of vegetables: these carrots start old and then get young. What I mean by this is that those babies begin as misshapen and/or damaged grown-up carrots that are run through an industrial tumbler to grind away deformities and cut them down to size. Then, they're transferred to gigantic peeling machines that smooth and shape them. The resulting identical baby fingers bear astoundingly little resemblance to an actual carrot. Just stop and take a hard look before you eat one. It may still have benefits, but there's nothing carrot-y about it.

In fact, if you look closely at the plastic package, you'll see the words "baby cut," which tells us they're masquerading as baby carrots. Also, as much of a carrot's goodness is in its skin and outer flesh, these question-able veggies have questionable nutritional benefits as well. You may think I've exag-gerated here, and maybe you're right, but I think it's important to emphasize the unfor-tunate fact that such overprocessd vegetables

are what many people think of as carrots.

But back to the carrots nature created, the kind your mother used to tell you that eating them could help you see in the dark. She wasn't wrong! Carrots are loaded with vitamin A, which can help protect vision, especially at night. Besides the obvious fiber benefits, there is simply nothing bad about a carrot. It's one of the richest sources of the aptly named carotenoid beta-carotene, a powerful antioxidant. Carrots are essential in my cooking and absolutely delicious. What more could you ask from one vegetable?

A NOTE ON...PICKLING

I always try to have pickled carrots in my refrigerator. They're the ultimate garnish for a Bloody Mary. I love the acidic punch that a pickled vegetable can give to almost any dish. At the restaurant we sometimes pickle vegetables and then cook them into dishes with unpickled veggies. On the plate the pickled vegetable becomes a delicious surprise, the flavor unexpected. I like to make a few different kinds of pickling liquids— Vegetable Pickling Liquid (page 185), Fruit Pickling Liquid (page 207), and *Escabeche* for Poultry and Fish (page 127).

Salt-Baked Carrots and Beets

A FEW YEARS AGO we were playing around in the kitchen with salt-crusted whole fish. We made all sorts of salt crusts, some with herbs, some with scraps of ham. Somewhere along the way, I came up with the idea of cooking vegetables the same way. I remembered having tried a dish in Spain years ago called *papas arrugadas,* or "wrinkled potatoes," and I seemed to recall the spuds were baked in the oven on a bed of salt. This recipe for many-colored carrots and beets takes that idea and then does what I like to do—drops a bunch of flavor into the mix. The spices and herbs make these roots rock out.

Makes enough to serve 4 as a nice side dish

1   **pound kosher salt**
    Zest of 1 lemon
2   **tablespoons pink peppercorns**
2   **tablespoons black peppercorns**
2   **branches fresh rosemary**
2   **branches fresh thyme**
1   **bunch small carrots, trimmed**
1   **bunch small beets, trimmed**

Preheat the oven to 350°. In a large roasting pan, combine the kosher salt, lemon zest, pink and black peppercorns, rosemary, and thyme and mix thoroughly. Add the carrots and beets and cover completely with the salt.

Bake until the veggies are cooked through and tender, 20–30 minutes depending on the size of the vegetables. Once thoroughly cooked, remove from the oven and scrape off the skin using a dish towel or the back of a paring knife.

Pickled Carrots

WHAT A WAY TO TAKE CARROTS to another level!
First we make them ridiculously tender in their
spa-worthy salt scrub, then they get a luscious
bath in pickling liquid. It's the ultimate detox, a
stress-melting treatment for today's urban carrot.
I like pickled carrots diced up in a summer salad,
or mixed with some shaved raw carrots in a
carrot salad. They make a perfect companion to a
plate of cured meats or good cheese.

VEGETABLE PICKLING LIQUID

This is the basic pickle that I use for vegetables;
it can be prepared ahead of time and kept in the
refrigerator for up to a month. I like to keep it
around for any last-minute pickling needs.
Makes 1 quart

2   cups cider vinegar
¼   cup sugar
1   tablespoon each mustard seed, black
    peppercorns, coriander seed, fennel seed,
    and *guindilla* pepper
2   sprigs fresh thyme
1   sprig fresh dill
2   cloves garlic

2   cups Salt-Baked Carrots (page 182)

For the pickling liquid, combine all the ingredi-
ents with 1 cup of water and bring to a boil.
Reduce the heat and simmer for 20 minutes.
Makes about 3 cups.

Cut the peeled salt-baked carrots into 1½-inch
pieces and place in a ceramic bowl. In a large
saucepan, bring the pickling liquid to a boil, then
pour over the carrots. Cover and set aside in the
refrigerator to cool.

The carrots can be served right away; however,
I like to let them macerate for at least 45 minutes
in the refrigerator.

Chilled Carrot Soup with Yogurt and Tarragon

CARROTS COME IN BEAUTIFUL COLORS, but the ones I like to use in this chilled soup are orange. A little fresh turmeric rubbed on a fine grater or a zester makes the color even more vibrant and lends a faraway romantic spice to this refreshing soup.

Serves 4

1	pound large carrots, peeled and cut into 1-inch chunks
	About ½ cup Arbequina or other good olive oil, plus more for drizzling
1	shallot, finely diced
1	clove garlic, finely diced
1	tablespoon cider vinegar
	Zest and juice of 1 orange
1	tablespoon grated fresh ginger
¼	teaspoon grated whole turmeric
	Salt
	Freshly ground black pepper
½	cup plain yogurt such as labne, a strained Middle Eastern yogurt
	Leaves of 1 bunch fresh tarragon, coarsely chopped (about 2 tablespoons)

Bring a large pot of well-salted water to a rolling boil. Add the carrots and blanch until tender, about 5 minutes (see Note, page 139). Remove the carrots from the boiling water and chill quickly in an ice bath.

Meanwhile, heat 1 tablespoon olive oil in a small skillet over medium-high heat. Add the shallots and sweat for 1 minute. Add the garlic and sweat for 1 more minute. Remove from heat.

Place the carrots in a Vitamix or blender with the shallots, garlic, vinegar, orange zest and juice, ginger, and turmeric and process at high speed. With the motor running, drizzle in about ½ cup cold water, to achieve a nice velvety consistency. Reduce the speed to its lowest setting and drizzle in ½ cup olive oil until it's fully incorporated. Adjust the seasoning with salt and pepper; if you like the flavor a bit more acidic, add more orange juice or vinegar.

Divide the soup among 4 chilled bowls and top each serving with a dollop of yogurt, a sprig of tarragon, a drizzle of olive oil, and a little fresh ground pepper.

Ice-Cold Carrots, Radishes, and Beets with Potted Anchovy and Lemon Butter

THIS IS A LITTLE TAKE on the Italian *bagna cauda,* the classic Piedmontese dish of vegetables dipped in a warm anchovy cream sauce. But instead of serving the carrots, radishes, and beets warm, I like them all cold and refreshing. The fresh snap of the carrots and the spice of the radishes are kept in check by our trusty friend, the anchovy. If you can't find goat butter, a good-quality sweet cream butter will work, but I love the grassiness of goat butter. What a great beginning to a wonderful picnic!

Makes a nice pile of goodies that will make 4 people (or 2 hungry people) happy

1	bunch French breakfast radishes
1	bunch Thumbelina or baby carrots
1	bunch baby beets
¼	cup kosher salt
1	bowl ice cubes
½	cup goat butter or sweet cream butter
2	fillets Homemade Potted Anchovies (page 82) or best-quality salted anchovies
	Zest of 1 lemon
1	tablespoon of your favorite chopped herbs (chives, basil, and parsley are all very nice)
	Freshly ground black pepper

I like to cut the vegetables into different shapes. For the radishes, it's nice to cut them in half lengthwise and then in half again to make quarter wedges. Depending on the size of the carrots, they can be cut into oblique inch-long pieces or if they're Thumbelina carrots simply halved length-wise. Since the beets are served raw, they've got to be cut thinly; the easiest way to do this is to slice them into little coins on a mandoline.

Once you've cut all your vegetables, sprinkle the kosher salt over the bowl of ice, toss in the vegetables, stir them together well, and set aside in the refrigerator to chill for a few minutes.

Meanwhile, combine the butter, anchovies, lemon zest, herbs, and freshly ground pepper in the food processor and process until everything is evenly incorporated and the butter is soft, whipped, and easily spreadable.

Put the butter in a small bowl or ramekin. Remove the vegetables from the fridge, drain, and serve over ice in another bowl. I love the intense contrast of the crisp, cold root vegetables dipped in the luxurious, soft, flavored butter. Yum.

chapter twelve

CORN

SUMMERY

✳ ✳ ✳

JOYFUL

✳ ✳ ✳

DELICIOUS

IF YOU START DOING ANY KIND OF RESEARCH on corn and health, the first thing you'll turn up is that corn could seem an unlikely choice to be a Hero in this book. Substances made from corn have raised health concerns linked to obesity, and some people even claim that corn is a trigger for people with RA. I was shocked to discover that something as seemingly innocuous and delicious as fresh corn could be damaging to me. In fact, if

"The more I studied corn, the more I understood how crucial the distinction is between corn the *food* and corn the *commodity*."

anything, I would have thought that sustainably and responsibly grown corn would help someone like me.

Then I learned how crucial it is to make the distinction Michael Pollan does in *The Omnivore's Dilemma,* between corn the *food* and corn the *commodity*. The curse and the joy of this remarkable grass is that although it is a whole grain and tastes like summer itself, it can be transformed into tens of thousands of things, including food products like high-fructose corn syrup and genetically modified sweet corn, that are responsible for the bad rap corn gets.

How can you not see the difference between a bag of corn chips and one steamed ear of sweet corn at the height of summer? And in fact, even if that fresh ear of sweet corn were to cause me a bit of discomfort, for me it's a good trade-off. I am simply unwilling to forego one of life's great pleasures—namely, my childhood memories with being a kid out of school about to devour corn on the cob from a huge pot of corn just picked from our fields. After all, just how unhealthy could an occasional ear

of sweet corn eaten only in season really be, compared with the life-pleasure it delivers?

To me, the opposite of stress is pleasure, and stress compromises your immune system's ability to deal with disease. So doesn't it make sense that pleasure and joy—even in small doses (like that ear of corn)—does just the opposite? Corn is, after all, a whole grain. Let's not turn it into something it's not.

I most certainly try to avoid processed corn products like high-fructose corn syrup and corn sugars (dextrose). And so should you. I'm not interested in highly refined corn products. I'm talking about the fleeting pleasure of an armload of the sweet stuff you get at your local farm stand during two precious months a year. Sometimes commonsense turns out to be the best medicine.

I like to use corn in my cooking so much that I've come up with a list of 10 Things to Do with Corn, opposite, that just may lengthen the season by giving you so many delicious things to try.

10 THINGS TO DO WITH CORN

1. Cut the kernels from fresh sweet corn and fold into grits at the last minute for a sweet surprise.

2. Save the cobs and dry them in a low oven (200°) overnight. Then put them on the coals of a grill to give grilled fish a light smoke.

3. Or simmer fresh cobs—with a few sweet onions, carrots, dried garbanzos, and lots of basil—in a large pot of water for an aromatic vegetable broth.

4. Steam sweet corn, cut it off the cob, and puree with butter, sea salt, and cracked pepper for an unusual corn butter for toast, grilled fish, or meat.

5. Wrap the husks from fresh corn around small portions of sea bass and a dab of corn butter (#4), sea salt, pepper, and tarragon. Tie and steam (over corn broth, of course).

6. Slice sweet corn kernels off the cob and sauté quickly over high heat with minced garlic, diced bacon, smoky pimentón, and a squeeze of lemon.

7. Blacken whole ears of husked corn in a cast iron skillet, cut the kernels off, and fold them into a cornmeal pancake batter for savory corn cakes.

8. Gently poach a few cobs in a light pickling liquid, cut the kernels off the cob, and serve with slivers of fresh raw scallops for a delicate summer *crudo*.

9. Steam husked ears and slather with *all i oli* for a Spanish take on a Mexican street food classic.

10. Lightly poach fresh kernels in butter and olive oil with diced summer squash, string beans, and basil for a delicate turn on the Iroquois' Three Sisters, three inseparable, complementary crops.

Corn and Crab Salad

TO MY PALATE, corn and crab are blood brothers. I have a hard time making a crab dish in the summer without at least thinking about corn. Frequently, the corn ends up stealing the show. Bright, sugary corn marries so well with the sweetness of crab. Corn also loves herbs like basil and tarragon and dill. If you find yourself on a summer weekend longing for the perfect dish for lunch in the garden, sunlight dappling through the trees, this is it.

Jump in the car (or bicycle, horse, or motorcycle...) and go as fast as is legal to the nearest farm stand for the sweetest corn you can find (I always try it raw first!). Then stop by the fishmonger for some fresh lump crabmeat (or a steamed lobster, diced up) and race home. This dish is so simple you can make all of that happen before lunchtime. I like to serve the salad family style, with country toast rubbed with garlic and olive oil.

Serves 4

4   ears white sweet corn, shucked
    Zest and juice of 1 lemon
1   tablespoon Champagne vinegar
1   clove garlic, grated
5   tablespoons olive oil
½   pound jumbo lump crabmeat, picked through
    to remove bits of shell
    **Handful Sun Gold tomatoes or other
    cherry tomatoes, halved**
1   English cucumber, skin on, halved and sliced
    into half-moons
¼   cup pickled shallots (TECHNIQUE, page 156)
1   avocado, diced
    Salt
    Freshly ground black pepper
    Aleppo pepper
    Handful fresh basil leaves, torn into large pieces
    Leaves of 1 branch fresh tarragon, torn into pieces

Bring a large pot of salted water to a boil. Blanch the corn for 2 minutes. Cut the kernels off the cob with a sharp knife.

In a large serving bowl, combine the lemon zest and juice, vinegar, and garlic and mix well, then whisk in the olive oil. Fold in the corn, crabmeat, tomatoes, cucumber, pickled shallots, and avocado and carefully mix together. Season with salt, black pepper, and Aleppo pepper and finish with the torn herbs.

Steamed Corn with Clams and Bacon

WHEN I WAS NINE, my uncle had a clam bake. He drove four hours in his banana-yellow 1965 Chevy pickup truck to the Massachusetts coast and filled the back with bushel baskets of clams packed in ice and seaweed. Then he returned to his house in Vermont where he'd invited about a hundred folks and hired a local rock band to play while he baked clams and steamed huge cauldrons of corn over big fire pits. It was a hot July night and just at dusk it began to rain so hard we had to put a tent over the fire pit, which made for delicious, smoky corn. This is just another one of the great rules of the kitchen, that from mishaps you often discover wonderful things. I know that gastro-nostalgic moment influenced the way I make corn. Sweet corn with smoky pimentón always take me back to that rainy July night.

Serves 4

½   cup diced slab bacon
4   cloves garlic, thinly sliced
24   littleneck clams
2   ears sweet corn, shucked and cut into 2-inch lengths
¾   cup dry white wine
2   teaspoons pimentón
    Aleppo pepper
    Handful fresh basil leaves, torn
    Healthy drizzle of olive oil

In a large heavy-bottomed pot, sweat the bacon over medium heat. Once it begins to render, about 2 minutes, add the garlic and sweat until translucent. Add the clams, corn, and white wine and stir in the pimentón. Increase the heat to high and cook, uncovered, for about 30 seconds, until the alcohol has evaporated. Reduce the heat to medium low, cover, and steam until all the clams have opened and the corn is tender, 5–8 minutes. Discard any clams that don't open.

I like to serve this dish in a large earthenware bowl, with a sprinkle of Aleppo pepper, torn basil, and a generous drizzle of fruity olive oil.

Best Grilled Corn, in the Husk

CORN, CORN LIQUOR, and a little bit of fire. Simple and damn good. Serve simply with a drizzle of olive oil, knob of sweet butter, or homemade *all i oli* (page 21).

Serves 4

1 cup bourbon
½ cup sugar
½ cup salt
8 ears sweet corn in their husks

In a large heavy-bottomed pot, mix the bourbon, sugar, and salt into a gallon of water and bring to a boil. Set aside to cool. Meanwhile, gently peel the corn husks back a few inches so you can easily remove the silk, and then replace the husks. Once the bourbon water is thoroughly cooled, add the corn in the husks and soak for at least a couple hours, or even overnight if you're thinking ahead.

Preheat the grill to high heat. Remove the corn from the water and drain. Grill the corn in the husks, turning, until the ears are charred and blackened on the outside and the corn is tender on the inside, about 3 minutes per side. Let the corn cool a few minutes. When you can comfortably handle them, shuck the cobs and serve.

Crispy Fried Hominy

THERE'S NO DOUBT ABOUT IT, this crunchy corn snack can take some time but the process is really simple. If you follow the steps, you'll be rewarded with an unusually delicious treat.

Culinary lime (the earliest form is referred to as *potash* or *culinary lye*) was used by Native Americans to make dried corn easier to digest and even tastier since long before European settlers arrived here. In the old days, they'd take the ash from their hardwood fires, mix it with water and use this liquid to simmer dried corn. Today, culinary lime is readily available. Just think how difficult this recipe would be if I made you start a campfire first just for the ashes!

As much as I love hominy, it's even better when it's fried: super crispy on the outside and chewy on the inside. Cilantro, chiles, and lime juice make this corn addictive. Don't confuse dried hominy corn with decorative, colored dried corn on the cob. I like the large-kernel hominy corn available at ansonmills.com or in Mexican groceries. Don't even think of using canned hominy.

Serves 4 (or 1 if it's for me)

⅓	cup culinary lime
1½	cups dried hominy corn
4	cups olive oil for frying
	Salt
1	serrano or jalapeño pepper, seeded and finely minced
1	bunch cilantro, Delfino if you can find it, chopped
4	limes, halved

To prepare the lime water, combine 10 cups water with the culinary lime in a large pot (it needs to be nonreactive, enamel or porcelain, because the lime will react with other metals). Bring to a rolling boil. Turn off the heat and set aside for a few hours.

After several hours, you'll see a thin skin on the surface of the water. You want neither that skin nor the sediment that settles to the bottom. So you need to strain them out. Place a fine-mesh strainer over another large nonreactive pot. Carefully strain the liquid through the strainer; discard the lime sediments.

Add the hominy to the strained liquid and bring to a boil over high heat. Turn off the heat, cover, and let stand overnight at room temperature so that the lime can do its job.

Bring the pot back to a boil, reduce the heat to low, and simmer, covered, for 3–4 hours. Drain the hominy well and set aside to cool.

While the hominy is cooling, heat the olive oil in a heavy-bottomed pot or tabletop fryer until it registers 340° on a candy thermometer. Working in small batches, drop the hominy kernels into the hot oil until they're crispy, 1–2 minutes. Drain on paper towels and transfer to a large mixing bowl. Toss with the salt, chile pepper, and cilantro and serve with a squeeze of fresh lime.

chapter thirteen

STONE FRUIT

LUSCIOUS

✳ ✳ ✳

COLORFUL

✳ ✳ ✳

RADIANT

WHEN THIS BOOK WAS COMING TOGETHER IN MY MIND, I was focused on cherries. But then I realized that their Auntie Peach and Uncle Apricot, their Cousin Plum, their Nephew Nectarine—the whole stone fruit family—are every bit as much Heroes as those cherries. So I started to embrace the entire clan. Just looking at those containers of apricots and plums of different sizes and colors, the succulent colors of their flesh,

even the first supermarket cherries of the season, can make me feel as buoyant as a sunny day.

I didn't really grow up around much stone fruit. We lived way too far north for those trees to thrive. It wasn't until I went to college in Michigan and started traveling to Traverse City, the heart of cherry country, that I really began to appreciate them. I couldn't believe my eyes, an entire landscape of cherry orchards planted on rolling green hills set against the banks of Lake Michigan. We'd visit the orchards,

buy baskets of cherries by the roadside, and gorge ourselves. That began what were probably my first experiments with cooking on my own. It may seem odd today, but at that time, cherries were to me an exotic ingredient. At first I'd just toss them into salads; then I got more daring and creative. I'd fold them into rice and sauté them with spinach and toasted nuts. I even remember stuffing a roast chicken with cherries and garlic.

I guess you could say cherries were kind of a gateway drug for me. I soon moved on

"Cherries were kind of a gateway drug for me. I soon moved on to the harder stuff like peaches, plums, and eventually apricots."

to the harder stuff like plums, peaches, and eventually apricots. Once I got high on stone fruit, there was no coming down.

I'm afraid I am a bit of a cliché: most of the desserts I love come right from my grandmother's green metal recipe box, stuffed with yellowing index cards that date from the 1950s. Growing up, we always had stewed plums with clotted cream (remember she's English) and her plum cake (page 212). My favorite breakfast was peaches in syrup with yogurt. Nowadays, I like to cook with stone fruit in somewhat more unconventional ways like pickled plums with lightly cured fluke (page 204) and stone fruit gazpacho (page 208).

I suppose that part of the allure of these fruit is not just their juicy sweet flavor; their gorgeous shapes and colors still astonish me. They're like precious jewels on the plate: shavings of white peaches over fresh ricotta with honey and pistachios (page 211) is a near-perfect summer dessert; a few seared plums can transform a traditional confit of

duck leg into a luxurious dinner (page 204), and a jar of pickled plums on the windowsill catches the morning sunlight like stained glass. In a way, stone fruit are too beautiful to be so smart!

In reality, they're a nutritionist's dream. There are vitamins that stone fruits don't have much of, but there can't be very many. Cherries have high concentrations of vitamin C and other antioxidants that may help protect against inflammatory conditions and are so necessary to maintaining a healthy immune system. And drinking tart and black cherry juice may help reduce inflammation. I've learned to worry about the state of my immune system as a way to help manage my health issues.

As I noted in Chapter 3, the almond is related to stone fruits, a fact that makes me feel good just thinking about it. It is reassuring, too, to know that my favorite fruits of summer are working really hard to help me get on with my life.

Confit of Duck Legs with Plums

THIS IS AN EASY, TASTY WAY to make duck legs: poach the legs in olive oil or duck fat; served with the acidity and sweetness of the plums. The sumptuous duck feels remarkably light without sacrificing any of the wonderful decadence of the bird. When I was little, my grandmother would prepare duck with grapes. I happen to prefer the tartness of plums. Crisping the skin of the duck legs in a hot pan after gently cooking them adds a whole other dimension to this dish.

Serves 4

1	cup salt
1	cup sugar
4	cloves garlic, lightly crushed
1	tablespoon coriander seeds
1	bunch fresh thyme
	Zest and juice of 1 orange
4	duck legs and thighs
3	cups olive oil or duck fat, plus 1 tablespoon olive oil
1	pound Italian plums, halved and pitted
	Salt
	Freshly ground black pepper
	Handful fresh basil leaves

Combine the salt, sugar, garlic, coriander seeds, thyme, and orange zest and juice in a nonreactive pan. Add the duck and thoroughly coat with the salt mixture. Cover with plastic wrap and refrigerate for 3–4 hours. Remove the duck legs, rinse thoroughly under cold water, and pat dry.

In a deep, heavy-bottomed pot, heat the olive oil or duck fat over medium heat until it registers 150° on a candy thermometer. Add the duck legs and gently poach them until the meat is tender but not quite falling off the bone, 30–35 minutes.

Meanwhile, heat the tablespoon of olive oil in a large cast iron pan over medium-high heat and sear the plums, cut-side down, for 2 minutes, until nicely caramelized and beginning to soften. Season the plums with salt and pepper and some torn fresh basil and set aside in a serving bowl.

Once the duck legs are cooked through, remove them to a pan lined with paper towels. Let the oil or duck fat cool and then carefully pour all but 1 tablespoon into a container to save for future cooking.

Heat the tablespoon of the duck cooking oil in a large skillet over medium-high heat and sear the duck legs, skin-side down, until golden and crispy, about 3 minutes. Serve with seared plums.

Lightly Cured Fluke with Pickled Plums

I AM OF THE OPINION that our local fluke from Long Island is one of the world's great fishes. I love it grilled, fried, pan-roasted, and especially raw. I'm a huge fan of raw fish, if it's well prepared. With all that, the real star of this dish is the pickled plums that help the fluke taste ever so elegant in your mouth.

Serves 4 as an appetizer

1	fillet sushi-grade fluke, cured for 10 minutes (TECHNIQUE, page 218)
16	slices pickled plums (page 207)
2	tablespoons Marcona almonds, coarsely chopped
	Generous drizzle olive oil
	Aleppo pepper
	Small handful fresh basil leaves, torn

Using a very sharp knife, slice the fluke fillet as thinly as possible, starting from tail and moving towards the top of the fillet. Gently toss the sliced fish in a mixing bowl with the pickled plums, almonds, and olive oil. Distribute among 4 chilled plates. Finish with a generous sprinkle of Aleppo pepper and garnish with the torn basil leaves.

Pickled Plums

PICKLED PLUMS ARE A VIBRANT ADDITION to salads and fish dishes, and a cool accompaniment to a cheese plate. I like to fold them into farro or even rice to add an unexpected pop of acidity. Raw and cured fish dishes (page 204) and oysters are wonderful with a fine sliver of pickled plums. Try to choose firm, slightly under-ripe plums for pickling so that they don't become mushy once you add the pickling liquid. I like to use red, purple, and golden sour plums in season. The pickling liquid works well with other stone fruit, too.

Makes about 2 jars

    2   **pounds of your favorite plums**
        Zest of 1 lemon cut in strips

FRUIT PICKLING LIQUID
    2   **cups sugar**
    1   **cup red wine vinegar**
    1   **tablespoon coriander seeds**
    1   **teaspoon black peppercorns**
    1   **bay leaf**

With a very sharp knife, carefully slice each plum away from its stone into nice segments. Discard the stones.

Sterilize a large canning jar or two and fill two-thirds full with the sliced plums. Add the lemon strips and a sprig or two of citrusy herbs like lemon thyme or lemon balm, if you like.

For the pickling liquid, combine the ingredients in a large saucepan, add 6 cups water, and bring to a boil. Simmer a moment, then pour over the plums in the jars. Let the liquid cool, then cover with the lids and refrigerate. The plums will be delicately pickled after a few hours, but if you want a more intense pickle you'll have to leave them in the fridge overnight.

The pickled plums will keep in the refrigerator for several weeks.

Stone Fruit Gazpacho with Scallops

SINCE I'VE SPENT SO MANY YEARS eating and cooking in Spain, I would be remiss if I didn't include a gazpacho in this book. But alas, this is not your *abuela*'s gazpacho. In this version, peaches, plums, and watermelon all come together in a bright, colorful, chilled soup that is topped with a single seared diver scallop. The tart sour plums allow the sweet plump scallop to feel a little less self-conscious in its summery dress. If you can't find sour plums, substitute sweet plums, preferably golden plums, plus the juice of 2 lemons.

Serves 4

1	pound white peaches, pitted
1	pound sour plums, pitted
2	cups cubed yellow (or red) seedless watermelon
1	clove garlic, coarsely chopped
1	shallot, coarsely chopped
1	tablespoon Champagne vinegar
1	cup plus 3–4 tablespoons fruity olive oil
	Salt
	Freshly ground black pepper
4	jumbo diver scallops
	Espelette pepper
	A few sprigs of fresh thyme (with blossoms if possible)

Combine the peaches, plums, watermelon, garlic, shallots, and vinegar in the Vitamix, blender, or food processor. Process on high until smooth and creamy, then reduce the speed and drizzle in the 1 cup olive oil until completely incorporated. Season with salt and pepper and set aside to chill in the refrigerator. Go ahead and chill 4 glass soup bowls while you're at it.

Preheat the oven to 325°. When the gazpacho is chilled, heat 2 tablespoons olive oil in an oven-proof skillet over medium-high heat. Season the scallops generously with salt and pepper. Once

the olive oil slips easily across the pan, carefully place the scallops in the pan and sear until golden brown. I like the scallops to be just barely cooked, so I only sear one side. After about 2 minutes on the stovetop, put the whole kit and caboodle in the oven, without flipping the scallops; they will need 2–3 minutes in the oven.

Fill each chilled soup bowl with a generous portion of gazpacho and nestle one scallop in each bowl, seared side up. A sprinkling of Espelette pepper and the thyme sprigs and blossoms and a drizzle of fruity olive oil is all you need.

White Peaches, Pistachios, Honey, and Ricotta

WHEN WHITE PEACHES are in season (which seems to only last about five minutes in New York), nothing is more truly summer than the one perfect peach I have every year. Once they start showing up in the farmers market I greedily buy them, and while I enjoy every white peach I eat, I really only ever have one perfect peach a year. When I find it, I scream and jump for joy, it's pure hedonistic indulgence. Luckily all those less-than-perfect-but-still-delicious peaches have value, too.

There is a lovely, traditional Catalan dessert called *mel i mató,* just fresh cheese drizzled with honey. Sometimes it might have fruit, too, but usually it's just cheese and honey. This is a little homage to the perfect peach by way of Catalunya. Using a sharp mandoline to slice the peaches gives you sweet slivers that fall off like flower petals. She loves me, she loves me not...

Serves 4

2   or 3 firm white peaches, plus a yellow one
    Juice of 1 lemon
1   pound fresh ricotta cheese
4   tablespoons honey
¼   cup shelled pistachios, toasted in a dry,
    hot pan for 30 seconds
2   tablespoons fruity olive oil

Quarter and pit the peaches, then slice into thin curls on a mandoline. Toss with the lemon juice in a bowl.

Divide the ricotta among 4 dessert bowls, drizzle a tablespoon honey on each, and toss on a handful of toasted pistachios. Top each with a few curls of the peach slices and a drizzle of olive oil and serve.

Spiced Stone Fruit Preserves

I ALWAYS GET SO EXCITED at the market in stone fruit season that I buy too many. Such plums! Such peaches! They all look so good, but inevitably the ones at the bottom of the basket get a bit soft. Preserves are a great use for Mother Nature's factory seconds. I always like savory spice in my sweet preserves, hence the bay leaf and peppercorns. Obviously you can spread these succulent preserves on toast. And while there's nothing wrong with that, may I suggest a dollop with fresh yogurt in the morning? Or, serve them with your favorite cheeses.

Makes 2 jars

2   pounds mixed pitted stone fruit: sour plums, Italian plums, peaches, nectarines, cherries
    Zest of 1 lemon, pith removed, cut into strips
    Juice of 1 lemon
⅓   cup sugar
1   teaspoon grated fresh ginger
    A cheesecloth sachet with 1 bay leaf, 2 *guindilla* peppers, generous chunk peeled ginger, 1 teaspoon black peppercorns, 1 teaspoon anise seeds, 1 teaspoon coriander seeds, 3 cloves, and 1 pod black or green cardamom

Cut the stone fruit into sections roughly 1 inch long. In a large saucepan, combine the lemon zest, lemon juice, sugar, ginger, spice sachet, and ¾ cup water. Simmer over medium heat for 10 minutes. Add the fruit and cook for 8–10 minutes, or until the fruit softens and the liquid begins to thicken. Remove from heat and ladle fruit first, then liquid, into 2 sterilized canning jars. Refrigerated, the preserves will keep about 1 month.

Plum Cake

WHEN I WAS GROWING UP IN Vermont, the summers were never hot enough for plums to get really sweet. Every year my grandmother would grow plums and every year she'd serve us bowl after bowl and we'd struggle to eat one or two, wincing at their sourness. Eventually she came up with the idea of baking them into a cake and suddenly no one could resist those plums. Thanks Mutti. When life gives you lemons, make plum cake.

Makes one 10-inch cake

2   cups all-purpose flour
2   teaspoons baking powder
½   teaspoon salt
2   eggs
1½   cups sugar
½   cup milk
6   tablespoons butter, melted
1   teaspoon vanilla
1   pound Italian plums, pitted and halved
1   teaspoon cinnamon
      Fresh herbs such as thyme or lemon verbena

Preheat the oven to 350°. Grease a 10-inch round terracotta baking dish or cake pan with butter.

Sift the flour and baking powder together in a mixing bowl. Add the salt and set aside. In a standing mixer fitted with a paddle, beat the eggs and 1 cup of the sugar until creamy. Add the milk, melted butter, and vanilla. Slowly add the dry ingredients until completely incorporated.

Spread the batter ¾ inch thick in the prepared pan. Arrange the plums evenly on top of the batter and sprinkle with the remaining ½ cup sugar mixed with the cinnamon. Bake for 25 minutes, until a cake tester or a knife poked in the center comes out clean. Garnish with some fresh herbs and serve with a scoop of vanilla ice cream, if you like.

chapter fourteen

GOOD FISH

SCARCE

✳ ✳ ✳

SUSTAINABLE

✳ ✳ ✳

SATISFYING

IT'S A SAD REALITY THAT THE CHOICES WE MAKE in the kitchen have an immediate environmental impact, but unfortunately they do, and no class of food is as threatened today as good fish. Bluefin tuna has been overfished to the point of endangerment, and if we continue to consume it at the current rate, we'll lose this magnificent creature forever. Other members of the tuna family, like yellowfin and bonito, are more

plentiful and just as delicious. Before we make a purchase in a fish market, or order fish in a restaurant, we must be vigilant and consider the provenance, culture, and health of its stocks.

And it's not just tuna. We have managed to greedily overfish our waters to the extent that once-common everyday fish, like trawl-caught Atlantic Cod, have become endangered species. People look to chefs to help them make the right choices about food, hoping that we know more than they do. I feel a great responsibility to make informed decisions about the food I put on the menu,

knowing that the choices we make in the restaurant influence the choices our guests make in the supermarket. We all remember the catastrophe with so-called Chilean sea bass: first it was found on high-end restaurant menus across the country after a huge surge in popularity, and within a decade it was found on the Monterey Bay Aquarium Seafood Watch's "Avoid" list.

So what can you eat? I suspect organic salmon is a marketing ploy—*organic* in this case refers to their feed, and says nothing about the conditions in which they're raised. The salmon that I'm convinced is OK to eat

"In the sweet rightness of things, it turns out that the fish I most like to cook happen to be the fish that are the best for me to eat."

is wild salmon when it's harvested responsibly in season. On the subject of wild versus farm-raised, it's a sticky wicket. It is heartening that there are credible people practicing aquaculture more and more every day. Most char and trout, for example, are farmed responsibly.

Fortunately it's becoming more common for our markets to state the provenance of their seafood. Take shrimp. Most folks don't know that the majority of the shrimp found in fish markets comes from Asia, where the growing conditions tend to be poor and unregulated and their feed is often of inferior quality. I much prefer wild Gulf shrimp properly frozen to the so-called fresh shrimp that's been tossed with preservatives to lengthen its shelf life. So, unless you're lucky enough to live near a fishing port and can buy catch right from the boat, you're better off with shrimp that's caught at sea and frozen immediately.

Fish is one of my favorite things to cook and I believe it should be revered. The way it's cooked says a great deal about the chef; the Japanese may often be accused of over-fishing, but when they get fish in the kitchen, no one has more reverence for fish than a Japanese chef. For a whole year I studied with the renowned sushi chef Toshio Suzuki. Besides slicing techniques, I learned how delicate fish is, that it should be touched as little as possible because the bacteria that lives on the outside of fish thrives in warm temperatures. (That's why good sushi chefs are constantly wiping down their cutting boards with cold—not hot!—water.)

We all know that fish is an excellent source of protein, is mostly low in cholesterol (except for shrimp and lobster), and oily fish such as salmon and anchovies are loaded with the crucial omega-3s that may help the body control inflammation and stiffness. And in the sweet rightness of things, the fish I love to eat turn out to be the best for me! The unassuming, mighty anchovy gets its own chapter in this book and I suggest good ways to cook sardines, trout, salmon, mackerel, black sea bass, and tuna—good fish all, most high in omega-3s, and environmentally safe, too.

A just-caught fluke is cut into 4 fillets, which helps it cure in the seasoned salt.

Curing Raw Fish

ONE OF MY FAVORITE WAYS to celebrate the freshest fish is to prepare it raw. Curing raw fish at home may seem a little daunting, but there are just a few simple things to keep in mind. First and foremost, find a fishmonger you can trust! Then ask for her recommendations on the freshest fish to eat raw. Have her pack it in ice and once you get home, replenish the ice and keep the fish in the fridge on the fresh ice. It's important to use a razor sharp knife (a dull knife won't cut precisely, causing raw fish to break down quickly). Make sure to use a non-porous cutting board (not wood!), washing it frequently with very cold water as you work. If you're cleaning your own fish, thoroughly wash the cutting board before slicing the fish.

Exposed to a curing mixture, raw fish takes on a pleasant texture in the mouth (the salt actually extracts excess moisture from the flesh, leaving nice firm fillets). The fish is perfectly seasoned and delicately perfumed by the herbs and spices in the cure. If you intend to eat the fish raw, as a crudo, then let it cure for 30–35 minutes. This technique, which cures 1 fish fillet, also works well if you're cooking the fish; just don't cure it longer than 10 minutes or it'll be too salty.

2   cups kosher salt
1   cup sugar
    Zest of 1 lemon
1   tablespoon toasted coriander seeds
1   tablespoon pink peppercorns
4   sprigs fresh thyme
1   fillet sushi-grade fish such as fluke, bonito, or yellowtail

Lightly Cured Summer Bonito

I LOVE BONITO, the smaller, lesser-known relative of the better-known tunas. It's full of flavor, nutritionally loaded, and so much more abundant than its overfished cousins. In the summer, when schools of bonito are bountiful off the coast of Long Island, I love to cure it this way. It's so simple, but has it all in one single bite: rich fattiness, bright acidity, and a kick of spice. For another way with cured fish, see Lightly Cured Fluke with Plums (page 204).

Serves 4 as an appetizer

1   tablespoon toasted pine nuts
1   serrano chile, seeds and stem removed, finely minced
    Small handful fresh green olives such as Castelvetrano, pitted and roughly chopped
1   fillet sushi-grade bonito, skin and any pinbones removed, cured for 10 minutes (TECHNIQUE, left)
¼   cup good fruity olive oil
2   tablespoons Pickled Shallots (TECHNIQUE, page 156)
    Squeeze of fresh lemon

In a small mixing bowl, combine the toasted pine nuts, serrano chile, and olives and set aside.

When the fish has cured for about 10 minutes, thinly slice it into bite-size pieces with a very sharp knife and add to the bowl with the pine nut mixture. Drizzle in the olive oil and carefully fold together with a spoon or rubber spatula. Taste a small piece of the fish to make sure it's seasoned well. If it needs a bit more salt, sprinkle on some coarse sea salt.

Divide the bonito among 4 chilled plates, evenly distributing all the goodies, and finish with a few rings of the pickled shallots and a squeeze of lemon on each plate.

Combine the salt, sugar, lemon zest, coriander, peppercorns, and thyme in a bowl and mix thoroughly. In a nonreactive baking dish, layer half the salt mixture and place the fillet on top, then cover completely with the remaining salt mixture. Set aside to cure in the refrigerator for 30–35 minutes, depending on the thickness of the fillet. You'll notice that after about 30 minutes the texture of the fish will become more resistant to the touch; I like it when it's slightly firm and one slice has an opaque, almost translucent appearance.

Discard the curing mixture, rinse the fillet very well under very cold running water, and pat dry with a paper towel. Refrigerate or use immediately in a recipe.

Pan Roast of Arctic Char with Sorrel Sauce

I REALLY LOVE WILD SALMON that's sustainably harvested; king, coho, and Copper River are all delicious, but their seasons are limited and they tend to be very pricey. Many years ago when I worked for Chef Floyd Cardoz, he introduced me to char and I think I actually may have grown to prefer it to salmon. Char is a close relative to both salmon and trout; like salmon, it can survive in both fresh and salt water and thrives in very cold (arctic) waters.

The flesh ranges from ivory to bright pink in color and is delicate and delicious. Much like salmon, char can easily be overcooked and, if you're not careful, it will quickly go from silky and moist to crumbly and dry. One simple way to avoid this is to cook it at a lower temperature. I like to score the char's skin to keep it flat. I start the fish in a hot pan on the stove to crisp the skin, then add some herbs and a pat of butter and finish it in a gentle oven. The end result is crispy, crunchy skin and luxurious flesh.

Serves 4

1   fillet arctic char, skin on, about 12 ounces
   Salt
   Freshly ground black pepper
2   tablespoons olive oil
4   sprigs fresh lemon thyme
4   small knobs butter, plus 1 tablespoon
   Handful bluefoot or other wild mushrooms
1   cup Sorrel Sauce (page 276)

Preheat the oven to 350°. With a sharp knife, cut the char fillet into 4 even portions and season liberally with salt and pepper on all sides. Heat 1 tablespoon of the olive oil in a well-seasoned cast iron pan over medium-high heat. Add the char skin-side down and sear until golden and crispy, about 3 minutes.

Carefully transfer the char with a spatula to a shallow roasting pan, skin-side down. Place a sprig of thyme and a knob of butter on top of each portion. Roast until just cooked through and perfectly medium rare, about 5 minutes.

Meanwhile, wipe out the cast iron pan with a paper towel, return to the heat, and add the remaining tablespoon butter. Once it begins to foam, toss in the mushrooms. Season with salt and pepper and sauté until tender, stirring, about 3 minutes.

Spoon a pool of sorrel sauce on each of 4 plates. Place a piece of char on the sauce, discarding the lemon thyme, and finish with a few mushrooms on each serving.

Line-Caught Atlantic Cod with Picada

THE TECHNIQUE OF USING a nut-based paste, *picada*, to thicken stews in Spain dates back to the time of the Romans and the 4th century AD original recipes of Apicius, one of the most important writers on cookery. *Suquet*, a fish stew similar to the French bouillabaisse and one of the most important dishes in Catalunya, would not be complete without *picada*. The silky, delicate Atlantic cod is a perfect companion to this nutty *picada*. Look for line-caught or gillnetted fish from the icy waters of the northeast Arctic and Iceland, and avoid trawl-caught fish, because much of the sea's ecosystem is severely damaged in the harvesting process.

Serves 4

- 1 pound mixed baby root vegetables such as baby carrots, fingerling potatoes, and small parsnips, peeled and cut into even-size pieces
- 1 cup *picada* (page 52)
- 1 cup fish, chicken, or vegetable stock, plus more if needed
- 1 teaspoon white wine vinegar
  Salt
  Freshly ground black pepper
- 12 ounces line-caught Atlantic cod fillet, cut into 4 equal portions
  Few leaves wild arugula or parsley
  Drizzle of fruity olive oil

Bring a large pot of well-salted water to a rolling boil and blanch the root vegetables until cooked through and tender, 6–7 minutes. Drain and set aside to cool. (When blanching potatoes, I prefer not to shock them in an ice bath because it makes the potato mealy.)

In a large, deep skillet big enough to fit all 4 portions of cod, whisk the *picada* and stock together over medium heat until thoroughly combined. You don't want the texture to be too soupy, but it shouldn't be too thick, either. If there's a lot of liquid, just let it reduce until you get the texture you like. Adjust the seasoning with the vinegar, salt, and pepper.

Season the cod with salt and pepper on all sides and add to the *picada* mixture. Ideally, the liquid should only partially cover the fish. Cover the pan, reduce the heat to a simmer, and braise the cod until almost cooked through, 4–6 minutes. As the fish is braising, you may need to add a little stock to keep the sauce from becoming too thick.

Add the blanched vegetables to the skillet and cook until they're warmed up and ready to serve, about 2 minutes.

Carefully remove the cod from the pan with two spoons or a fish spatula and set aside on a plate. Divide the vegetables and sauce evenly among 4 warm, shallow bowls. Top each bowl with a portion of cod and a sprig or two of arugula or parsley. Finish with a drizzle of fruity olive oil and serve immediately.

Preserving Tuna

Growing up, I was indifferent to tuna in a can, but the first time I had canned tuna in Spain, I completely changed my tuna tune. The Spanish are fanatical about their canned seafood, and tuna is no exception. In recent years, high-quality Spanish tuna has become available in the United States; however, it is surprisingly easy to make your own when high-quality yellowfin is available. And as I've said earlier, we must be careful to choose the right tuna (i.e., not bluefin).

I like to fold preserved tuna with homemade *all i oli* and sliced cucumbers for a delicious tuna salad sandwich. Even a piece of preserved tuna on toast is great. Or toss it in a salad with cherry tomatoes, feta cheese, walnuts, and arugula.

Makes 4 jars

- 1 **pound kosher salt**
- 1 **pound sugar**
- 1 **tablespoon pimentón**
- 1 **pound freshest available yellowfin or bonito tuna**
- 4 **cups olive oil**
- 4 **cloves garlic**

4   sprigs fresh thyme
8   *guindilla* peppers
     Zest of 4 lemons, shaved with a
     vegetable peeler

Combine the salt, sugar, and pimentón in a bowl
and add the tuna, covering thoroughly with the
salt and sugar mix. Cover and refrigerate for 1 hour
to cure. Thoroughly rinse the tuna and pat dry.

Combine the olive oil, garlic, thyme, *guindilla*,
and lemon zest in a large pot and heat over very

low heat to 125° on a candy thermometer. Add the
tuna and gently cook for 10 minutes, until the tuna
is just cooked through but not dry.

Remove the fish to a plate lined with a paper
towel and let both fish and oil cool.

Divide the fish among 4 small, sterilized
canning jars with flip-top lids and top with the
olive oil and herb cooking mixture. Cover the
jars and process in boiling water for a minute
to seal. The tuna will keep in the refrigerator
for about 3 weeks.

A NOTE ON...
TROUT

Vermont is landlocked, that's a pretty indisputable fact. I grew up loving fishing as most boys do, but unfortunately our waters didn't have a whole lot of variety: only bass, sunfish, pickerel, pike, and mostly trout. Without question, to my palate trout is the tastiest of all those fish. Of course most of the other fish I had growing up was frozen and frankly not very good, so trout won by default. I've been lucky enough since to eat some of the best fish in the world, but I always come back to trout, and it only seemed right to dedicate a whole section of this chapter to one of my favorite fish.

Unless you're going to catch your own, all of the trout available in our fish markets is farm-raised. And that's not necessarily a bad thing. It certainly means trout is one of the most sustainable fish. Some trout are raised in open streams, ensuring the fresh-ness of the water, and are fed a natural diet. Beware of trout that comes to market already deboned and butterflied. It's probably not as pristine and fresh as we'd like it to be. A good fishmonger should know where his fish is coming from. Ask how he receives his trout. We want it to be cleaned on the spot!

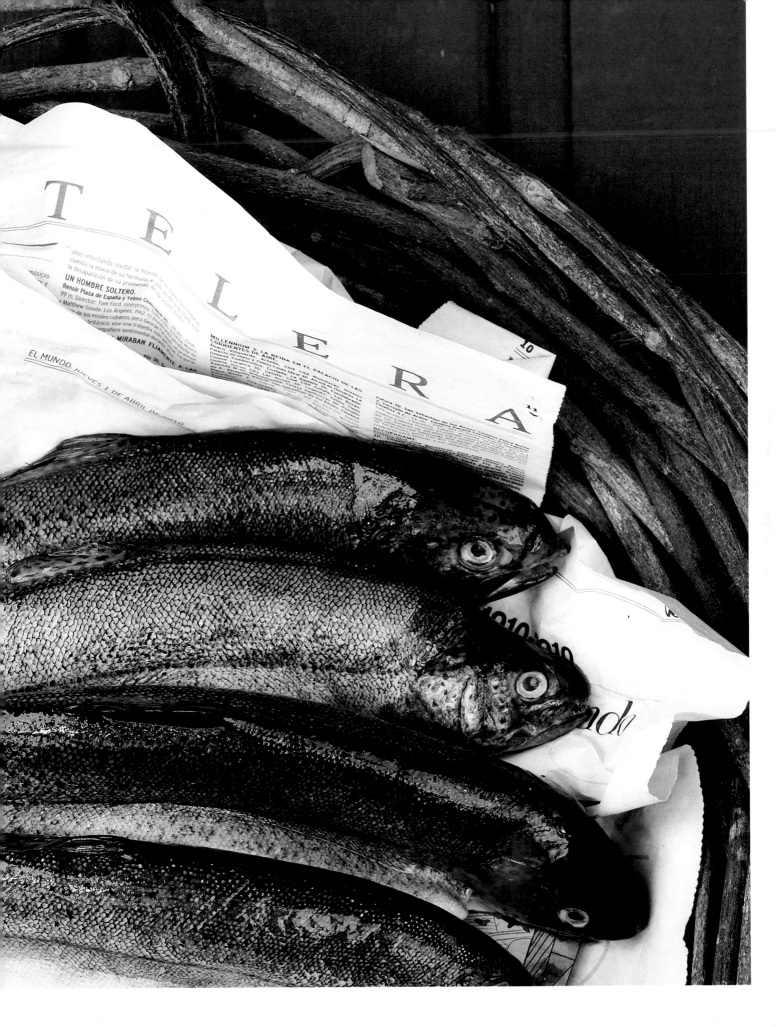

Trout a la Navarra

AFTER SWITZERLAND, Spain is the most mountainous country in Europe, and all those fast-flowing mountain streams mean wonderful trout. No place in Spain is as famous for trout as the kingdom of Navarra, on the border of France, where beautiful icy water runs down from the Pyrenees. This could be the national dish of Navarra: crispy trout, salty ham, nothing better. Ask your fishmonger to butterfly the trout with the head and tail on, bones and gills removed.

Serves 4

2 tablespoons olive oil
2 large rainbow trout, butterflied
  Salt
  Freshly ground black pepper
6–8 thin lemon slices
1 small bunch kale, coarsely chopped
1 clove garlic, finely minced
  Drizzle lemon juice
6 thin slices serrano ham

Preheat the oven to 350°. Heat 1 tablespoon of the olive oil in a large cast iron skillet over medium-high heat. Season the trout with salt and pepper on all sides and sear it in the pan, skin-side down, until crispy, about 4 minutes. Carefully transfer the trout, skin-side down, to a large roasting pan. Top each fish with a few slices of lemon and place in the oven. It will take 5–7 minutes to cook through, depending on the size of the fish.

While the fish is roasting, wipe out the cast iron pan with a paper towel, heat the remaining 1 tablespoon olive oil over medium heat, and toss in the kale. Gently wilt for 2–3 minutes before adding the garlic, then finish with salt, pepper, and a drizzle of lemon juice.

Once the fish is finished (if you touch it with your finger, it should be firm but still give off a little moisture), arrange on 2 serving platters and top each fish with a generous portion of kale and several slices of serrano ham. Serve immediately.

Mutti's Pan-Fried Troutlings

WHEN I WAS A KID, this was the first dish my grandmother taught me to cook. We would make it with trout that I caught in the stream that runs by our house: hence troutlings, because regardless of how big my first fish loom in my memory, Mutti never lets me forget they were really cigar-size. Ideally this dish is prepared with a whole bunch of tiny spring troutlings (6–7 inches long), served family-style and eaten with your fingers. Otherwise, use the smallest trout you can find. If the fish are small enough, refry the bones and eat them as crispy little treats.

Serves 4 as an appetizer

4 whole brook troutlings, smallest available, gutted, gills removed
  Salt
  Freshly ground black pepper
¼ cup all-purpose flour
4 tablespoons butter
4 tablespoons capers
  Lemon halves
  Fresh parsley, coarsely chopped

Season each troutling with salt and pepper on all sides and inside the cavities as well, then dust with the flour. Heat 1 tablespoon of the butter in a cast iron pan over medium-high heat until it begins to brown, then add 1 trout and pan-fry on all sides until golden brown, 5–7 minutes depending on the size of the fish. Just before removing the fish from the pan, toss in 1 tablespoon of capers and a healthy squeeze of lemon juice.

Transfer the fish to paper towels. Wipe out the pan and repeat until you've pan-fried all the trout. I like to serve the fish family-style on a platter with a sprinkling of chopped parsley.

How to Smoke a Trout

HOMEMADE SMOKED TROUT is rewarding and surprisingly easy. All you need is a large pot with a lid and a rack, some aluminum foil, and a handful of wood chips or dried fruitwood twigs. I like to just barely cook the trout through so that it's warm and moist, but nicely medium rare, to serve immediately. If you're smoking it to preserve it, however, you'll want to cook it longer.

The trout is best smoked outside. Line a very large pot with foil and arrange the wood chips or twigs in a small pile inside the pot on top of the foil. Ignite with a kitchen torch or a lighter until you have a nice little fire going. Cover the pot only part way, leaving room for air so the fire will keep burning.

Meanwhile, season 2 skin-on trout fillets with salt, pepper, and a little lemon zest. (I like to keep the skin on while I'm smoking the fish, then peel it off once it's finished.) Place the fillets on a rack that will easily fit inside the pot. Cover the pot tightly and wait a minute for the flame to go out, then quickly slip in the trout on the rack, trying not to let much smoke escape. About 5 minutes of smoking is long enough if you're serving the trout right away.

If you're planning on thoroughly smoking the fish, remove the fish from the pot and start another little fire. Then return the fish to the pot and smoke it for another 10–15 minutes.

Warm Smoked Trout with Pickled Onions

THIS MAKES A WONDERFUL little snack/appetizer/party dish. I love eating the fish while it's still warm from the smoker and the crème fraîche is ice cold.

Serves 6 as an appetizer

1   cup Vegetable Pickling Liquid (page 185)
1   red cippolini onion, sliced into paper-thin rings on a mandoline
½   cup crème fraîche
1   teaspoon fresh ground horseradish
6   pieces country bread, toasted
2   fillets warm smoked trout (TECHNIQUE, opposite), each cut into 3 small pieces
    Coarse sea salt
    Freshly ground black pepper
    Fresh fennel blossoms, fennel fronds, or sprigs of dill
    Drizzle of fruity olive oil

Heat the pickling liquid in a small saucepan (see photograph, opposite) over medium-high heat. Add the onion rings, and simmer for 5 minutes. Set aside to cool in the liquid.

In a small bowl, fold together the crème fraîche and the horseradish. Smear a dollop on each toast, top with a piece of smoked trout, and a few rings of pickled onions. Finish with coarse sea salt, pepper, fennel blossoms, and a drizzle of olive oil. Serve family style on a platter while the trout is still warm.

Gently Roasted Brown Trout with Summer Squash

MY FRIEND FRANCA Tantillo's amazing farm in the Catskills, Berried Treasures, is the source of the most incredible produce she sells at the Greenmarket in New York City's Union Square. Sometimes when I'm lucky, she'll also bring down some fresh German brown trout from a fishery nearby. I prepare these fish with herbs from her garden, both raw and lightly cooked summer squash, and lemon zest. Steaming the fish on top of the squash keeps it moist and delicately infuses the trout with summery flavor.
Serves 4

2 German brown trout, filleted, skin on
   Salt
   Freshly ground black pepper
½ pound mixed heirloom summer squash,
   cut into ½-inch pieces
   Small handful cherry tomatoes (I love sweet
   Sun Gold cherry tomatoes)
1 shallot, quartered and separated into petals
   Zest and juice of 1 lemon, plus additional juice
   for the shaved squash
   Leaves of 1 sprig fresh lemon thyme
   Leaves of 1 bunch fresh summer savory
   Leaves of 1 sprig fresh oregano
4 or 5 leaves fresh basil, torn
1 teaspoon Aleppo pepper or hot red pepper flakes
4 tablespoons olive oil
1 tablespoon dry white wine
   Few pieces baby summer squash, sliced into
   ribbons on a mandoline

Preheat the oven to 350°. Season the trout fillets with salt and pepper on all sides.

In a large mixing bowl, combine the cut-up squash with the tomatoes, shallots, lemon zest and juice, herbs, and Aleppo pepper; season with salt and pepper. Toss with 1 tablespoon of the olive oil and the white wine. Evenly distribute on a rimmed cookie sheet and slide the pan into the oven.

While the squash is in the oven, heat 2 table-spoons of the olive oil in a large cast iron pan over medium-high heat. Add the trout fillets, skin-side down, and sear until golden and crispy, about 3 minutes. Carefully remove the fish from the pan and place them, skin-side up, on top of the vegetables in the oven. Finish cooking the trout in the oven until just cooked through, another 5 minutes. The squash should be bright in color and barely cooked, with a bit of toothiness.

In a small bowl, season the raw squash ribbons with salt, pepper, the remaining 1 tablespoon olive oil, and lemon juice to taste.

Divide the cooked vegetables evenly among 4 warm plates. Place a fillet atop each bed of vegetables and scatter each plate with a few raw squash ribbons. Serve immediately.

In Spain salt cod comes in many different cuts. Clockwise from top, *migas*, or small pieces; *lomo*, or loin; *filete*, the full fillet; and *tripa*, the tripe or sounds. Scenes from La Casa del Bacalao in Barcelona, right.

LA CASA DEL BACALAO
sólo vende
AUTÉNTICO BACALAO
sin aditivos ni conservantes,
sólo sal

Desalinating Salt Cod

SOAKING *BACALAO* (SALT COD) to wash away the curing salt is a judgment call, the timing depends upon the quality and amount of salt that was used in the drying process—soak it for too short a time and the fish will still be overly salty; soak it too long and the fish will lose its distinctive flavor. For a large piece or a whole fillet, I believe that cod should soak in cold water in the fridge for at least 12 hours, changing the water every 6 hours. After 12 hours, I cut off a tiny piece of fish and taste it. If it's still very salty, I give it another 6–12 hours, tasting as I go. Twenty-four hours is the standard, but some *bacalao* soaked that long can be bland, so it's a good idea to check it periodically. Another way to check the salinity inside the fish is to insert a sharp knife into the fish, then pull it out and touch it to your tongue. If you can still taste the salt, it needs more soaking time.

Salt Cod with Garbanzo Beans and Spinach

EVEN THOUGH REFRIGERATION has made the art of salting, desalinating, and cooking cod unnecessary, something magical happens to the flavor of the fish during the salting process that makes the flavor of fresh cod pale in comparison. It's been over one hundred years since we stopped *needing* to salt our fish to make it last, but the incredibly flavorful ingredient became so tightly woven into the fabric of many cuisines that nothing else can match it.

My introduction, formal education, and finishing school of salt cod took place in the kitchens of Spain. In every Spanish market there are multiple stalls dedicated exclusively to the sale of myriad varieties, cuts, and preparations of salt cod and it seems as though refrigeration hasn't done much to close down these *bacalao* shops.

Bacalao can be a bit daunting at first, but it's really not that difficult to work with and the results are amazing. For this dish I use two different cuts of salt cod; the fillet and the "sounds," also called "tripe." Cod tripe may not seem all that appetizing, nor is it easy to find, but believe me, it's incredibly flavorful, with a very high level of gelatin that lends a lovely creaminess to the garbanzo beans. If you can't find cod tripe, cod skins can be finely diced and folded into the beans for a similar effect.

Salt cod is generally packed and stored in wooden boxes which can seem a little off-putting and very unfoodlike, but don't worry, once you've gotten the salt cod home and soaked it, it becomes a fish again! When buying cod, try to open the boxes and check the cod. Avoid fillets that look yellow and/or too flat. Once desalinated properly, the fish should be tender and delicate, never mushy. It helps to let the fillets dry in the refrigerator uncovered for a few hours after you remove them from the soaking water.

Serves 4

2   tablespoons olive oil
1   onion, thinly sliced
4   cloves garlic, thinly sliced
1   cup cod tripe, desalinated (TECHNIQUE, page 235) and finely minced, or 2 tablespoons finely minced cod skin
2   cups dried garbanzo beans, soaked overnight and drained
½   cup white wine
    Bay leaves
    A few sprigs fresh thyme
4   *guindilla* peppers
    Salt
    Freshly ground black pepper
    Handful cherry tomatoes, tossed in olive oil and roasted in the oven at 275° for 2 hours
    Handful or two of fresh spinach
1   pound salt cod fillets, desalinated (TECHNIQUE, page 235) and cut into 4 portions
    Drizzle of fruity olive oil

Heat the olive oil in the pressure cooker and gently sauté the onions and garlic until tender. Add the cod tripe or skins, garbanzo beans, white wine, bay leaves, thyme, and *guindilla* peppers. Add water to cover and fit the lid on. Bring the temperature up to high until it begins to boil, then reduce to a simmer and cook until the beans are very tender, about 1 hour. Alternately, you can do this in a large, heavy-bottomed pot, you'll just need to cook the beans for 2½ hours or so until they're tender.

Remove the lid and season with salt and pepper. Fold in the tomatoes and spinach and nestle in the fillets of salt cod. Gently simmer, uncovered, until the fish is just flaky, about 6 minutes. Finish with a healthy drizzle of fruity olive oil.

AUTUMN

IN VERMONT

CH. 15: Squash EARTHY ✳ ABUNDANT ✳ AUTUMNAL

CH. 16: Mushrooms WOODSY ✳ MEATY ✳ MELLOW

CH. 17: Greens HEARTY ✳ VIBRANT ✳ HEALTHY

CH. 18: Good Meat JUICY ✳ TENDER ✳ GRASSFED

239

My childhood friend
Ben Machin, above,
raises heritage Tunis
lamb on his farm,
Tamarack Tunis. Top
left, a flock on the
hillcrest at Ben's
farm in Corinth,
Vermont. Freshly
slaughtered lambs,
left, hang in our barn.
Far left, my chef pal
Zak Pelaccio and I
rinse lacy caul fat.

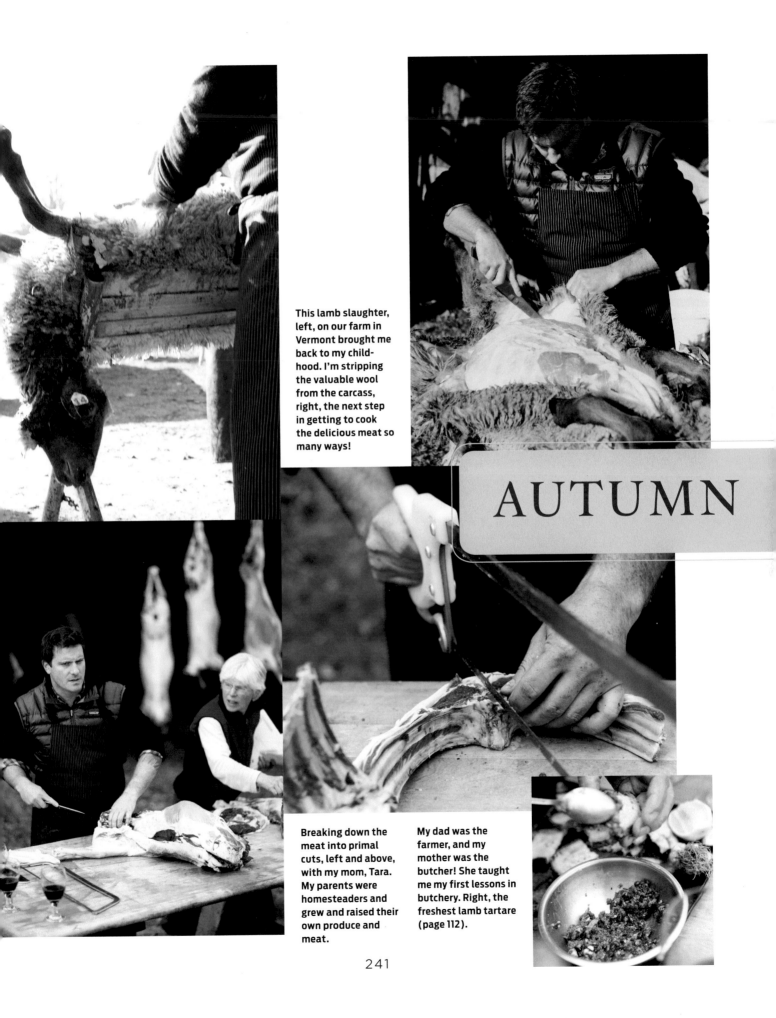

This lamb slaughter, left, on our farm in Vermont brought me back to my childhood. I'm stripping the valuable wool from the carcass, right, the next step in getting to cook the delicious meat so many ways!

AUTUMN

Breaking down the meat into primal cuts, left and above, with my mom, Tara. My parents were homesteaders and grew and raised their own produce and meat.

My dad was the farmer, and my mother was the butcher! She taught me my first lessons in butchery. Right, the freshest lamb tartare (page 112).

Cleaning a fresh rack of lamb, left. My front-of-the-house partner at Tertulia, Gil Avital, far left. Pan-frying lamb kidneys, left, and a succulent mixed grill of the freshest lamb chops and kidneys, right. Above, roasting lamb shoulder in the fragrant heat of the wood-fired oven.

AUTUMN

The dinner of the lamb: around the table with my whole family and some close friends, above, sharing a toast with my grandmother Mutti, as my nephew Will looks on. My niece Marlow supervises from my brother Nils's shoulders, right, and at the lamb-laden dinner table, far right.

chapter fifteen

SQUASH

EARTHY

✳ ✳ ✳

ABUNDANT

✳ ✳ ✳

AUTUMNAL

WINTER SQUASH IS NOT AN EASY THING FOR A KID TO LOVE, and I was no exception. It seems to me that the way squash is typically treated as a food reflects more the way it looks on the outside than the way it tastes on the inside. It might sound pretentious, but I didn't really fall in love with the stuff until I started to cook it myself as a chef. I never liked the heavy-handed way that squash is typically prepared: clumpy purees,

bland roasted acorn squash, canned pumpkin pie mix—none of these things do justice to the beautiful, nuanced flavors of squash when it's properly prepared.

I only started to appreciate squash when I learned to think about it in nontraditional ways. When I was working at Mugaritz in the Spanish Basque Country, the chef/owner Andoni Luiz Aduriz created a dessert that not only was atypical for a dessert in that it involved squash, it was atypical for a squash dish in the way it was prepared: a large

winter squash was cut into 8-inch crescents about ½ inch thick. Those slices were poached in a simple syrup until tender. Then they were moved to the griddle where they were caramelized. These crisped slices were served with a vanilla-scented truffle foam.

One of the things I liked most about Andoni's dessert was the way it straddled sweet and savory. But another important idea came through to me: squash didn't have to be a puree or a soup, it could be handled in much the same way we would treat a fruit

"It seems to me that the way squash is typically treated reflects more the way it looks on the outside than how it tastes on the inside."

like an apple. In fact, of course, squash, with its seeds on the inside, is technically a fruit. This got me thinking that if we could prepare squash as a dessert, why couldn't we do other things with it, like make crunchy squash chips? Or squash pickles. Or even a béchamel with squash for croquettes.

A few years later, when I had my own restaurant, we had a dish in the late summer that was garnished with lightly pickled radishes. As the weather began to get colder and radishes became fewer and farther between, I didn't want to take the dish off the menu. I needed a substitute and suddenly, it occurred to me: squash! I cut a large Hubbard squash in half, threw it on the meat slicer, and ripped off a few paper-thin ribbons. First I tried blanching the slices in boiling water with the intention of pickling them afterward, but they fell apart. Then I tried heating them up in a pickling liquid and presto, the pickled squash that I use in Autumn Squash Salad (page 248) was born.

Besides these unexpectedly delicious sides of squash, it turns out that squash has significant health benefits for me. It's a high-fiber, low-calorie, nutrient-dense food. Richly colored red, orange, and yellow squashes—particularly these winter varieties—contain an impressive amount of antioxidants like beta carotene, which forms vitamin A. In fact, winter squash just may be the prince of the carotene antioxidants, alpha and beta, which may help in combatting inflammation and may aid our immune system by interrupting the harmful chain reaction that results when free radicals form.

The seeds of squash, like pumpkin seeds, themselves contain beneficial fatty acids; they're irresistible when roasted on a baking sheet with a bit of olive oil in a cool oven (around 225°) for about 20 minutes, until they become crunchy and flavorful.

I've learned quite a few lessons from squash. Interestingly enough, a vegetable I didn't think I liked that much turns out to be something I love; the secret was to approach it differently. When we venture beyond the expected, we sometimes arrive at an unusual and exciting new place.

Autumn Squash Salad

I SEE NO REASON WHY salads should be limited to greens. This one has a ton of different textures and flavors and is as visually rewarding as it is delicious. Vermont is famous for its fall color, so when I thought of this dish, I wanted all the components to come together on a platter in the same way that autumn leaves fall together in a collage of color on the forest floor. There are bits of roasted squash, blanched squash, pickled squash, and even toasted squash seeds. While I don't like dishes that are so fussy and manipulated they look less like food and more like art, I can't deny that we eat first with our eyes.

Serves 4

1   cup Vegetable Pickling Liquid (page 185)
    Few thin ribbons Hubbard squash, skin on,
    cut on a mandoline
1   kabocha squash, cut into large wedges
    Salt
    Freshly ground black pepper
    Healthy drizzle plus ¼ cup olive oil
¼   cup cider vinegar
1   teaspoon honey
1   clove garlic, grated
1   bunch Tuscan kale, stems removed
1   delicata squash, halved and cut into half-moons,
    then blanched in salted water for 30 seconds
1   watermelon radish, sliced paper-thin, plus greens

Few slices *jamón serrano*, **prosciutto,
or cured country ham**
¼   **cup toasted** *pepitas* **(pumpkin seeds)**
Leaves from 1 bunch fresh cilantro

Preheat the oven to 375°. Heat the pickling liquid over medium-high heat in a medium saucepan and add the Hubbard squash ribbons. Simmer until tender, about 5 minutes. Set aside to cool in the liquid.

In a medium-sized roasting pan, toss the kabocha squash wedges with salt, pepper, and a drizzle of olive oil. Roast until tender, about 15 minutes. Set aside.

For the dressing, whisk together the vinegar, honey, and grated garlic in a bowl and slowly add the ¼ cup olive oil until well mixed.

Here, our fingers are our best tools. Wash your hands and tear the kale into bite-sized pieces and distribute on a platter. Layer on the pickled Hubbard squash, roasted kabocha squash, blanched delicata squash, and the watermelon radish slices. Drizzle on the dressing, then gently run your fingers through the salad to distribute the dressing without breaking the delicate squash slices. Lace a few slices of ham over the top and scatter the toasted pumpkin seeds and cilantro.

Roasted Winter Squash

I LOVE LATE SEPTEMBER, when the last light of summer is waning and farmers markets proudly display their colorful squash of all shapes and sizes. There are so many amazing different varieties, each with a distinct flavor. This is a simple and easy way to prepare all kinds of winter squash, either one kind or many of them. I always make extra squash and snack on it cold.
Serves 8

6	pounds mixed autumn squash, unpeeled butternut, kabocha, delicata, spaghetti, pumpkin, and/or Hubbard
	Salt
	Freshly ground black pepper
½	cup olive oil
½	cup maple syrup
1	bunch fresh rosemary
1	bunch fresh thyme
1	bunch fresh sage
1	bunch fresh oregano
1	head garlic, cloves lightly crushed
	Zest of 2 lemons

Preheat the oven to 375°. Cut the squash into similar size pieces, but do not peel. Remove the seeds and arrange the squash cut-side up in a large roasting pan. Season thoroughly with salt and pepper, drizzle with the olive oil and maple syrup, and evenly scatter with the herbs, garlic cloves, and lemon zest.

Roast until tender, 35–50 minutes, depending on the size of the squash pieces. Serve immediately on a large platter. Any leftover squash is delicious cut up and tossed in a salad or just for nibbling.

Winter squash are as beautiful on the outside as they are tasty inside. Big blue pumpkins, striped spaghetti squash, riotously colored turbans, smooth butternuts, kuris, kabocha, and blue Hubbard.

Stuffed Spaghetti Squash

YOU'D NEVER GUESS by looking at its smooth exterior that when you roast the aptly named spaghetti squash and run a fork along the insides, the flesh will fall away in thin strands. In Spain it's called *cabello de angel*, "angels' hair," and it's usually served candied as a sweet. This stuffed squash is a wonderful side dish, but hearty enough to be a delicious main course.

Serves 4

1	medium-to-large spaghetti squash, halved, seeds removed
	Salt
	Freshly ground black pepper
8	sprigs fresh thyme
1	bunch fresh sage
	Generous drizzles of olive oil
	Drizzle of honey
½	pound hen-of-the-woods mushrooms, coarsely chopped
½	cup Marcona almonds, coarsely chopped
1	clove garlic, grated
2	tablespoons Champagne vinegar
1	cup finely grated Idiazábal cheese

Preheat the oven to 375°. Place the squash, cut sides up, in a large roasting pan. Season the flesh with salt, pepper, a sprig each of thyme and sage, a drizzle of olive oil, and a drizzle of honey. Roast until tender, about 40 minutes.

Finely chop the remaining herbs and toss with the mushrooms, Marcona almonds, and garlic. Season with the vinegar, another splash of olive oil, and salt and pepper.

Once the squash is tender, scrape out the flesh with a fork into a large bowl, reserving the skin intact; if it's cooked through, the flesh should have the texture and appearance of al dente spaghetti. Toss the squash together with the mushroom mixture and spoon back into the skins. Cover each squash half with the grated cheese and bake for another 10 minutes, until the cheese is melted and the mushrooms are cooked through. Serve piping hot.

Butternut Squash Soup with Smoked Trout

I'M A SUCKER FOR BUTTERNUT SQUASH SOUP; it is definitely one of my comfort foods. Sometimes I make this creamy, delicate soup and live off it for days; and sometimes I add homemade smoked trout and crème fraîche to make it just a little bit sexier.

Serves 4

1	shallot, finely diced
1	clove garlic, thinly sliced
2	tablespoons plus ¼ cup olive oil, plus more to drizzle
2	pounds butternut squash, peeled and cubed
1	tablespoon Champagne vinegar
¼	cup white wine
	Zest of 1 lemon
	Salt
	Freshly ground black pepper
¼	cup crème fraîche
¼	pound smoked trout (TECHNIQUE, page 230)
	Handful fresh basil leaves

In a large heavy-bottomed pot, sweat the shallots and garlic in the 2 tablespoons olive oil over medium heat until translucent, about 5 minutes. Add the squash and deglaze with the vinegar and white wine. Add just enough water to cover and bring to a simmer. Cook until the squash is very tender, about 20 minutes.

With a rubber spatula, carefully transfer to a blender or food processor and process until smooth. With the motor running, drizzle in the ¼ cup olive oil. Add the lemon zest and adjust the seasoning with salt and pepper.

Divide the soup among 4 warm bowls. Top each serving with a little island of crème fraîche and scatter the smoked trout around the island. Finish with some coarsely ground pepper, basil leaves, and a drizzle of olive oil. Serve immediately.

chapter sixteen

MUSHROOMS

WOODSY

✳ ✳ ✳

MEATY

✳ ✳ ✳

MELLOW

I'VE ALWAYS BEEN MAD ABOUT MUSHROOMS. I grew up hunting morels and chanterelles with my mom in the thick stand of maples near our house where they popped up among the spring green ferns after a heavy rain. I thought I knew mushrooms, but at the Boqueria market in Barcelona, I realized I was a fungal neophyte. I'd never seen so many varieties: saffron milk caps, trumpets of death, mousserons. When I cooked at

"Mushrooms may stimulate the immune system. They're vitamin-rich and contain phytonutrients. And you thought they were just cellulose and water."

the restaurant Alkimia, I had a ritual on my day off: I'd forage at the market (way more productive than the Vermont woods) and then run home to cook my booty.

I always liked mushrooms for their meaty flavor, particularly dried mushrooms, but it wasn't until I went to Japan for *The Next Iron Chef* that I really understood them. Competing in Japan, our judge was Dr. Yukio Hattori, a noted authority on Japanese gastronomy, who had appeared on the original Japanese *Iron Chef* in the 1990s. Dr. Hattori explained the near-spiritual reverence for the mushroom in Japan, where matsutakes (or pine mushrooms) can be as expensive as truffles. It turns out that mushrooms, particularly dried mushrooms, have an extremely high glutamic acid content. This is the amino acid responsible for umami, one of the five basic tastes and loosely translated as "deliciousness." Dr. Hattori is a huge proponent of umami, and, as it turns out, I am too.

Over the years, as I've gone deep into both Spanish and Japanese cooking, I've been surprised by their parallels. In both traditions, dishes are not cluttered with ingredients but rather focus on a few flavors. In both cuisines, the mushroom is a stellar ingredient. When I was working at the Michelin two-star restaurant Abac in Barcelona, one of our most popular dishes was simply grilled porcini mushrooms tossed with a mushroom vinaigrette (page 262). While there is something intensely Spanish about this dish, I could easily imagine eating it in Japan.

In Chinese medicine, mushrooms have been used for thousands of years to treat a whole range of ailments. Western doctors seem to have a hard time coming to terms with Chinese medicine. But I believe thousands of years of trial and error have produced results that cannot be ignored. Emerging studies suggest that ordinary button mushrooms (cremini) may have an effect on inflammation. It turns out that mushrooms contain *terpenoids*, phytonutrients with may have anti-inflammatory effects. Mushrooms are also known for their antioxidant benefits, and are a good source of some B vitamins, vitamin D, and several minerals. In addition, some mushrooms have soluble fiber. They're

And like so many Heroes, it is important to handle them delicately and not overcook them, which could compromise the very qualities we love about them.

A NOTE ON...
CLEANING MUSHROOMS

The best way to clean mushrooms is to wipe them down with a damp towel. Unfortunately, many wild mushrooms like chanterelles and black trumpets are full of pine needles and bits of dirt that make them difficult to clean this way. What I suggest, if they're really dirty, is to give them a quick soak in a bowl of ice water for 2 or 3 minutes, then spread them on a kitchen towel to dry. What you don't want to do is to scrub them and damage their delicate surface. Don't wash the mushrooms until immediately before preparing them. Otherwise they'll retain moisture, become soggy, and spoil quickly.

For large mushrooms like porcini, hedgehog, or king oyster, you may not even need to clean them. Just use a sharp paring knife to trim the bottom of the stem and carefully scrape away the thinnest possible outside layer of skin. Hen-of-the-woods are cultivated mushrooms and are usually quite clean. They have a woody stem where the petals of the mushroom come together; just trim off the bottom of the stem, which can be a bit woody.

The best way to store mushrooms is in a small basket in the refrigerator, uncovered. Plastic bags are the worst way to store mushrooms—moisture will turn them slimy.

low in calories and sodium, and are cholesterol- and fat-free. And you thought mushrooms were nothing more than water and cellulose!

Of course, some mushrooms are inedible and deadly toxic whereas others are the essence of nourishment. As far as I'm concerned the potential for inflammation blocking + antioxidants + over-the-top deliciousness all add up to mushrooms-as-Hero.

Warm Mushroom Salad

THE ORIGINAL VERSION OF THIS SALAD was conceived amongst the mushroom stands at the Boqueria market in Barcelona and executed in my tiny, poorly appointed kitchen in the Gothic Quarter. One thing I always do when I'm cooking with mushrooms is to strain the liquid the mushrooms inevitably give off as they cook and use that liquid in a vinaigrette or sauce. It creates a whole other layer of flavor.

Serves 4

¼	cup paper-thin slices raw celery root
½	pound king oyster mushrooms, sliced paper thin lengthwise
4	tablespoons olive oil
	Zest and juice of 1 lemon
	Salt
	Freshly ground black pepper
½	pound hen-of-the-woods mushrooms, torn into small pieces
¼	pound wood ear mushrooms, sliced into thin strips
1	clove garlic, thinly sliced
2	tablespoons dry sherry wine
	Small bunch dandelion greens
	Small handful fresh parsley leaves
½	cup Warm Mushroom Vinaigrette (page 262)
2	tablespoons finely grated horseradish
¼	pound Idiazábal or Manchego cheese, sliced paper-thin with a vegetable peeler

In a large mixing bowl, toss the celery root and king oyster mushrooms together with 2 tablespoons of the olive oil and the lemon juice; season with salt and pepper and set aside to macerate.

Meanwhile, heat the remaining 2 tablespoons olive oil in a large skillet over medium-high heat. Give the hen-of-the-woods and the wood ear mushrooms a lively sauté for 3–4 minutes before adding the garlic. Season with salt and pepper, add the sherry wine, and sauté for 1 minute more. Set a fine-mesh sieve over a small skillet and drain the mushrooms, reserving the liquid for the vinaigrette.

Gently mix the sautéed mushrooms with the celery root and king oyster mushrooms in a large salad bowl; toss together with the dandelion greens and parsley.

Pour the warm vinaigrette over the salad—the greens should pleasantly wilt, ever so slightly. Adjust the seasoning with salt and pepper and divide among 4 salad plates. Finish each plate with the lemon zest, fresh horseradish, and a few shavings of cheese. Serve while the salad is still warm.

Juanito's signature smile at Bar Pinotxo. It's my favorite spot for breakfast in the Boqueria market.

Warm Mushroom Vinaigrette

THIS IS A LOVELY VINAIGRETTE that brings out the real depth of flavor in Warm Mushroom Salad (page 261). It can also be tossed over roasted potatoes for an incredible earthy flavor or drizzled on top of a simple grilled steak. Why do mushrooms and steak work so well together and appear in so many recipes (and inferior bottled sauces)? Because they both contain a large amount of glutamic acid, the amino acid responsible for the fifth taste, umami. If you don't have the juice from sautéed mushrooms, just soak a tablespoon or two of dried mushrooms (like shitakes, you don't need costly morels) with ½ cup hot water for 10 minutes. Strain the mushrooms and reduce the liquid in a small pan by half for a rich essence of mushroom.

Makes about 1 cup

½   cup plus 1 tablespoon olive oil
1   shallot, finely minced
1   clove garlic, finely minced
¼   cup sweet sherry vinegar
½   cup mushroom liquid from sautéed mushrooms, or ¼ cup reduced liquid from soaked dry mushrooms
    Salt
    Freshly ground black pepper

In a small skillet over medium-low heat, heat the 1 tablespoon olive oil, add the shallots, and sweat for a minute. Add the garlic, sweat a minute, then add the sherry vinegar. Lightly reduce for another minute to mellow the acidity. Pour in the mushroom liquid, increase the heat, and whisk in the ½ cup olive oil. Season with salt and pepper.

If using with the mushroom salad, heat the vinaigrette until you can barely stand the temperature with your finger—about 120°—then pour over the salad and serve immediately.

Flatbreads of King Oyster and Shitake Mushrooms

FLATBREADS ARE ANOTHER one of those things in the restaurant, like meatballs, that no matter the topping, if they're on the menu, they fly out the door. This is a simple flatbread dough that can be used with many different toppings, like chorizo and cheese or grilled radicchio and ricotta; see page 90 for a version with anchovies. The mushrooms' meaty texture is a great contrast to the crispy flatbread.

Serves 4 as an appetizer

2   tablespoons olive oil
½   pound shitake mushrooms, stems removed
½   pound king oyster mushrooms, sliced into coins
½   pound black trumpet mushrooms
½   pound hen-of-the-woods mushrooms
2   shallots, quartered and separated into petals
1   clove garlic, thinly sliced
1   tablespoon cider vinegar
1   tablespoon butter
    Leaves from 2 sprigs fresh parsley, coarsely chopped
    Salt
    Freshly ground black pepper
    Grilled Flatbreads (page 90)
1   pound fresh ricotta cheese

In a large skillet, heat the olive oil over medium-high heat and vigorously sauté all the mushrooms, the shallots, and garlic together for 3–4 minutes. Add the vinegar and reduce for 30 seconds. Add the butter, parsley, and salt and pepper and sauté for 1 minute more. Transfer to a mixing bowl.

When grilling the flatbreads, evenly distribute one-fourth of the mushroom mixture and the ricotta on top of each flatbread immediately after turning it on the grill. Then finish grilling until the bread is cooked through and nicely charred. Remove from the grill, cut each flatbread into 3 or 4 pieces, and serve immediately.

Pickled Mushrooms

THESE MUSHROOMS MAKE an excellent condiment for cured meats, work well with a variety of cheeses on a cheese board, or can be easily be incorporated into other dishes like Pickled Chanterelles with Mackerel in Escabeche (page 266) and Farro Salad with Preserved Tuna (page 69).

Makes 2 jars

2 tablespoons unsalted butter
2 cloves garlic, sliced
½ pound mixed wild mushrooms such as chanterelles, morels, hen-of-the-woods, and/or oyster mushrooms
   Salt
   Freshly ground black pepper
1 cup Vegetable Pickling Liquid (page 185)
   About 2 cups extra-virgin olive oil

Heat the butter in a medium-sized skillet over medium-high heat. Once the butter begins to foam, add the garlic and mushrooms and season with salt and pepper. Sauté vigorously for 5 minutes, until the mushrooms start to wilt. Add the pickling liquid, increase the heat, and cook until the liquid simmers. Remove the pan from the heat and let stand for 10 minutes.

Drain the mushrooms and distribute evenly among 2 canning jars. Pour in olive oil to cover and close the lids. Refrigerated, the mushrooms will keep for a week or so.

Cremini Mushrooms al Ajillo

THERE ARE TONS OF VARIATIONS of dishes *al ajillo*, or "with a little garlic," all over Spain. This is an extremely easy and tasty dish that can be served as a side or as a nice little tapa. Pile these mushrooms, hot or cold, into little ceramic dishes, stick a toothpick in each, and you're on your way to your own tapas party. I also love them tossed in a salad.

Serves 4–6 as a tapa

¼ cup olive oil
1 pound small cremini mushrooms, whole, lightly wiped down with a damp cloth
3 cloves garlic, thinly sliced
2 *guindilla* peppers, or 1 teaspoon red pepper flakes
2 tablespoons Champagne or white wine vinegar
½ cup dry white wine
   Salt
   Freshly ground black pepper
¼ cup coarsely chopped fresh parsley

In a large saucepan, heat the olive oil over medium-high heat. Add the mushrooms and roll them around in the pan with a rubber spatula to brown evenly on all sides. Once the mushrooms are nice and seared, reduce the heat to medium low and add the garlic while continuing to stir. Add the peppers or pepper flakes and sauté for 3 minutes, until the garlic starts to wilt, but not brown. Once the garlic has softened in flavor and texture, add the vinegar and increase the heat to medium high to glaze the mushrooms.

Pour in the white wine and braise the mushrooms until tender, 8–10 minutes. Season with salt and pepper and finish with a scattering of chopped parsley.

Llorenz Petras is the go-to Mushroom Man, renowned in Barcelona's Boqueria market for his encyclopedic knowledge.

Pickled Chanterelles with Mackerel in Escabeche

THIS IS ONLY ONE of the thousand-plus uses for pickled chanterelles, but it's a great one. These juicy pickles cut right through the richness of the fish. And oh my! Hasn't mackerel gotten the shaft over the years? High in omega-3s, rich in protein, low on the food chain, and to me, very delicious, mackerel deserves a bit of a revival. Because mackerel is so oily, if the fish is not really fresh, it can get a bit funky. Be sure to look for fish that is firm to the touch and has clear eyes.

Serves 4

2   fresh mackerel, filleted, pin bones removed
    Salt
    Freshly ground black pepper
2   cups *Escabeche* for Pickling Poultry or Fish
    (page 127)
2   cups Pickled Mushrooms (page 265),
    such as chanterelles
    Handful coarsely chopped fresh herbs,
    such as parsley and basil

Season the fillets liberally with salt and pepper. In a medium saucepan, heat the *escabeche* (making sure there are enough vegetables to create a nest to support the fillets. Add the mackerel skin side up and gently poach until just cooked through, 4–6 minutes depending upon the size of the fish.

Serve the mackerel warm on top of the pickled mushrooms, garnished with a handful of scattered fresh herbs.

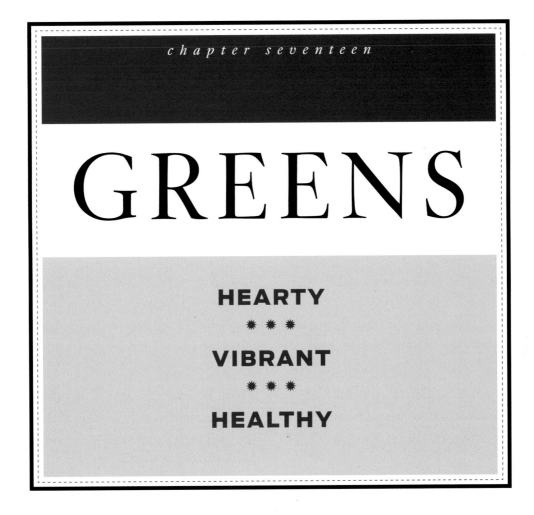

chapter seventeen

GREENS

HEARTY

✳ ✳ ✳

VIBRANT

✳ ✳ ✳

HEALTHY

JUST TAKE A WALK THROUGH THE PRODUCE AISLES of your grocery store or stroll through your farmers market and in almost every season you'll behold stacks of rich dark leafy greens: bundles of Swiss chard piled as high as a small child; black kale and purple kale and curly kale; mustard greens; tender little spinach leaves and sandy big ones; and of course the whole range of Asian greens like bok choy and tatsoi, mizuna and water

"It's one thing to make the claim that greens are among the healthiest foods you can eat; it's quite another to want to eat them."

spinach. Just looking at them can make you feel healthy. But is it enough to "eat your greens"? Are they always that tasty? Frankly most of the greens I recall eating in my life have been pretty bland.

My dad always told my brother and me to eat our "roughage" when we were growing up, and so we did. He was (and still is) a huge fan of the nutrient-rich, but not so user-friendly stinging nettles. Nettles grew rampant on our farm and there was never any shortage of them on our dinner table where they ranked at the top of the things I most hated to eat. Many years later, when I was cooking in San Francisco, we had nettles on the menu.

At first, I was understandably dubious of those nasty plants (we had to wear two pairs of latex gloves just to handle them raw!). Once I tried them, however, I was amazed. I didn't just like them, I loved them. The chef simply rendered and then glazed some bacon, then sautéed the nettles with garlic and fresh thyme in the same pan. A little white wine, a splash of chicken stock, and

after 10 minutes the nettles underwent a transformation from coarse and stringy to rich and tender. I've come to realize that most greens suffer from "nettle syndrome": we know they're good for us, but it's one thing to make the claim that greens are among the healthiest foods you can eat; it's quite another to actually want to eat them. Since it's widely known that most Americans don't come close to eating their recommended share of veggies, I feel responsible for making you want to "cook your greens." I think of my job in the kitchen as figuring out ways to make those vegetables really shine. I'm not suggesting that we deconstruct greens or mask their flavor with other ingredients. Each vegetable has its own particular charm.

Just imagine a silky soup of pureed collard greens cooked with a smoked ham hock, finished with a dollop of yogurt and served with some pickled collard green stems. Or some lightly blanched mustard greens, pureed and folded into potatoes fork-mashed with olive oil. Or what about delicate green raviolis, where a stuffing of minced shrimp

and pork is wrapped in chard leaves and steamed until tender. All of these dishes are a welcome departure from the usual simple steamed or stewed or sautéed greens—which can be fine, too. Just not particularly inspiring. Sometimes a simple splash of good vinegar or lightly sautéed good bacon is all you need to elevate those simple greens into something crave-worthy.

Just as with squash, it helps to think outside the box about cooking with greens. Have you ever thought of grilling greens? One of my favorite recipes in this chapter is for Crispy Tuscan Kale on the Grill (page 275). Not exactly ordinary. Or what about braising some Swiss chard in olive oil, garlic,

and white wine instead of water and folding it into some beaten eggs and cooked potatoes for an unconventional omelet? Are you a big fan of brunch? What about reinventing eggs Benedict, scrapping the Canadian bacon for some braised kale? And on the subject of kale, I happen to like it raw in a salad with shaved radishes, carrots, summer squash, and a buttermilk vinaigrette.

Of course you'd have to look very hard to find a single food as nourishing and delicious as the wide spectrum of greens. Dark, leafy greens are among the healthiest of all vegetables. Most are rich in vitamins A, K, and folate. Many are good sources of minerals and calcium as well as powerful disease-fighting antioxidants. I include greens in this book to demonstrate how they can become so much more than the obligatory healthy vegetable.

Spicy Rapini with Almonds

I'M A BIG FAN OF BITTER GREENS and none gets me going like rapini (also called broccoli rabe). One of my all-time favorite vegetables, it has a natural spiciness that's similar to Brussels sprouts. The horseradish here just enhances that flavor. The sweet quince paste, *membrillo,* is a classic condiment to serve with cheese in Spain, but it's so delicious I don't like to limit it and serve it with many things. Here it mellows the greens in a very elegant way.

Serves 4

2	tablespoons olive oil
2	bunches rapini, each stalk cut in half length-wise
¼	cup Marcona almonds, roughly chopped
2	cloves garlic, thinly sliced
1	tablespoon freshly ground horseradish
1	tablespoon red pepper flakes
	Salt
	Freshly ground black pepper
2	tablespoons diced quince paste
	Juice of 1 lemon

Heat the olive oil over high heat in a large skillet. Add the rapini and quickly sauté—I like to brown it a little bit in the pan. Once the greens begin to wilt, about 2 minutes, toss in the almonds, garlic, horseradish, and red pepper and season with salt and pepper.

Continue cooking for 2 more minutes, then transfer to a large serving platter. Sprinkle with the diced quince paste and lemon juice and serve right away.

TECHNIQUE

Steaming Greens

STEAMING IS A HEALTHY WAY to prepare greens and retain much of their food value, but just plain steamed greens can be a bit tasteless. To ratchet up the flavor of ordinary greens when steaming, I like to pre-season my cleaned greens (such as rapini, kale, collards, spinach, or mustard): Put the greens in a large mixing bowl, add a healthy splash of olive oil, a couple cloves of sliced garlic, and a few thin slivers of lemon, along with a generous sprinkle of salt and pepper and toss well. Place the dressed greens in a steamer basket fitted into a saucepan over an inch or so of water. Cover and steam over medium-high heat until they're tender and bright green. For a little bit more flavor, add a splash of white wine to your steaming liquid.

Crispy Tuscan Kale on the Grill

WHEN I GAVE THIS RECIPE to *Food & Wine* magazine recently it became an instant hit. People contacted me on Facebook from every corner of the world, telling me how much they loved grilling kale. Who knew? The truth is, kale done this way is pretty damn tasty, quite easy to make, and a great beginning to a barbecue. As well as being a great snack, you can break the grilled kale leaves into large pieces and toss them in a salad.

Makes 1 healthy stack

1	cup olive oil
2	tablespoons balsamic vinegar
2	cloves garlic, finely minced
	Zest and juice of 1 lemon
2	bunches Tuscan kale, stems and all, washed and spun dry
	Salt
	Freshly ground black pepper

Preheat the grill to high or build a small fire in a charcoal grill. In a large mixing bowl, combine the olive oil, vinegar, garlic, and lemon zest and juice and mix well. Add the kale leaves. Season with salt and pepper and gently toss until kale is evenly coated.

When the grill is hot, carefully lay the kale leaves, as many as will fit, side-by-side in a single layer on the grill. In about 2 minutes the leaves will crisp. Turn them and grill on the other side for another 1–2 minutes. Repeat with the rest of the leaves.

Pile the grilled kale leaves in a big stack on a large platter or cutting board and serve them up.

Sorrel Sauce

GROWING UP IN VERMONT, we used to pick wild sorrel and toss it into our salads. After I went away to high school I totally forgot about sorrel until many years later when I worked at Mugaritz in San Sebastián. There, we young cooks had to get up early every morning to forage for wild vegetables, one of which was oxalis, a form of wild wood sorrel that reminded me of the sorrel of my childhood.

I love this sauce with salmon or char, and it's just as good with roasted pork belly. If you can't find sorrel, make the sauce with watercress and it will be as tasty, it just won't have sorrel's characteristic sourness. In fact, it's just that slightly sharp, mouthwatering tingle that makes sorrel such a wonderful sauce for rich food.

Makes about 1 cup

- 1 tablespoon olive oil
- 1 bunch sorrel, thoroughly washed
- 1 shallot, finely diced
- 1 tablespoon white wine
- 2 tablespoons drained plain yogurt or labne
   Salt
   Freshly ground black pepper

Heat the olive oil in a skillet over medium-high heat and quickly sauté the sorrel and shallots together until the sorrel begins to wilt.

Transfer the sorrel to the Vitamix or blender and process with the white wine and yogurt; season with salt and pepper. If you find the sauce to be a bit thick you can thin it out with a splash or two of water.

Xató Salad

THIS IS MY TAKE ON a Catalan specialty, a salad of bitter escarole (add frisée if you like) and nutty Romesco that comes together beautifully. *Xató* is probably derived from the French word chateau (another version of this salad is on page 89).

One of the things I like to teach my cooks about plating salads is to be delicate, to create a sense of volume, and to leave space between the ingredients. There are a number of salty things going on here, so if you're particularly salt-sensitive feel free to omit some ingredients. This a real, old-world dish with full, intense flavors and begs to be paired with wine. I'd suggest an ice-cold glass of fino sherry.

Serves 4

- 1 head escarole
- ¼ cup Romesco Sauce (TECHNIQUE, page 55)
- 1 tablespoon sherry vinegar
- ¼ cup fruity olive oil, plus more for drizzling
   Freshly ground black pepper
- 6 fillets best-quality salted anchovies or Homemade Potted Anchovies (page 82)
- 2 ounces salt cod, desalinated (TECHNIQUE, page 235) and cut into paper-thin slices
- ¼ cup Arbequina olives or other black olives
   A few slices Ibérico ham or best-quality cured ham

Clean the escarole, separate the leaves, and tear into small pieces, discarding the bitter tips and reserving the white and yellow parts. In a large mixing bowl, combine the Romesco with the vinegar, drizzle in the olive oil, and whisk together. Add the escarole, toss to thoroughly coat with the vinaigrette, and season with black pepper.

Divide the escarole among 4 small bowls and evenly lace in the anchovies, salt cod, and olives. Top with the ham. Finish each bowl with a final drizzle of fruity olive oil.

Pan-Roasted Brussels Sprouts

BRUSSELS SPROUTS MUST BE the meatballs of the vegetable world because whenever I put them on the menu folks can't seem to get enough. People want their Brussels sprouts! A little chorizo and some lemon juice go a long way to perk up these little cabbages.

Serves 4

1	tablespoon good olive oil
1	pound Brussels sprouts, preferably baby Brussels sprouts
½	pound dried chorizo, diced
1	cup chicken stock
1	tablespoon lemon juice
	Salt
	Freshly ground black pepper
2	tablespoons chopped fresh parsley

Heat the olive oil over medium-high heat in a large cast iron skillet. Add the Brussels sprouts and cook until gently browned, about 3 minutes depending on size. Shake the pan occasionally to brown them on all sides. Add the chorizo and cook for about 2 minutes; the sprouts will take on a nice rosy color from the sausage. Add the stock, lemon juice, and salt and pepper. Simmer for about 5 minutes, or until the liquid is reduced and the sprouts are tender.

Finish with a sprinkling of chopped parsley and serve.

Early Girl's greens.
Patty Gentry, above,
harvesting kale on her
Long Island farm.

Chard Croquettes

EATING A CRUNCHY HOMEMADE CROQUETTE is a wholly satisfying experience. Croquettes are not difficult, there are just a lot of steps involved in the preparation. Once you come to terms with that, they're really pretty straightforward. In fact, nearly every grandmother in Spain makes croquettes—*croquetas*—at home with no complaints. I would just suggest you read all the way through this recipe before you begin.

Serves 6

4	tablespoons olive oil, plus more for frying
1	bunch chard including stems, finely chopped
2	cloves garlic, finely chopped
	Salt
	Freshly ground black pepper
1	tablespoon Champagne vinegar
1½	cups milk
4	tablespoons unsalted butter
6	tablespoons all-purpose flour
2	eggs, lightly beaten
½	cup finely ground dried bread crumbs

Lightly oil a large rimmed cookie sheet. In a large saucepan, heat 2 tablespoons of the olive oil over medium-high heat. Add the chard and garlic and sauté vigorously until wilted and tender, about 2 minutes. Season with salt and pepper and mix in the vinegar. Transfer the chard to a large mixing bowl and set aside to cool.

In a medium saucepan, heat the milk to a simmer. Clean the saucepan used for the chard and return to the stove. Add the remaining 2 tablespoons olive oil and the butter and cook over medium heat until the butter begins to foam. Sprinkle in 4 tablespoons of the flour, a little at a time, stirring constantly to make a roux. Slowly add the warm milk, a little at a time, and whisk to thoroughly incorporate. Cook the mixture for 10 minutes, until thickened, stirring constantly to prevent lumps. Once you have a thick, smooth consistency, fold in the chard and mix thoroughly, Add salt and pepper and check the seasoning, you want the croquettes to be highly seasoned.

Pour the mixture onto the cookie sheet and spread evenly, ideally to a depth of about ¾ inch. Wrap the tray in plastic wrap and transfer to the freezer for 2–3 hours, until frozen solid.

For the breading procedure you'll need 3 separate shallow bowls; one with the 2 remaining tablespoons flour, one with the beaten eggs, and one with the dried bread crumbs.

Once the croquette mixture is frozen through, cut the mixture into 1-inch squares with a sharp knife. If cutting the croquettes becomes difficult, warm the blade of the knife under hot running water for a few seconds.

Coat each croquette individually, first lightly in the flour, then in the eggs, and finish by thoroughly coating with the bread crumbs by rolling them around in the bread crumb bowl. This process will get a bit messy, so just wash your hands periodically. After the croquettes are breaded, set them aside on large cookie sheets so that they are not touching. Cover with plastic wrap and keep in the freezer until you're ready to fry them.

Heat the oil for frying in a table-top deep fryer or deep heavy-bottomed pot over medium-high heat to 350°. Working in small batches, fry the croquettes until golden brown and heated all the way through, about 4 minutes each. A good way to check if the croquettes are thoroughly cooked is to insert a knife tip into the center and make sure it comes out hot. Drain on paper towels and serve immediately.

chapter eighteen

GOOD MEAT

JUICY

✳ ✳ ✳

TENDER

✳ ✳ ✳

GRASSFED

I'M AN UNABASHED MEAT MAN—I've been cooking at New York's meat-centric food festival "Meatopia" every year for the past five years—but for me, being a meat man doesn't necessarily mean that I eat tons of the stuff. It means that when I do eat meat, I eat really *good* meat. It's the way I was raised and I hold that intense food memory in common with every American who grew up on a farm or a ranch or in a community

"We have become so disconnected from the source of our food that we no longer associate a cut of meat with the animal it came from."

where pastured animals yielded the best-tasting meat. What's so sad to me is how that taste memory is just that, something distant and vaguely recalled. For much of the meat raised in this country today lacks the quality I knew. (And most of the Moms out there aren't butchers like mine!).

In Spain recently I was lucky enough to observe the famous Ibérico pigs roaming in near-wilderness, foraging for acorns on the leafy floor of dappled oak forests, total strangers to growth hormones and anti-biotics. The ham made from these animals has a flavor like no other. The meat is rich in oleic acid, a healthy monounsaturated fat, and it is beyond delicious. But here's my point: even though this ham is in fact pretty good for us, I still would not advocate eating or serving more than a few slices of it in one sitting.

If you remember nothing else of what I have to say about meat, remember this: traditionally, we've built our meals around meat—a steak dinner, a leg of lamb, a stand-ing rib roast. But I believe we must consider eating meat in smaller portions. I'm con-vinced we need to understand how to use meat as just another tasty ingredient. Good pork, responsibly raised, is so flavorful and can take so many directions, but this does not mean we should consume obscenely massive portions of it. Let's use pork sparingly, to deepen the flavor of a vegetable dish like Pan-Roasted Brussels Sprouts (page 279), or to add an earthy balance to seafood.

As for beef, you'll notice there's little of it in this book. Some studies show that eating a lot of red meat may contribute to inflam-mation in RA sufferers. I enjoy a good steak as much as other folks, but I do not make the decision to eat that steak lightly. It's really important that I know where and how the beef was raised. I'm not sure we fully under-stand the realities about the quality of life and diet of feedlot-raised, factory-farmed animals, all in the name of cheap meat.

We have become so disconnected from the provenance of our food that we no longer associate a cut of beef, vacuum-packed in plastic in the supermarket, with the animal it came from. Sanitizing and decoupling the meat from the animal has made it easier for

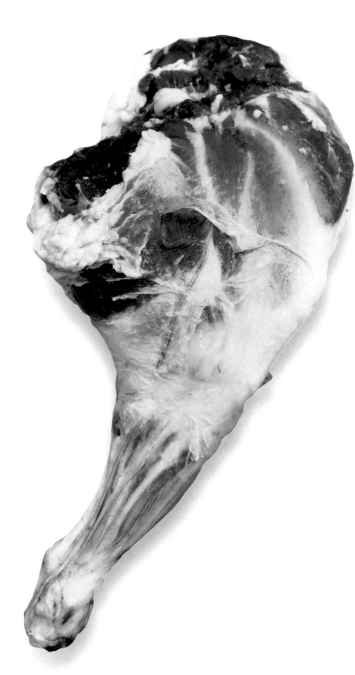

us to consume larger quantities. My stomach turns at supermarket "meat products" like chicken fingers that begin with inferior meat, then use additives to preserve and flavor it, and process it until it is unrecognizable as something originally animal. Somehow, this has become OK.

I'm not advocating that we go out and kill our own animals. When you look at some of the photographs from the lamb slaughter we did in Vermont (pages 240 to 243), I understand how they might be a bit hard to take. But rest assured the images from a nearby processing plant would be *truly* disgusting.

I fantasize about a simpler way of eating meat: we go to the butcher shop and we ask what's fresh that day. And sometimes that might be an off cut, like beef shins or hanger steak (which happens, too, to be better-priced). But if that's what's available—because we know it's fresh and we know its origin—that's what we cook.

Slow-Roasted Lamb Shoulder

I WAS 18 YEARS OLD and a little drunk, red wine from the *porrón* my host father had pressed into my hand streaking across my fanciest dress shirt. There was a familiar thick, lanoline smell of lamb in the early spring air. I was in a small town in Castilla y León at a family winery, roasting whole lamb for *Semana Santa,* Holy Week. Castilla y León is the heart of lamb country in Spain and no festival is complete without lamb roasted over hot coals. Easter week is certainly no exception. It was probably the first time I'd ever been drunk with adults, and definitely the first time I'd been drunk at 11 o'clock in the morning.

The day before, we had stopped at the butcher shop to pick up four whole suckling lambs and brined them overnight with olives, herbs, and preserved lemons. Every time I have roast lamb, I think of that incredible Easter Sunday, my first of many memorable Easters in Spain. If you can't get lamb shoulder, leg of lamb will work nicely, just cook it a little longer.

Serves 6

- 1 **cup good-quality black olives, pits removed**
- 6 **slices Quick-Cured Lemons (page 18)**
- 4 **cloves garlic, peeled and lightly crushed**
  Generous handful mixed fresh herbs, like rosemary, oregano, sage, parsley, and/or thyme
- ½ **cup good olive oil**
- 1 **lamb shoulder, roughly 4–6 pounds, ask your butcher to debone it**
  Salt
  Freshly ground black pepper

In a large mortar and pestle or in a food processor, work together the olives, cured lemons, garlic, herbs, and olive oil into a nice, rustic paste. If you're using a food processor, be careful not to overprocess it; you want the paste a bit coarse.

Open the lamb shoulder up on a cutting board (right) and use a sharp knife to trim any connecting meat to form a nice square. Rub the lamb all over with the paste you've just made. Carefully roll the whole thing up so that it looks like a Yule log and truss it with butcher's twine every inch

and a half. Refrigerate the lamb for a few hours or overnight to allow all the wonderful flavors to come together.

Remove the lamb from the refrigerator and let it come to room temperature, about 45 minutes. Preheat the oven to 300°.

Place the lamb on a rack fitted in a roasting pan. Roast for 1 to 1½ hours. You're looking for an internal temperature of about 148°. I like to tie a few branches of rosemary together with string to make a nice herb brush and use that to baste the lamb with the drippings every 20 minutes or so. Once the lamb is done, set it aside in a warm place to rest for 10 minutes before serving.

While the lamb is resting, I like to wilt some bitter greens like puntarelle or dandelion greens in a hot skillet with some of the drippings from the lamb pan. It only takes a couple of minutes and works really well with the lamb.

Carefully remove the butcher's twine. With a sharp knife, carve the shoulder into thin slices. Serve the sliced shoulder family style with a platter of the wilted greens.

A NOTE ON...
LAMB

Believe it or not in this rich country of ours, our markets are flooded with lamb imported from halfway around the world. While New Zealand and Austrailan lamb have gained renown over the years, it doesn't make any sense to me when we have such great lamb right here at home. Sure, you have to search out the good producers, but it is more than worth the effort. Finding local grassfed lamb can be much easier and more affordable than finding good beef.

Here's our Vermont lamb, that I just butchered into these wonderful cuts: clockwise from top left: caul fat, neck, shanks, shoulders, legs, loins, caul-wrapped tenderloins, chops, and breast.

So I wonder, why do folks buy those little packages of frozen lamb chops, when a fresh leg of local lamb or a shoulder roast can be a fraction of the price and has so much more flavor?

In recent years, the pig seems to be the animal chefs like to go on about when it comes to nose to tail cooking. But let's not forget the greatness of unsung lamb cuts like the neck, the kidneys, the liver, and even the tongue.

Homemade Lamb Bacon with Kale and an Egg

I LOVE LAMB. So did Lyle Felch, a third-generation farmer who would come to our farm twice a year to slaughter our lambs when I was a kid. Apparently I used to badger him with so many questions that he'd ask my mother if her little radio had an "off" switch. I still get really excited when it's time to slaughter!

We had a lamb slaughter recently on our farm in Vermont. This time the lambs were raised by one of my oldest friends, Ben Machin. Ben, after a career jumping out of planes as a forest fire-fighter, switched to the slightly safer job of shepherd. He took over the flock he inherited from his grandfather—an old breed call Tunis—and grazes them on Vermont hillsides. Their meat is fatty and grassy, and when I was butchering the lamb, the breasts reminded me of pork belly, which gave me the idea of making lamb bacon. Unlike traditional pork bacon, I only lightly cure and smoke the lamb (in a real smoker or improvised outdoor grill), then gently cook it in olive oil to keep it juicy.

Ask your butcher for lamb breast; it's becoming more commonly available and usually comes with the ribs connected. Granted bacon-making is a bit of a process, but it is extremely rewarding. Once you've cooked the lamb in the oil, make sure you save the oil to use again. In the unlikely event that you have bacon leftover, it can be sliced into strips and crisped up to make the best BLT ever!

Serves 4

FOR THE LAMB BACON

- 2   **pounds fresh lamb breast**
- ½   **pound kosher salt**
- ½   **pound sugar**
-     **Wood chips for smoking**
- 5–6 **cups olive oil (nothing fancy)**
- 4   **branches fresh thyme**
- 2   **branches fresh oregano**
- 1   **head garlic, halved**
- 2   **bay leaves**

Trim the lamb of excess fat. Combine the salt and sugar in a large roasting pan. Add the lamb breast, thoroughly cover with the mixture, and set aside to cure in the refrigerator for 2 hours.

After about 1½ hours, preheat the oven to 300° and set up a smoker outside. It's very easy to use an outdoor grill to make a smoker, all you need is some moist wood chips—I use apple or cherry. Start a small fire in the bottom of the grill just as you would if you were grilling. Since you're not actually grilling the lamb bacon, just using the smoke to flavor it, you only need a small pile.

Once you've got some glowing hot coals, you're ready to smoke the lamb. Remove the meat from the fridge, thoroughly rinse off the salt mixture under cold running water, and pat dry. Cover the coals with a handful of moist wood chips until they begin to smolder and give off a pleasant smoke. Place the lamb on the grill rack and cover the grill. Depending upon the intensity of the smoke, you'll need to leave the lamb on for 15–25 minutes for a nice, smoky flavor.

Place the lamb in a large, ovenproof pot with a lid and cover with the olive oil. Add the thyme and oregano branches, garlic, and bay leaves. Cover and slowly bake in the oven for about 2 hours, until tender. Transfer the lamb from the oil to a pan with a rack. Strain and reserve the oil.

Once the bacon cools, it's ready to use. It can be sliced into strips and crisped just like regular bacon or portioned into larger pieces and served as an entrée.

Whatever you do, don't throw out the oil! It's now infused with a delicious smoky, lamb flavor and is great for cooking vegetables. Refrigerate it after it cools down. I like to freeze the oil and reuse it every time I make lamb bacon; each time it just gets better.

FOR THE KALE

- 2   tablespoons oil from cooking the lamb bacon
- 1   shallot, finely minced
- 1   clove garlic, finely minced
- 1   healthy bunch Tuscan kale, roughly chopped
- 1   teaspoon Champagne vinegar
-    Salt
-    Freshly ground black pepper

Heat the oil in a large skillet over medium heat. Add the shallots and sweat for a minute, then add the garlic and kale and cook until the kale starts to wilt, about 2 more minutes. I find the bitterness of kale is nicely offset by a little Champagne vinegar; add just a splash. Lower the temperature to medium low, the kale will sweat off some liquid, wilt, and become tender. After 3 minutes, the kale should be tender but retain its bright color. Season with salt and pepper and then divide among 4 plates.

TO FINISH THE DISH

- ½   cup oil from cooking the lamb bacon
- 4   slices lamb bacon
- 4   fresh pullet eggs

While the kale is cooking, heat up 2 pans, one over high heat to sear the bacon, and the other over low heat to gently cook the eggs. I like to use a well-seasoned cast iron pan for the bacon so I need no oil to crisp it on both sides.

Heat the oil in the pan over low heat to 140° and poach the eggs gently (see Eggs Poached in Olive Oil, page 22). Meanwhile, in the other pan, crisp the portions of bacon about 1–2 minutes a side.

Place a piece of crispy bacon on each plate next to the kale and top each serving with an olive oil–poached egg.

Lamb Meatballs in Tomato Sauce with Ricotta

MEATBALLS—it doesn't seem to matter in what form, are always a top seller at the restaurant. Whether it's duck meatballs, or veal or lamb, our guests never tire of them. I like lamb meatballs with sheep's milk ricotta, but if you can't find it, fresh cow's milk ricotta is just fine.

Serves 6–8

FOR THE MEATBALLS

- 4   pounds ground lamb breast
- 1   pound ground lamb top round
- 1   cup cubed bread, soaked in 1 cup milk
- ½   cup chopped mixed fresh herbs like parsley, mint, oregano, rosemary, and/or thyme
- 2   tablespoons red wine
- 4   cloves garlic, minced
- 1   tablespoon *guindilla* pepper
- 1   tablespoon ground black cumin
- 1   tablespoon ground coriander seed
- 1   teaspoon ground fennel
- 4   tablespoons kosher salt
- 1   teaspoon black pepper
- 4   eggs

Combine the ground lamb, bread, herbs, red wine, garlic, *guindilla,* cumin, coriander seed, fennel, salt, and black pepper in a standing mixer fitted with a paddle or a dough hook. Process for 1 minute at medium speed (or mix by hand like a bread dough), then slowly add the eggs one at a time until thoroughly incorporated. Form into meatballs about an 1½ inches in diameter (they'll shrink a bit in cooking).

TO FINISH THE DISH

- 4   pounds fresh plum tomatoes, slowly roasted, or 2 (28-ounce) cans good-quality tomatoes, drained
- ½   cup olive oil
- 4   cloves garlic, minced
- 2   *guindilla* peppers
- 1   bunch fresh basil, leaves crushed by hand, a few leaves reserved for serving
       Leaves from 1 large bunch fresh oregano
- 2   bay leaves
       Salt
       Freshly ground black pepper
       Good ricotta cheese
       Leaves of fresh parsley for serving

If you're using fresh tomatoes, layer them in a baking sheet with olive oil, garlic cloves, and whatever herbs you have on hand. Roast in a 300° oven for 45 minutes. Peel the skins and discard.

In a large heavy-bottomed pot, heat the olive oil over medium-high heat. Working in batches, add the meatballs a few at a time and roll around until they're golden brown. Once the meatballs are all nicely browned, remove them from the pot to a large plate lined with paper towels.

Reduce the heat under the pot and add the garlic, *guindilla* peppers, basil, oregano leaves, and bay leaves. Crush the roasted or canned tomatoes by hand, one by one, into the pot. Slowly cook down until the sauce takes on a rich, sweet tomato flavor and comes together nicely, about 1 hour. Season with salt and pepper.

Return the meatballs to the pot, reduce to a simmer, and cook until just heated through, about 8 minutes. Serve the meatballs and sauce in small bowls with generous dollops of ricotta and a few torn leaves of basil and parsley.

Lamb Loin Wrapped in Caul Fat and Herbs

CAUL FAT, OR *crépine*, is a fatty membrane that surrounds the innards of many animals. It may look like lacy, meaty lingerie, but its flavor is hardly racy. Caul fat is actually quite mild and has been used for many years as a natural casing for sausages. Here, it makes a nice herby crust for lamb loin, protecting the moist meat inside from the high heat of the pan. Have your butcher order the caul fat.

Serves 4

2   **lamb loins, cut in half lengthwise**
1   **clove garlic, halved**
    Salt
    Freshly ground black pepper
4   **(10 by 10-inch) pieces caul fat**
    Generous handful fresh sage leaves and thyme sprigs
2   **tablespoons olive oil**

Rub each piece of lamb with the cut garlic and season with salt and pepper. On a large, clean cutting board, spread out one piece of the caul fat. At the edge closest to you, make a nice layer of herbs and place a lamb loin on top and cover with more hebs. Roll up the loin in the caul fat away from you, just as if you're rolling a cigar. Cut a 24-inch piece of butcher's twine and truss the loin every inch and a half. Repeat with the other three loins.

Heat the olive oil in a large cast iron pan over medium-high heat. Add the lamb rolls and carefully sear on all sides, about 4 minutes total. Let the rolls rest for 2–3 minutes, then slice and serve.

Alternate plan for a mixed grill.
Kidneys, tenderloin in caul fat, and a piece of the saddle all ready to be roasted.

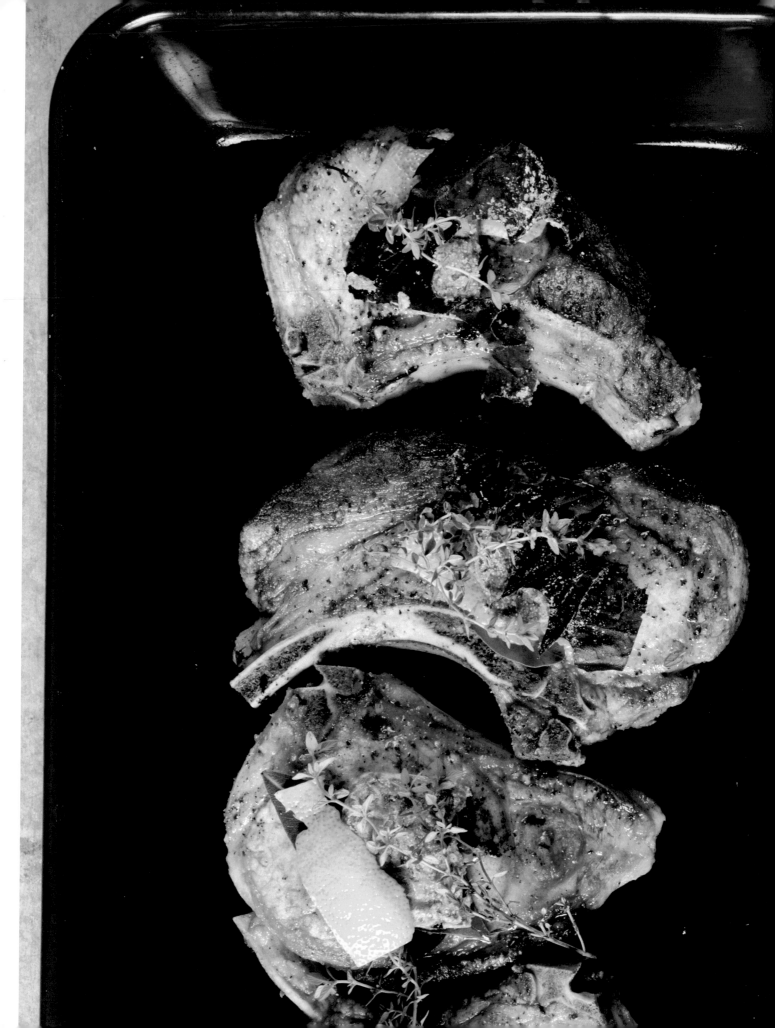

Brining Meat and Poultry

I'M A BIG FAN OF BRINING. By soaking a pork chop (or a bird or a pork loin or pork belly) overnight in a salty, aromatic liquid, you season the meat all the way through, rather than just on the surface as you do when you sprinkle on salt before roasting. I think of a brine as a way to add more nuanced flavor to the meat. Making a pork chop with roasted apples? Throw a few roughly chopped apples into the brine. For a nice, lemony, herby roasted chicken, add a handful of herbs from the garden.

There aren't too many hard and fast rules to brining, but the one thing I do recommend is to remove the meat from the liquid and allow it to air dry before cooking. With a bird, it's best if you can let it dry for a few hours in the fridge to help extract moisture from its skin and make it crispy and delicious. The best way to do this is just to leave it uncovered on a rack in a roasting pan.

It's very important when brining to completely dissolve the salt and sugar in the water, but then you must make sure the water is cold before adding the meat. A simple way to accomplish both is to heat up a cup or two of water and dissolve the salt and sugar into that water, then mix the solution with 6 cups cold water.

Here's a very, very basic brine. Feel free to get creative with the aromatics—toss in orange slices, hot chiles, a splash of bourbon, whatever feels right. I believe that 12 hours is plenty of time for meat to stay in the brine, but even 3 or 4 hours will make a big difference in a small piece of meat.

½ cup kosher salt
½ cup granulated sugar
1 onion, roughly chopped
1 carrot, roughly chopped
2 bay leaves
1 tablespoon mixed spices in cheesecloth (I like coriander, mustard, and fennel seeds)
A few branches of fresh herbs such as thyme, cilantro, basil, and tarragon

In a large pot, bring 2 cups of water to a boil, add the sugar and salt, mix well to dissolve. Transfer to a large bowl, add 6 cups cold water and the aromatics. Add the meat, cover, and refrigerate overnight. Remove the meat, pat dry, and let dry, uncovered, in the refrigerator before cooking.

English-Cut Pork Chops with Borlotti Beans

A PORK CHOP either transports me to another planet of taste, or else it's just blah. It's true with anything you cook: you can't make good food with bad ingredients, but insipid pork chops? Unacceptable! I'm mad about pork and I've been lucky to develop relationships over the years with a few pig farmers who care mightily about the pigs they raise. Pork from a heritage breed, given a natural diet with no hormones or anti-biotics, and left free to root around in the woods is a remarkable thing. Naturally raised pork is more expensive than commodity pork and with good reason: it's costly to raise such an animal.

Good pork chops should be saved for special occasions. They're a cause for celebration, and worth every penny. A chop that's English-cut means that the deckle, the cap of meat and fat that runs along the rib of the chop, isn't removed in butchering. It makes for a larger, more moist, and rustic chop, one with old world charm.

Serves 2–4

FOR THE BEANS

1½   cups fresh borlotti beans
2   medium carrots, cut into ½-inch pieces
2   shallots, quartered
1   bay leaf
     1½ cups Caldo del Día (page 128), or chicken stock
1   large chunk fresh pork belly or slab bacon
2   tablespoons salt
     Freshly ground black pepper
¼   cup crumbled Cabrales cheese

Combine all ingredients except the cheese in a pressure cooker with 1½ cups water. Cover, bring to a boil, then reduce to a simmer and cook for 55 minutes, until the beans are cooked through and creamy. Alternately, put all the ingredients in a large heavy-bottomed pot and cook, covered, for 2 hours, until soft. With a rubber spatula, gently fold in the crumbled cheese.

FOR THE CHOPS

2   large or 4 small English-cut pork chops, brined overnight (TECHNIQUE, page 297)
1   tablespoon olive oil
     Salt
     Freshly ground black pepper
4   cloves garlic, lightly crushed
4   *guindilla* peppers
4   bay leaves
     Zest of 1 lemon or orange, cut into 4 strips
2   branches fresh thyme
2   branches fresh oregano
2   branches fresh mint
     Rind scraps from blue cheese
1   large Winesap or other sweet apple, cut with a melon baller
1   tablespoon butter

Preheat the oven to 350°. Remove the chops from the brine and let them dry out in the fridge or pat them well with a paper towel. In a large heavy-bottomed pan, heat the olive oil over high heat. Season the chops with salt and pepper and sear until golden brown on both sides, about 3 minutes per side.

Carefully place the chops on a rack set in a roasting pan. Cover each chop with a clove of garlic, a *guindilla* pepper, a bay leaf, a few pieces of orange peel, and 1 branch each of thyme, oregano, and mint. Crumble the scraps of blue cheese over the chops and herbs. Transfer the pan to the oven and roast for about 15 minutes, or until a thermometer inserted in the center of the meat registers 150°. Set aside in a warm place to rest for 10 minutes before serving. Reserve the drippings and drizzle over the beans.

In a small skillet, saute the apple balls in the butter over medium heat until browned, about 15 minutes. Season with salt and pepper.

Serve the pork chops on a board with the apple balls and a lovely pot of beans.

Spice-Rubbed Hanger Steak on the Grill

TEN YEARS AGO, riding my motorcycle across Mexico, I fell in love with *arrachera,* hanger steak. There it's marinated, grilled, and served with lime. Until recently hanger steak was the cow's best-kept secret; an inexpensive, relatively tender, flavorful cut that could be roasted or grilled like any other steak, but at a fraction of the cost. Then damn chefs like me started putting it on their menus and butchers got wise.

The cut is called *hanger steak* because it sort of hangs down off the steer's diaphragm, near the kidneys. I'm a huge fan of this cut, but it can be chewy, so I suggest lightly pounding it to tenderize it before grilling. Or you can marinate it overnight in herbs, onions, garlic, and olive oil. The pomegranate seeds here give a punchy acidity that reminds me of the fresh lime of the Mexican *arrachera.*

Serves 4

- 1 **tablespoon dried pomegranate seeds**
- 1 **tablespoon ground coriander**
- 1 **teaspoon ground fennel seeds**
- 1 **teaspoon sesame seeds**
- 2 **pounds hanger steak, trimmed of excess fat and silverskin**
   Salt
   Freshly ground black pepper
- 2 **pounds Yukon Gold potatoes, unpeeled**
- ¼ **cup fruity olive oil, plus more for drizzling**
- 1 **cup Cerignola olives, pitted and coarsely chopped, or other meaty, fresh, green olives**
   Grated fresh horseradish
   Juice of 1 lemon
- 1 **tablespoon finely chopped chives**

Preheat the grill to high or light a medium fire in a charcoal grill. Combine the pomegranate seeds, coriander, fennel seeds, and sesame seeds in a mixing bowl. Season the steak generously with salt and pepper, rub thoroughly with the spice mixture, and set aside.

Cut the potatoes into 1-inch pieces, place in a large pot, and cover with cold water; add enough kosher salt until the water tastes like sea water. Bring to a simmer over medium-high heat and simmer until the potatoes are cooked through and creamy, about 20 minutes.

Grill the steak over high heat, turning frequently to char evenly; I like to serve my hanger steak slightly on the rare side, about 8 minutes on a hot grill. Once you've cooked the steak to your liking, set it aside to rest.

Meanwhile, while the steak is grilling, drain the potatoes, then crush them roughly with a potato masher, mixing in the olive oil as you mash. Fold in the olives, horseradish to taste, lemon juice, salt, and pepper.

With a sharp knife, slice the steak diagonally against the grain, which makes it a little less chewy. Serve the steak on a bed of the potatoes on a large platter, and finish with a drizzle of olive oil and a sprinkling of chives.

Roasted Marrow Bones

TRADITIONALLY THOUGHT OF as brain food, bone marrow is said to contain many nutrients and beneficial oils. But for me, bone marrow is simply one of my favorite indulgences. As with any other meat, be mindful of the source of those bones. Marrow bones, often called pipe bones, are usually 3-inch pieces cut from the shank of the calf or steer. I ask my butcher to run the bones through his bandsaw, halving the bones to look like dugout canoes filled with rich cargoes.

A spoonful of Spiced Stone Fruit Preserves (page 212) or Currant Glaze (page 171) makes a beautiful contrast with the mellow marrow.
Serves 8–12

8	marrow bones, cut lengthwise into 3-inch pieces
3	tablespoons kosher salt
1	bunch rosemary
1	clove garlic
¼	cup olive oil
	Freshly ground black pepper
	Several branches fresh rosemary
	Drizzle of *saba* or aged balsamic vinegar
	Good bread, toasted or grilled

Place the bones in a large pot, add 2 tablespoons of the salt, and cover with ice water. Refrigerate for 12 hours. The salt will help extract any residual blood in the bones.

Preheat the oven to 425°. Combine the garlic and olive oil in a mortar and pestle or food processor and process until smooth.

Remove the bones from the water, pat dry and place in a large roasting pan, cut-side up. Season the marrow liberally with salt and pepper. With a pastry brush, baste on the olive oil–garlic mix. Top each bone with some rosemary.

Roast until golden and bubbly, about 15 minutes. Serve with a drizzle of *saba* or balsamic vinegar and lots of grilled toast.

ACKNOWLEDGMENTS

THERE ARE SO MANY PEOPLE I am indebted to for all the support and love I've gotten over the years, it's impossible to list them all. But I would particularly like to thank my editor and producer, Dorothy Kalins, for keeping me on track, for pushing me when I needed to be pushed, and for believing in me when I needed to be believed in. My publisher, Kirsty Melville, I am so grateful for your vision and support: What would have happened if I never stopped by your table that night in the restaurant?

To Colin Clark, lifelong friend and tremendously talented photographer; Lynn Juang, the most incredible partner I could ask for; my parents, my loving grandmothers, my brother Nils and Daria, Will, and Marlow. To all the Spanish chefs who have been so generous and supportive over the years, particularly Jordi Vilà and Andoni Luis Aduriz.

To the kind folks from Aceites Valderrama, the whole Despaña family, Ben Machin, the trusted Dr. Harry Fischer, my wise friend Robert Gordan, my wise counsel Steve Sheppard, Saori Kawani and Korin Japanese Trading Corp. To Mario, Genna, Louis, Nick, and all my boys. To Gil Avital. To Patty Gentry and her Early Girl Farm, Pierless Fish, and Franca Tantillo of Berried Treasures Farm.

To the *Hero Food* book team, the incomparable Don Morris, whose design makes these pages come alive, the eyeballs of Carol Helms, the helping hands of Roger Sherman and Tyler Viggiano. To the team at Andrews McMeel: Jean Lucas for herding cats, John Carroll, David Shaw, and the impeccable Deri Reed. Thanks to Kate Spingarn for recipe magic, to my tireless researchers, Jeanne Koenig and Kathy Brennan, and to Stevie Pierson for juicy words. Special thanks to the award-winning food and nutrition author (and registered dietitian), Roberta Duyff for reading the manuscript and giving this book her blessing.

To my fellow New York chefs, all part of this brilliant and wacky community of people who care so much about food: Amanda Freitag, Akhtar Nawab, Marco Canora, and twice to Zak Pelaccio. And to Jason Hua, Andrew Carmellini, Bill Telepan, Julian Alonzo, Floyd Cardoz, Michael Anthony, Wylie Dufresne, Johnny Iuzzini, and George Mendes.

And to the beautiful city of New York, my home.

METRIC CONVERSIONS & EQUIVALENTS

APPROXIMATE METRIC EQUIVALENTS

Volume	Metric
¼ teaspoon	1 milliliter
½ teaspoon	2.5 milliliters
¾ teaspoon	4 milliliters
1 teaspoon	5 milliliters
1¼ teaspoons	6 milliliters
1½ teaspoons	7.5 milliliters
1¾ teaspoons	8.5 milliliters
2 teaspoons	10 milliliters
1 tablespoon (½ fluid ounce)	15 milliliters
2 tablespoons (1 fluid ounce)	30 milliliters
¼ cup	60 milliliters
⅓ cup	80 milliliters
½ cup (4 fluid ounces)	120 milliliters
⅔ cup	160 milliliters
¾ cup	180 milliliters
1 cup (8 fluid ounces)	240 milliliters
1¼ cups	300 milliliters
1½ cups (12 fluid ounces)	360 milliliters
1⅔ cups	400 milliliters
2 cups (1 pint)	460 milliliters
3 cups	700 milliliters
4 cups (1 quart)	0.95 liter
1 quart plus ¼ cup	1 liter
4 quarts (1 gallon)	3.8 liters

Weight	
¼ ounce	7 grams
½ ounce	14 grams
¾ ounce	21 grams
1 ounce	28 grams
1¼ ounces	35 grams
1½ ounces	42.5 grams
1⅔ ounces	45 grams
2 ounces	57 grams
3 ounces	85 grams
4 ounces (¼ pound)	113 grams
5 ounces	142 grams
6 ounces	170 grams
7 ounces	198 grams
8 ounces (½ pound)	227 grams
16 ounces (1 pound)	454 grams
35.25 ounces (2.2 pounds)	1 kilogram

Length	
⅛ inch	3 millimeters
¼ inch	6 millimeters
½ inch	1¼ centimeters
1 inch	2½ centimeters
2 inches	5 centimeters
2 ½ inches	6 centimeters
4 inches	10 centimeters
5 inches	13 centimeters
6 inches	15¼ centimeters
12 inches (1 foot)	30 centimeters

METRIC CONVERSION FORMULAS

To Convert	Multiply
Ounces to grams	Ounces by 28.35
Pounds to kilograms	Pounds by .454
Teaspoons to milliliters	Teaspoons by 4.93
Tablespoons to milliliters	Tablespoons by 14.79
Fluid ounces to milliliters	Fluid ounces by 29.57
Cups to milliliters	Cups by 236.59
Cups to liters	Cups by .236
Pints to liters	Pints by .473
Quarts to liters	Quarts by .946
Gallons to liters	Gallons by 3.785
Inches to centimeters	Inches by 2.54

OVEN TEMPERATURES

To convert Fahrenheit to Celsius, subtract 32 from Fahrenheit, multiply the result by 5, then divide by 9.

Description	Fahrenheit	Celsius	British Gas Mark
Very cool	200°	95°	0
Very cool	225°	110°	¼
Very cool	250°	120°	½
Cool	275°	135°	1
Cool	300°	150°	2
Warm	325°	165°	3
Moderate	350°	175°	4
Moderately hot	375°	190°	5
Fairly hot	400°	200°	6
Hot	425°	220°	7
Very hot	450°	230°	8
Very hot	475°	245°	9

COMMON INGREDIENTS & THEIR APPROXIMATE EQUIVALENTS

1 cup uncooked white rice = 185 grams

1 cup all-purpose flour = 140 grams

1 stick butter (4 ounces · ½ cup · 8 tablespoons) = 110 grams

1 cup butter (8 ounces · 2 sticks · 16 tablespoons) = 220 grams

1 cup brown sugar, firmly packed = 225 grams

1 cup granulated sugar = 200 grams

Information compiled from a variety of sources, including *Recipes into Type* by Joan Whitman and Dolores Simon (Newton, MA: Biscuit Books, 2000); *The New Food Lover's Companion* by Sharon Tyler Herbst (Hauppauge, NY: Barron's, 1995); and *Rosemary Brown's Big Kitchen Instruction Book* (Kansas City, MO: Andrews McMeel, 1998).

INDEX

A

Aleppo pepper, 51, 87, 142, 148, 195, 196, 204, 232
almonds
    10 Things to Do with Almonds, 58
    Ajo Blanco with Sardine Confit, 50–51
    Almond Sablé, 59
    Blackberry and Almond Crumble, 171
    hero food, 47–49
    Pork and Almond Stew, 52
    Romesco Sauce, 55
    Salbitxada, 57
    Spicy Rapini with Almonds, 272
    Stuffed Spaghetti Squash, 254
    superhero, 49
ancho chiles, 18, 28, 39, 45, 57, 65, 69, 74, 89, 119
anchovies
    Anchoas y Escalivada, or Anchovies and Charred Vegetables, 85
    Caramelized Cauliflower with Anchovies, 87
    cleaning technique, 81
    Ensalada of Preserved Anchovies, 89
    Flash-Fried Anchovies with Crispy Lemons and Sage, 89
    hero food, 77–79
    Homemade Potted Anchovies, 82
    Ice-Cold Carrots, Radishes, and Beets with Potted Anchovy and Lemon Butter, 189
    Lightly Smoked Sardines on Toast, 86
    note on preserving of, 82
    omega-3s and selenium in, 79
    Soft-Cooked Gribiche with Pickled Anchovies on Toast, 108
    Two Kinds of Anchovies, One Kind of Flatbread, 90
    Xató Salad, 276
artichokes
    Cazuela of Mongetes and Clams, 39
    Crispy Fried Artichokes, 27
    Preserved Artichokes, 18
    Verdina Bean Salad, 35
arugula, 35, 69, 223, 224
asparagus
    Grilled Asparagus and Leeks with Romesco Sauce, 54–55
    Squid with Baby Favas, Mint, and Basil, 144–45
Atlantic cod, 216
Autumn Squash Salad, 238–39, 248–49
avocado, 195

B

bacon. See also pork
    Caldo del Día, 128
    Creamy Grits with Slow-Cooked Pork Loin, 70
    Duck Liver Toasts and Pickled Raisins, 122
    English-Cut Pork Chops with Borlotti Beans, 298
    Flageolets with Autumn Greens and Fresh Bacon, 45
    Homemade Lamb Bacon with Kale and an Egg, 290–91
    Risotto of Irish Oats, 66
    Spice-Rubbed Hanger Steak on the Grill, 301
    Steamed Corn with Clams and Bacon, 196
    Truffled Lentils and Eggs, 40
banana, 58, 155
bass. See sea bass
beans, dried
    Caldo del Día, 128
    Cazuela of Mongetes and Clams, 39
    Chicken and Seafood Paella, 134–35
    English-Cut Pork Chops with Borlotti Beans, 298
    Flageolets with Autumn Greens and Fresh Bacon, 45
    garbanzo beans, 117, 141, 236
    Gently Scrambled Eggs with Wild Vegetables, 103
    hero food, 30, 32–33
    note on black beans, 36

    Pea Tendrils a la Catalana, 141
    Salt Cod with Garbanzo Beans and Spinach, 236
    note on salting of, 33
    note on soaking of, 33
    Sopa de Enfermos, 128
    Squid with Baby Favas, Mint, and Basil, 144–45
    technique for making in a pressure cooker, 35
    Tolosa Bean Soup, 36
    Truffled Lentils and Eggs, 40
    Verdina Bean Salad, 35
    White Bean Salad with Preserved Tuna and Parsley Vinaigrette, 159
beef
    brining of, 297
    notes on good meat, 282–85
    Roasted Marrow Bones, 302
    Spice-Rubbed Hanger Steak on the Grill, 301
beets
    Ice-Cold Carrots, Radishes, and Beets with Potted Anchovy and Lemon Butter, 189
    Salt-Baked Carrots and Beets, 182
bell peppers
    Anchoas y Escalivada, or Anchovies and Charred Vegetables, 85
    Grilled Asparagus and Leeks with Romesco Sauce, 54–55
    Sofrito, 65
berries
    Blackberry and Almond Crumble, 171
    Currant Glaze for Pork, 171
    hero food, 162, 164
    Mutti's Blueberry Boy Bait, 167
    Raspberries and Yogurt with Buttermilk Crêpes, 168
    A Real Smoothie, 155
    Strawberry Ice Cream, 168
Best Grilled Corn, in the Husk, 198
birds. See also chicken, duck, guinea hen
black sea bass, 146

Blackberry and Almond Crumble, 171
blanching
    note on, 139
Bomba rice, 132, 135
    note on, 73
Brining Meat and Poultry, 297
Brussels sprouts, 279
Buttermilk Crêpes, 168–69
Butternut Squash Soup with Smoked Trout, 254

C

cabello de angel (angels' hair), 254
Caldo del Día, 128
Caramelized Cauliflower with Anchovies, 87
carrots
    Chilled Carrot Soup with Yogurt and Tarragon, 186–87
    Creamy Grits with Slow-Cooked Pork Loin, 70
    Crispy Guinea Hen, 131
    English-Cut Pork Chops with Borlotti Beans, 298
    Farro Salad with Preserved Tuna, 69
    hero food, 179–81
    Ice-Cold Carrots, Radishes, and Beets with Potted Anchovy and Lemon Butter, 189
    Pickled Carrots, 185
    pickling of, 181
    Poached Long Island Duck Breasts with Farro, 119
    Preserved Artichokes, 18
    Salt-Baked Carrots and Beets, 182
    Sopa de Enfermos, 128
    vitamins in, 181
cauliflower, 87
Cazuela of Mongetes and Clams, 39
char
    aquaculture of, 217
    Pan Roast of Arctic Char with Sorrel Sauce, 220
Chard Croquettes, 280
chickpeas. See garbanzo beans
chicken
    brining of, 297
    Caldo del Día, 128
    Chicken and Seafood Paella, 134–35

Escabeche for Pickling Poultry or Fish, 127
factory vs. farm, 115–17
note on chicken stock, 117
Salbitxada with grilled, 57
Sopa de Enfermos, 128
Sunday Roast Chicken, 130
Chicken and Seafood Paella, 134–35
Chilean sea bass, 216
Chilled Carrot Soup with Yogurt and Tarragon, 186–87
Chilled Sweet Pea Soup, 147
cleaning techniques
anchovies, 81
mushrooms, 259
rack of lamb, 242
raw fish, 218
squid, 83
cod. *See also* salt cod
Line-Caught Atlantic Cod with Picada, 223
Confit of Duck Legs with Plums, 204
corn
10 Things to Do with Corn, 193
Best Grilled Corn, in the Husk, 198
Corn and Crab Salad, 195
Creamy Grits with Slow-Cooked Pork Loin, 70
Crispy Fried Hominy, 199
as food vs. commodity, 192
hero food, 190, 192
Steamed Corn with Clams and Bacon, 196
vitamins in, 192
crab, 195
Creamy Grits with Slow-Cooked Pork Loin, 70
Cremini Mushrooms al Ajillo, 265
crêpes
Raspberries and Yogurt with Buttermilk Crêpes, 168
Crispy Fried Artichokes, 27
Crispy Fried Hominy, 199
Crispy Guinea Hen, 131
Crispy Tuscan Kale on the Grill, 275
Currant Glaze for Pork, 171
cutting techniques
duck, 120–21
grating tomatoes, 64
quail egg, 126

D

Deep-Frying an Egg in Olive Oil, 107
desalinating, of salt cod, 235
desserts
Almond Sablé, 59
A Real Smoothie, 155
Blackberry and Almond Crumble, 171
Mutti's Blueberry Boy Bait, 167
Plum Cake, 212
Raspberries and Yogurt with Buttermilk Crêpes, 168

Strawberry Ice Cream, 168
White Peaches, Pistachios, Honey, and Ricotta, 211
Deviled Eggs, 104
duck
Confit of Duck Legs with Plums, 204
cutting technique for, 120–21
Duck Liver Toasts and Pickled Raisins, 122
Homemade Duck Sausage, 124–25
Poached Long Island Duck Breasts with Farro, 119

E

eggplant, 85
eggs
Almond Sablé, 59
Chard Croquettes, 280
cutting of quail egg, 126
Deep-Frying an Egg in Olive Oil, 106–7
Deviled Eggs, 104
Eggs Poached in Olive Oil, 22
Ensalada of Preserved Anchovies, 89
factory vs. farm, 100–101
Farro Salad with Preserved Tuna, 69
Five-Minute Eggs with Romesco, 104
Fork-Crushed Sweet Potatoes with Sobrassada and a Fried Egg, 108
Gently Scrambled Eggs with Wild Vegetables, 103
hero food, 98, 100–01
Homemade Lamb Bacon with Kale and an Egg, 290–91
Lamb Meatballs in Tomato Sauce with Ricotta, 293
Lamb Tartare with Spring Pullet Eggs, 112
Raspberries and Yogurt with Buttermilk Crêpes, 168
Soft-Cooked Gribiche with Pickled Anchovies on Toast, 108
Tortilla Española, 111
Truffled Lentils and Eggs, 40
vitamins in, 101
English-Cut Pork Chops with Borlotti Beans, 298
Ensalada of Preserved Anchovies, 89. *See also* Xató Salad
escabeche
Escabeche for Pickling Poultry or Fish, 127
Pickled Chanterelles with Mackerel in Escabeche, 266

F

Farro Salad with Preserved Tuna, 69
fava beans
Chicken and Seafood Paella, 134–35
Gently Scrambled Eggs with Wild Vegetables, 103
Squid with Baby Favas, Mint, and Basil, 144–45
fennel
Anchoas y Escalivada, or Anchovies and Charred Vegetables, 85
Chicken and Seafood Paella, 134–35
Lightly Cured Wild Salmon with Pea Salad, 148
fish (Atlantic cod, black sea bass, char, fluke, salmon, salt cod, sardines, tuna). *See also* anchovies; seafood; trout
Ajo Blanco with Sardine Confit, 50–51
aquaculture of char, 217
char compared with salmon, 220
cleaning and curing technique, 218–19
desalinating technique for salt cod, 235
Deviled Eggs, 104
endangered, 214, 216, 224
Farro Salad with Preserved Tuna, 69
hero food, 214–17
Lightly Cured Fluke with Pickled Plums, 204
Lightly Cured Wild Salmon with Pea Salad, 148
Lightly Smoked Sardines on Toast, 86
Line-Caught Atlantic Cod with Picada, 223
Pan Roast of Arctic Char with Sorrel Sauce, 220
Preserving Tuna, 224–25
salt cod cuts, 234
Salt Cod with Garbanzo Beans and Spinach, 236
sea bass steamed in corn husks, 193
smoked olive oil for, 22, 86
Sorrel Sauce with, 276
Sweet Potato Chips and Whipped Salt Cod, 28
White Bean Salad with Preserved Tuna and Parsley Vinaigrette, 159
Whole Black Sea Bass with Pea and Butter Sauce, 146
wild vs. farm-raised salmon, 217
Xató Salad, 276
Five-Minute Eggs with Romesco, 104
Flash-Fried Anchovies with Crispy Lemons and Sage, 89

flatbread
Flatbreads of King Oyster and Shitake Mushrooms, 262
Two Kinds of Anchovies, One Kind of Flatbread, 90
Flageolets with Autumn Greens and Fresh Bacon, 45
flowers, edible, 142
fluke, 204
Fork-Crushed Sweet Potatoes with Sobrassada and a Fried Egg, 108
fruit
Blackberry and Almond Crumble, 171
in brine, 297
Confit of Duck Legs with Plums, 204
Currant Glaze for Pork, 171
Fruit Pickling Liquid, 207
Lemon Butter, 189
Lightly Cured Fluke with Pickled Plums, 204
Mutti's Blueberry Boy Bait, 167
Parsley Juice, 155
Pickled Plums, 207
Plum Cake, 212
Quick-Cured Lemons, 18
Raspberries and Yogurt with Buttermilk Crêpes, 168
A Real Smoothie, 155
seasonal, 164
smoothie with, 58
Spiced Stone Fruit Preserves, 212
stone fruit as hero food, 201–03
Stone Fruit Gazpacho with Scallops, 208
Strawberry Ice Cream, 168
vitamins in, 152–55
vitamins in stone fruit, 203
White Peaches, Pistachios, Honey, and Ricotta, 211

G

game birds, 116–17
garbanzo beans
in chicken stock, 117
cooking of, 141
Pea Tendrils a la Catalana, 141
Salt Cod with Garbanzo Beans and Spinach, 236
Spanish varieties of, 141
Gently Roasted Brown Trout with Summer Squash, 232–33
Gently Scrambled Eggs with Wild Vegetables, 103
grains
Bomba rice, 73, 132, 135
Chicken and Seafood Paella, 134–35
Creamy Grits with Slow-Cooked Pork Loin, 70
Crispy Guinea Hen, 131
hero food, 60, 61–63
Farro Salad with Preserved Tuna, 69

grains (continued)
    Poached Long Island Duck
      Breasts with Farro, 119
    Rice with Squid and Green
      Beans, 74–75
    Risotto of Irish Oats, 66
    Sofrito, 65
    vitamins, 62–63
grating technique, for toma-
    toes, 64
green beans, 74–75
greens
    Autumn Squash Salad,
      248–49
    Chard Croquettes, 280
    Crispy Tuscan Kale on the
      Grill, 275
    Flageolets with Autumn
      Greens and Fresh
      Bacon, 45
    hero food, 269–71
    Homemade Lamb Bacon
      with Kale and an Egg,
      290–91
    nettles, 270
    nutrients and omega-3s, 271
    Pan-Roasted Brussels
      Sprouts, 279
    Pork and Almond Stew, 52
    sorrel, 128, 220, 276
    Sorrel Sauce, 276
    Spicy Rapini with Al-
      monds, 272
    steaming of, 272
    Xató Salad, 276
Grilled Asparagus and Leeks
    with Romesco Sauce, 54–55
Grilled Flatbread, 90
grits
    corn kernels with, 193
    Creamy Grits with Slow-
      Cooked Pork Loin, 70
guindilla peppers, 18, 22, 28,
    39, 57, 69, 82, 89, 119, 122,
    156, 185, 212, 225, 236, 265,
    293, 298
guinea hen
    Crispy Guinea Hen, 131

H

hazelnuts, 57
herbs
    note on torn, 148
Homemade Duck Sausage,
    124–25
Homemade Lamb Bacon with
    Kale and an Egg, 290–91
Homemade Potted Anchovies,
    82
How to Smoke a Trout, 230

I

Ibérico ham, 9, 35, 40, 276, 284
    note on, 43
Ice-Cold Carrots, Radishes,
    and Beets with Potted
    Anchovy and Lemon
    Butter, 189
Iroquois' Three Sisters, 193

J

jalapeño peppers, 112, 199

K

Kefir Vinaigrette, 148

L

labne, 85, 186, 276. See also
    yogurt
lamb
    brining of, 297
    Homemade Lamb Bacon
      with Kale and an Egg,
      290–91
    Lamb Loin Wrapped in
      Caul Fat and Herbs, 294
    Lamb Meatballs in Tomato
      Sauce with Ricotta, 293
    Lamb Tartare with Spring
      Pullet Eggs, 112
    note on, 288
    rack of, 242
    Slow-Roasted Lamb
      Shoulder, 287
leeks, 54–56
lemons
    Ensalada of Preserved
      Anchovies, 89
    Flash-Fried Anchovies with
      Crispy Lemons and
      Sage, 89
    Homemade Potted
      Anchovies, 82
    Lemon Butter, 189
    Preserving Tuna, 224–25
    Quick-Cured Lemons, 18
    Raspberries and Yogurt
      with Buttermilk Crêpes,
      168
    Sunday Roast Chicken, 130
Lightly Cured Fluke with
    Pickled Plums, 204
Lightly Cured Summer Bonito,
    219
Lightly Cured Wild Salmon
    with Pea Salad, 148
Lightly Smoked Sardines on
    Toast, 86
lobster, 134–35

M

mackerel
    escabeche for, 127
    Pickled Chanterelles with
      Mackerel in Escabeche,
      266
    shopping for, 266
meat, 282–85. See also specific
    animal
    hero food, 282, 284–85
    Salbitxada with grilled, 57
mushrooms
    Cremini Mushrooms al
      Ajillo, 265
    Crispy Guinea Hen, 131
    Farro Salad with Preserved
      Tuna, 69
    Flatbreads of King
      Oyster and Shitake
      Mushrooms, 262
    Gently Scrambled Eggs
      with Wild Vegetables,
      103
    hero food, 258–59
    note on cleaning, 259
    Pickled Chanterelles with
      Mackerel in Escabeche,
      266
    Pickled Mushrooms, 265
    Risotto of Irish Oats, 66
    Stuffed Spaghetti Squash,
      254
    vitamins in, 258
    Warm Mushroom Salad, 261
    Warm Mushroom
      Vinaigrette, 262
Mutti's Blueberry Boy Bait, 167
Mutti's Pan-Fried Troutlings,
    229
My Favorite Vinaigrette, 21

N

nettles, 270
Notes on
    black beans, 36
    blanching, 139
    Bomba rice, 73
    chicken stock, 117
    cleaning mushrooms, 259
    Ibérico ham, 43
    lamb, 288
    paella, 132
    pickling, 181
    preserving anchovies, 82
    salting beans, 33
    smoking sardines, 86
    soaking beans, 33
    sobrassada, 108
    Spanish olive oil, 16
    torn herbs, 148
    trout, 226
    txakoli, 147
ñora peppers, 52, 55, 65, 74, 131
nuts. See also almonds
    Ensalada of Preserved
      Anchovies, 89
    Lightly Cured Summer
      Bonito, 219
    Octopus and Parsley Salad,
      160
    Pea Tendrils a la Catalana,
      141
    Pork and Almond Stew, 52
    Salbitxada, 57
    Squid with Baby Favas,
      Mint, and Basil, 144–45
    walnuts, feta, and pre-
      served tuna, in salad,
      224
    White Peaches, Pistachios,
      Honey, and Ricotta, 211

O

oats, 62
    Blackberry and Almond
      Crumble, 171
    Risotto of Irish Oats, 66
octopus
    Octopus and Parsley Salad,
      160
    technique for cooking, 160
olive oil
    10 Things to Do with
      Almonds, 58
    Ajo Blanco with Sardine
      Confit, 50–51
    Best Grilled Corn, in the
      Husk, 198
    Chard Croquettes, 280

Cremini Mushrooms al
    Ajillo, 265
Crispy Fried Artichokes, 27
Crispy Fried Hominy, 199
Crispy Guinea Hen, 131
Crispy Tuscan Kale on the
    Grill, 275
Deep-Frying an Egg in
    Olive Oil, 107
Eggs Poached in Olive
    Oil, 22
Escabeche for Pickling
    Poultry or Fish, 127
Five-Minute Eggs with
    Romesco, 104
Flash-Fried Anchovies with
    Crispy Lemons and
    Sage, 89
hero food, 15
Homemade Lamb Bacon
    with Kale and an Egg,
    290–91
Homemade Potted Ancho-
    vies, 82
note on Spanish Olive
    Oil, 16
Preserved Artichokes, 18
Preserving Tuna, 224–25
Quick-Cured Lemons, 18
Salbitxada, 57
Smoked Olive Oil, 22
Sunday Roast Chicken, 130
Truffled Lentils and Eggs,
    40
Two Kinds of Anchovies,
    One Kind of Flatbread,
    90
Verdina Bean Salad, 35
Xató Salad, 276
olives
    Ensalada of Preserved
      Anchovies, 89
    Lamb Tartare with Spring
      Pullet Eggs, 112
    Octopus and Parsley Salad,
      160
    Slow-Roasted Lamb Shoul-
      der, 287
    Spice-Rubbed Hanger Steak
      on the Grill, 301
    Xató Salad, 276
omega-3 fatty acids
    anchovies, 79
    disease relief via, 3–4, 15, 63,
      79, 190, 276, 284
    eggs, 101
    fish, 217, 266
    Ibérico ham, 282, 284
    mackerel, 266
    sardines, 5, 50, 79
oranges
    Blackberry and Almond
      Crumble, 171
    in brine, 297
    Chilled Carrot Soup with
      Yogurt and Tarragon,
      186–87
    Confit of Duck Legs with
      Plums, 204
    Creamy Grits with Slow-
      Cooked Pork Loin, 70
    English-Cut Pork Chops
      with Borlotti Beans, 298
    Homemade Duck Sausage,
      124–25

Poached Long Island Duck Breasts with Farro, 119

P

paella
Chicken and Seafood Paella, 134–35
note on, 132–33
outdoors, 94–97
Pan Roast of Arctic Char with Sorrel Sauce, 220
Pan-Roasted Brussels Sprouts, 279
parsley
hero food, 153
nutrients in, 152–53
Octopus and Parsley Salad, 160
Parsley Juice, 155
Parsley Vinaigrette, 159
A Real Smoothie, 155
Salad of Marble Potatoes, 156
Salsa Verde, 155
White Bean Salad with Preserved Tuna and Parsley Vinaigrette, 159
Pea Tendrils a la Catalana, 141
peaches, 211
peas
blanching technique for, 139
Chilled Sweet Pea Soup, 147
hero food, 136, 138
Lightly Cured Wild Salmon with Pea Salad, 148
nutrients in, 138
Pea Tendrils a la Catalana, 141
Simply Sweet Peas, 142
Squid with Baby Favas, Mint, and Basil, 144–45
Sugar Snap Pea Salad, 142
Whole Black Sea Bass with Pea and Butter Sauce, 146
peppers
Aleppo, 51, 87, 142, 148, 195, 196, 204, 232
ancho chiles, 18, 28, 39, 45, 57, 65, 69, 74, 89, 119
bell, 54–56, 65, 85
guindilla, 18, 22, 28, 39, 57, 69, 82, 89, 119, 122, 156, 185, 212, 225, 236, 265, 293, 298
jalapeño, 112, 199
ñora, 52, 55, 65, 74, 131
serrano chiles, 219
Picada
Line-Caught Atlantic Cod with Picada, 223
Pork and Almond Stew, 52
Sopa de Enfermos, 128
pickling
of anchovies, 108
of carrots, 181, 185
Escabeche for Pickling Poultry or Fish, 127
Fruit Pickling Liquid, 207
Lightly Cured Fluke with Pickled Plums, 204
of mushrooms, 265
Pickled Carrots, 185

Pickled Chanterelles with Mackerel in Escabeche, 266
Pickled Mushrooms, 265
Pickled Plums, 207
Pickled Shallots, 156
note on, 181
of raisins, 122
Soft-Cooked Gribiche with Pickled Anchovies on Toast, 108
summer crudo, 193
Vegetable Pickling Liquid, 185
Warm Smoked Trout with Pickled Onions, 231
pigs. *See also* bacon; pork
Ibérico, 43
naturally raised American, 298
pine nuts
Ensalada of Preserved Anchovies, 89
Lightly Cured Summer Bonito, 219
Pea Tendrils a la Catalana, 141
Pork and Almond Stew, 52
Squid with Baby Favas, Mint, and Basil, 144–45
Plum Cake, 212
Poached Long Island Duck Breasts with Farro, 119
pomegranate seeds, 301
pork. *See also* bacon
Autumn Squash Salad, 248–49
brining of, 297
casing for Homemade Duck Sausage, 124–25
Chicken and Seafood Paella, 134–35
Creamy Grits with Slow-Cooked Pork Loin, 70
Currant Glaze for Pork, 171
English-Cut Pork Chops with Borlotti Beans, 298
Ibérico ham, 9, 35, 40, 43, 276, 284
Pan-Roasted Brussels Sprouts, 279
Pork and Almond Stew, 52
Tolosa Bean Soup, 36
Verdina Bean Salad, 35
Xató Salad, 276
potatoes. *See also* sweet potatoes
Ensalada of Preserved Anchovies, 89
Octopus and Parsley Salad, 160
Salad of Marble Potatoes, 156
Spice-Rubbed Hanger Steak on the Grill, 301
Tortilla Española, 111

Q

quail eggs
cutting technique, 126
Quail en Escabeche with Fried Quail Eggs, 127
Quick-Cured Lemons, 18
quince paste

Fork-Crushed Sweet Potatoes with Sobrassada and a Fried Egg, 108
Spicy Rapini with Almonds, 272

R

RA. *See* rheumatoid arthritis
radishes
Autumn Squash Salad, 238–39
Ice-Cold Carrots, Radishes, and Beets with Potted Anchovy and Lemon Butter, 189
raisins
Duck Liver Toasts and Pickled Raisins, 122
Pea Tendrils a la Catalana, 141
ramps, 54, 103
rapini, 272
ras el hanout, 156
Raspberries and Yogurt with Buttermilk Crêpes, 168
Real Smoothie, 155
rheumatoid arthritis (RA), 3–4, 15, 79, 190, 284
rice
Bomba rice, 73, 132, 135
paella, 94–97, 132–33, 134–35
Rice with Squid and Green Beans, 74–75
ricotta
Flatbreads of King Oyster and Shitake Mushrooms, 262
Lamb Meatballs in Tomato Sauce with Ricotta, 293
Sugar Snap Pea Salad, 142
Two Kinds of Anchovies, One Kind of Flatbread, 90
White Peaches, Pistachios, Honey, and Ricotta, 211
Risotto of Irish Oats, 66
Roasted Marrow Bones, 302
Roasted Winter Squash, 251
Romesco Sauce, 55
Five-Minute Eggs with Romesco, 104
Grilled Asparagus and Leeks with Romesco Sauce, 54–55
Xató Salad, 276

S

salads
Autumn Squash Salad, 238–39, 248–49
Corn and Crab Salad, 195
Ensalada of Preserved Anchovies, 89
Farro Salad with Preserved Tuna, 69
Lightly Cured Wild Salmon with Pea Salad, 148
Octopus and Parsley Salad, 160
plating of, 276
Salad of Marble Potatoes, 156
Verdina Bean Salad, 35

White Bean Salad with Preserved Tuna and Parsley Vinaigrette, 159
Xató Salad, 276
Salad of Marble Potatoes, 156
Salbitxada, 57
salmon
char compared with, 220
Lightly Cured Wild Salmon with Pea Salad, 148
omega-3s in anchovies compared to, 79
Sorrel Sauce with, 276
wild vs. farm-raised, 217
salmonella, 116
Salsa Verde, 155
salt cod
cuts of, 234
desalinating technique, 235
endangered, 216
Salt Cod with Garbanzo Beans and Spinach, 236
Sweet Potato Chips and Whipped Salt Cod, 28
Xató Salad, 276
Salt-Baked Carrots and Beets, 182
salting, of beans, 33
sardines
Ajo Blanco with Sardine Confit, 50–51
Lightly Smoked Sardines on Toast, 86
note on smoking sardines, 86
omega-3 fatty acids, 5, 50, 79
smoked olive oil for, 22, 86
sausage, homemade, 124–25
scallops
Stone Fruit Gazpacho with Scallops, 208
summer crudo, 193
sea bass
in 10 Things to Do with Corn, 193
Chilean sea bass, 216
steamed in corn husks, 193
Whole Black Sea Bass with Pea and Butter Sauce, 146
seafood. *See also* anchovies; fish
Cazuela of Mongetes and Clams, 39
Corn and Crab Salad, 195
lobster stock, 134
Octopus and Parsley Salad, 160
octopus cooking technique, 160
paella, 94–97, 132–33, 134–35
Rice with Squid and Green Beans, 74–75
squid cleaning technique, 83
Squid with Baby Favas, Mint, and Basil, 144–45
Steamed Corn with Clams and Bacon, 196
Stone Fruit Gazpacho with Scallops, 208
selenium, 79

serrano chiles, 219
shallots
	pickling technique, 156
shrimp
	Chicken and Seafood
		Paella, 134–35
	ocean fresh frozen, 217
Simply Sweet Peas, 142
Slow-Roasted Lamb Shoulder,
	287
Smoked Olive Oil, 22
soaking
	of beans, 33
	of poultry and meats in
		brine, 297
sobrassada
	note on, 108
Sofrito, 65
	in paella, 132
Soft-Cooked Gribiche with
	Pickled Anchovies on
	Toast, 108
Sopa de Enfermos, 128
sorrel
	Pan Roast of Arctic Char
		with Sorrel Sauce, 220
	Sopa de Enfermos, 128
	Sorrel Sauce, 276
	watercress instead of, 276
soups
	Butternut Squash Soup with
		Smoked Trout, 254
	Caldo del Día, 128
	Chilled Carrot Soup with
		Yogurt and Tarragon,
		186–87
	Chilled Sweet Pea Soup, 147
	Sopa de Enfermos, 128
	Stone Fruit Gazpacho with
		Scallops, 208
	Tolosa Bean Soup, 36
Spiced Stone Fruit Preserves,
	212
Spice-Rubbed Hanger Steak on
	the Grill, 301
Spicy Rapini with Almonds,
	272
squash
	Autumn Squash Salad,
		248–49
	Butternut Squash Soup with
		Smoked Trout, 254
	Gently Roasted Brown
		Trout with Summer
		Squash, 232–33
	hero food, 245–47
	Roasted Winter Squash, 251
	Stuffed Spaghetti Squash,
		254
	sweets made with, 246–47,
		254
	vitamins and omega-3s
		in, 247

squid
	cleaning technique, 83
	Rice with Squid and Green
		Beans, 74–75
	Squid with Baby Favas,
		Mint, and Basil, 144–45
Steamed Corn with Clams and
	Bacon, 196
Steaming Greens, 272
stone fruits. See also fruit
	Confit of Duck Legs with
		Plums, 204
	hero food, 201–3
	Lightly Cured Fluke with
		Pickled Plums, 204
	Pickled Plums, 207
	Plum Cake, 212
	Spiced Stone Fruit Pre-
		serves, 212
	Stone Fruit Gazpacho with
		Scallops, 208
	vitamins in, 203
	White Peaches, Pistachios,
		Honey, and Ricotta, 211
strawberries, 164
	Strawberry Ice Cream, 168
Stuffed Spaghetti Squash, 254
Sugar Snap Pea Salad, 142
summer crudo, 193
Sunday Roast Chicken, 130
sweet potatoes
	Fork-Crushed Sweet Pota-
		toes with Sobrassada
		and a Fried Egg, 108
	hero food, 177
	Sweet Potato Chips and
		Whipped Salt Cod, 28

T

techniques
	brining meat and poultry,
		297
	cleaning anchovies, 81
	cleaning squid, 73
	cooking garbanzo beans,
		141
	cooking octopus, 160
	cutting a quail egg, 126
	cutting up a duck, 120
	curing raw fish, 218
	deep-frying an egg in olive
		oil, 107
	desalinating salt cod, 235
	Escabeche for Pickling
		Poultry or Fish, 127
	grating tomatoes, 64
	how to smoke a trout, 230
	making dried beans in a
		pressure cooker, 35
	making Romesco sauce, 55
	making sofrito, 65

pickled shallots, 156
	preserving tuna, 224
	smoked olive oil, 22
	steaming greens, 272
Tolosa Bean Soup, 36
tomatoes
	Corn and Crab Salad, 195
	grating technique for, 64
	Lamb Meatballs in Tomato
		Sauce with Ricotta, 293
	Romesco Sauce, 55
	Sofrito, 65
	Sunday Roast Chicken, 130
	Two Kinds of Anchovies,
		One Kind of Flatbread,
		90
Tortilla Española, 111
Tristar strawberries, 164
trout
	Butternut Squash Soup with
		Smoked Trout, 254
	Gently Roasted Brown
		Trout with Summer
		Squash, 232–33
	How to Smoke a Trout, 230
	Mutti's Pan-Fried Trout-
		lings, 229
	note on, 236
	Trout a la Navarra, 229
	Warm Smoked Trout with
		Pickled Onions, 231
Truffled Lentils and Eggs, 40
tuna
	Deviled Eggs, 104
	endangered, 214, 224
	Farro Salad with Preserved
		Tuna, 69
	Preserving Tuna, 224–25
	Spanish tuna, 224
	White Bean Salad with
		Preserved Tuna and
		Parsley Vinaigrette, 159
Two Kinds of Anchovies, One
	Kind of Flatbread, 90
txakoli, 39, 146
	note on, 147

V

Vegetable Pickling Liquid, 185
Verdina Bean Salad, 35
vinaigrette
	of fresh almonds and
		sherry vinegar, 58
	Kefir Vinaigrette, 148
	mushroom liquid for, 261
	My Favorite Vinaigrette, 21
	Parsley Vinaigrette, 159
	Salbitxada modified as, 57
	smoked olive oil for, 22
	Warm Mushroom
		Vinaigrette, 262

vitamins
	almonds, 49
	anchovies, 79
	berries, 152–55
	carrots, 181
	corn, 192
	eggs, 101
	greens, 271
	mushrooms, 258
	peas, 138
	squash, 247
	stone fruits, 203
	whole grains, 62–63

W

walnuts
	Octopus and Parsley Salad,
		160
	in salads, 224
Warm Mushroom Salad, 261
Warm Mushroom Vinaigrette,
	262
Warm Smoked Trout with
	Pickled Onions, 231
wheat berries, 131
White Bean Salad with Pre-
	served Tuna and Parsley
	Vinaigrette, 159
White Peaches, Pistachios,
	Honey, and Ricotta, 211
Whole Black Sea Bass with Pea
	and Butter Sauce, 146
wild game birds, 116–17

X

Xató Salad, 276. See also
	Ensalada of Preserved
	Anchovies

Y

yogurt
	Anchoas y Escalivada, or
		Anchovies and Charred
		Vegetables, 85
	Chilled Carrot Soup with
		Yogurt and Tarragon,
		186–87
	Chilled Sweet Pea Soup, 147
	labne made from, 85, 186,
		276
	Lightly Cured Wild Salmon
		with Pea Salad, 148
	Minted Yogurt, 27
	Raspberries and Yogurt
		with Buttermilk Crêpes,
		168–69

Z

za'atar, 160

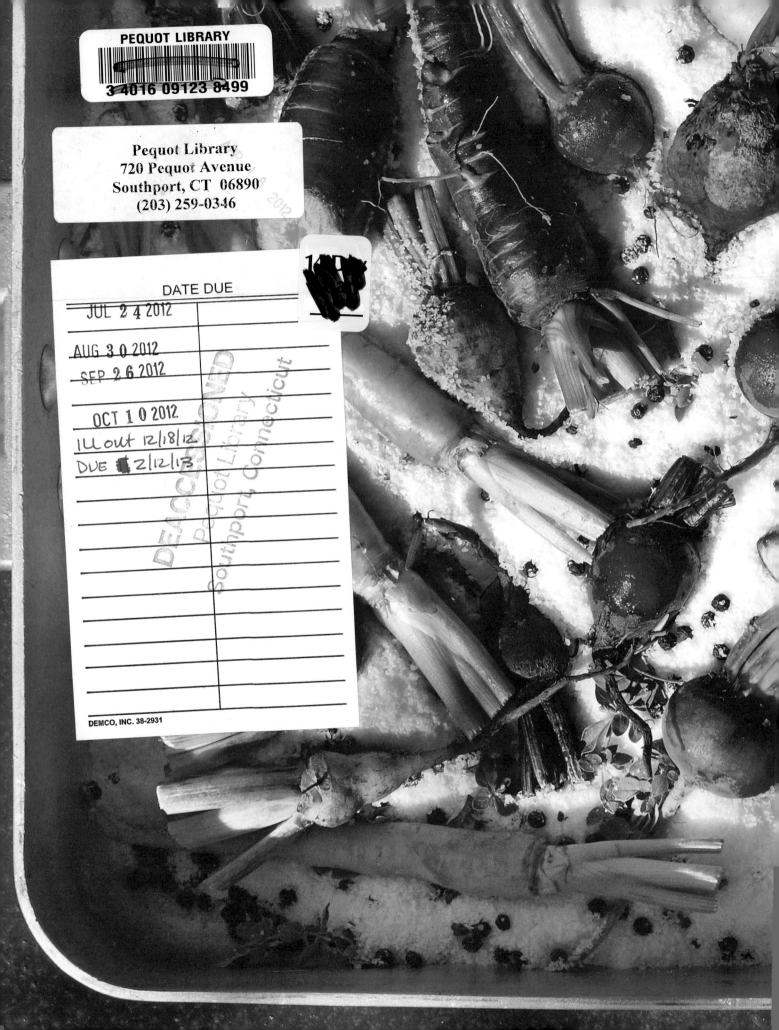